INSULATING YOUR HOUSE

A DIY GUIDE

INSULATING YOUR HOUSE

A DIY GUIDE

Andy McCrea

THE CROWOOD PRESS

First published in 2011 by
The Crowood Press Ltd
Ramsbury, Marlborough
Wiltshire SN8 2HR

www.crowood.com

© Andy McCrea 2011

British Library Cataloguing-in-Publication Data
A catalogue record for this book is available from the British Library.

ISBN 978 1 84797 266 8

Disclaimer
The author and the publisher do not accept responsibility, or liability, in any manner
whatsoever for any error or omission, nor any loss, damage, injury, or adverse outcome
of any kind incurred as a result of the use of the information contained in this book, or
reliance upon it. Readers are advised to seek professional energy efficiency advice relating
to their particular property, project and circumstances before embarking on any building or
related work.

Unless otherwise stated, all photographs and drawings are by the author.

Typeset and designed by D & N Publishing
Baydon, Wiltshire

Printed and bound in Malaysia by Times Offset (M) Sdn Bhd

Contents

Dedication

To my wife, Shirley, without whom this would not have been possible.

Acknowledgements

Thanks are due to my many colleagues, industry associates and organizations who offered advice, images and information used throughout this book. The captions associated with the figures and images detail the name/type of the product/system/service and the name of the company which manufactures/supplies or operates it, where appropriate. Acknowledgements are also made throughout the text, where pertinent, to other sources from which images and information have been adapted or taken. Details of relevant organizations and companies are given on pp. 181–183.

CHAPTER 1

Insulation – Why is it such a Good Idea?

Fitting insulation to a home will reduce fuel bills and increase comfort year on year, over the lifetime of the property. For the environmentally aware, fitting insulation is an excellent way to reduce your carbon footprint.

PURPOSE OF THIS BOOK

The costs of owning and living or working in a building are increasing steadily and one of the main contributory factors is energy bills. Fuel costs are rising and the reality is that most buildings waste energy needlessly. Undertaking a range of no-cost and low-cost measures, such as fitting insulation, can reduce this waste and provide significant savings in energy bills. Fitting insulation will also increase the comfort levels of a home, making it warmer and draught-free. As an additional benefit, reducing energy consumption will also result in lower emissions of harmful gases, such as carbon dioxide, into the environment.

The aim of this book is to bring a greater insight to people who want to know more about insulating

Measure	Installed whole-house cost	Approximate annual saving	Simple payback (years)
External wall insulation	£4,500	£450	Around 10 years
Internal wall insulation	£4,000	£400	Around 10 years
Cavity-wall insulation	£300	£120	Around 2.5 years
Suspended floor insulation	£90	£45	Around 2 years
Solid-floor insulation	£100*	£45 to £50	Around 2 years
Fillings cracks in floors	£25	£20	Roughly 1 year
Loft insulation (full 270mm)	£250	£150	Roughly 2 years
Loft insulation top-up (from 200mm)	£180	£45	Around 5 years
Draught-proofing windows and doors	£200	£25	Around 8 years
Fitting energy-efficient glazing	£2,000 to £4,000**	£135	Around 15 to 20 years
Insulating tanks and pipework	£50 to £70	£25	Around 2 years

Table 1: Approximate costs and savings from installing a range of energy-efficient measures in the home.
* If installed at the same time as laying a new solid floor.
** Based on a range of factors, including style of frames and glazing.
Note: These figures are for guidance only; obviously, costs and savings will be hugely dependent on individual properties. They are based on Energy Saving Trust information where available at the time of writing.

their home and to give them the information that will allow them to make cost savings by taking practical steps to do the work. Many of the jobs can be tackled easily through DIY and, with the reasonably modest costs involved, the savings in money (and emissions) can be very significant over the lifetime of the building.

Simple No-Cost or Low-Cost DIY Energy-Saving Hints

- Close your curtains at night to keep in the heat.
- Never leave hot water running.
- Defrost fridges and freezers regularly and never leave the fridge door open.
- Use the shower if you have one, rather than the bath.
- Only heat as much water as you need when boiling the kettle (but always make sure to cover the element of an electric kettle).
- Turn off lights when they are not required.
- Place tape over keyholes in external doors to prevent draughts.
- Never leave mobile phones on charge overnight.
- Make sure computer equipment is completely switched off and plugged out when not in use.
- Electrical appliances on standby could be costing you up to £99 per annum – switch off!
- Steamer pots reduce heat usage.
- Use 'task' lighting rather than whole-room lighting when only a small amount of light is required.
- Do not put warm or hot food straight into the fridge or freezer – let it cool down first.
- Put lids on pots and turn down the heat when the water starts to boil. The lids not only keep heat in the pot but also reduce condensation in the kitchen.
- The oven is expensive to use – try to use it as sparingly and as efficiently as possible. Where possible, use it for more than just one item and remember you can cook at a higher temperature at the top of the oven, and simultaneously at a lower temperature at the bottom.
- Do not open the oven door to check cooking – every time you do so you lose 20 per cent of the heat.

The emphasis in this book is on the DIY aspect of insulating a home and, in recent years, this type of work has been encouraged by government support, both through a variety of grant programmes

The Living Planet Report of the World Wildlife Fund. (wwf.org.uk)

and through awareness-raising activities by various organizations. With reasonable care and attention to health and safety precautions, in most cases insulation materials and products can be simply and effectively installed in the home. It is essential, however, to stress the importance of using the proper tools and equipment, protective clothing and the correct products for the application. When planning work around the home, the Building Regulations are a good place to start. A number of planned revisions will bring forward significant improvements in the standard of insulation for new buildings, but the challenge of improving the existing housing stock remains. This book has a role for homeowners who want to improve the insulation of their existing houses and buildings through DIY, as well as for those who are thinking of building an extension, roof-space conversion or even a new home.

There is also a good deal of interest, fuelled by the media (and with regards to the weather), in the subject of climate change and many people want to know how they can do their bit to reduce their carbon footprint. According to the World Wildlife Fund, the planet's resources are being used at a rate that would need three Earths to sustain:

In the UK we are currently living a 'three-planet lifestyle' and the report indicates that the world's ecological footprint – the demand people place upon the natural world – has more than tripled since 1961 and that rising carbon dioxide emissions are the biggest cause of our ecological impact on the planet. (Source: WWF's 'Living Planet' report 2006).

The insulation materials and products necessary to carry out the jobs described in this book are widely available. They are also affordable and their proper application and installation in the home, or in businesses, will deliver effective savings in fuel and electricity bills for many years to come.

THE SHAPING OF THE MODERN HOME

Until the 1960s most dwellings and buildings in the United Kingdom (UK) and the Republic of Ireland (RoI) had very little insulation, if any at all. There was a pressing need to build homes for the 'post-war boom' families and the standard of the fabric used for those houses came second. Houses did not have cavity walls as standard until the 1930s and the normal building method involved solid, outer-wall construction.

Homes were traditionally heated by an open-hearth coal fire, which could also be used to burn a variety of other fuels, including peat or wood. Some houses, even relatively modest ones, had two or more fireplaces. After the post-war austerity of the 1950s and early 1960s, central-heating systems began to appear in newer homes and by the end of 1960s they were almost *de rigueur*. A new house constructed in the 1970s would probably include an open fire, a central-heating system, fuelled with heating oil, gas or coal, and cavity-spaced external walls.

The 'price hikes' or sudden upward surges in the cost of fuel oil in the 1970s, and again in the 1980s, brought into sharp focus the reality that fossil fuels were a depleting, polluting source of energy and that their price was likely to remain highly volatile for some considerable time. The issue of the security and availability of these fuels became much more significant due to the political instability of many of the countries where they were most abundant. The exploitation since the 1970s of oil and

House with solid external walls (no cavity).

Victorian terraced houses from early 1890s. These houses are being lived in well over a hundred years after they were built.

gas from deposits in the seas around the British Isles, particularly in the North Sea and off the coast of Ireland, has provided a temporary respite in the supply of these fuels from elsewhere. Many people took advantage of the availability of oil to install oil-fired boilers, although coal was still available and remained popular. Coal-fuelled central-heating systems were more labour-intensive, but the fuel did have a price advantage over oil from time to time. By the early 1990s, the way in which buildings and homes were heated, and the relative price of the different fuels, assumed a whole new importance.

Roll of non-allergenic, itch-free, non-irritant loft insulation, 85 per cent made from recycled materials.

Polystyrene beads as used in cavity-wall insulation.

TOWARDS 2020 – LOOKING TO THE FUTURE

As fuel and electricity prices rise – as they inevitably will – the cost savings resulting from the installation of insulation will be greater year on year, and the time to pay back the initial investment will reduce. The savings given in these chapters are based on energy prices in 2009/2010; as prices rise, savings and payback times will improve steadily. At the same time, it is expected that the cost of installing insulation and the price of the materials will reduce, or at least keep pace with inflation.

Most governments around the world, including the UK and RoI, have committed to reduce their burning of fossil fuels, and to increase their use of renewable energy in an attempt to reduce carbon dioxide emissions and move to a lower-carbon future.

The European Union's (EU) 2009 Renewable Energy Directive sets a binding target of 20 per

Carbon Dioxide Emissions in the UK

In 2008, the UK's net emissions of carbon dioxide were estimated to be 532.8 million tonnes (Mt). This was around 2.0 per cent lower than the 2007 figure of 543.6Mt. There were decreases in emissions of 2.9 per cent (6.3Mt) from the energy supply sector; 2.9 per cent (3.9Mt) from the transport sector; and 3.0 per cent (2.7Mt) from the business sector. However, there was an increase of 3.2 per cent (2.5Mt) in emissions from the residential sector. One way to reduce emissions from the residential sector is to encourage the insulation of new and existing buildings.

The overall decrease in emissions has primarily resulted from continued fuel switching from coal to natural gas for electricity generation, combined with lower fossil fuel consumption by industry and the road transport sector. The increase in residential emissions has been attributed to the increased use of fossil fuels for domestic heating.

(Source: DECC Greenhouse Gas Emissions Report, 2008)

Glass-fibre loft insulation made largely from recycled plastic bottles and suitable for loft insulation top-up. The insulation is 150mm thick and can be applied over insulation that may already exist in the loft.

cent of the EU's energy consumption coming from renewable sources by 2020. The UK commitment to this target is to generate 15 per cent of its energy from renewable sources. The UK objective is to be on track by 2020 towards achieving an 80 per cent reduction in carbon emissions by 2050. In July 2009, the UK published a renewable energy strategy (RES), which sets out the comprehensive policy framework within which these objectives will be achieved. The UK Government's 2020 vision for the switch towards a low-carbon economy and society is set down in the RES and in the UK Low Carbon Transition Plan. Increased insulation and energy efficiency, combined with renewable energy from the wind, water, the sun and sustainable bio-energy, will have central roles in achieving the objectives.

The strategy proposes that over 30 per cent of electricity could come from renewable sources, compared with 5.4 per cent in 2008. This could be made up of 29 per cent large-scale electricity generation, and 2 per cent small-scale electricity generation. Considering heat demand, 12 per cent could come from renewable sources and also 10 per cent of energy used in transport could come from renewable sources.

Heating accounts for 47 per cent of the UK's carbon dioxide emissions and 60 per cent of average domestic energy bills. In homes this heat is used to keep warm, for hot water and for cooking. It can, of course, also be used for industrial processes. Insulation of buildings can dramatically reduce the carbon dioxide emissions resulting from domestic heating.

Data from 2007 shows that approximately 69 per cent of the UK's heat is produced from gas. Oil and electricity account for 11 per cent and 14 per cent respectively, solid fuel 3 per cent and renewables just 1 per cent. Heat sold – that is, heat that is produced and sold under the provision of a contract (including CHP plants and community heating schemes) – accounted for 2 per cent of the total.

(Sources: www.decc.gov.uk/en/content/cms/what_ we_do/uk_supply/energy_mix/renewable/res/res. asp

www.decc.gov.uk/en/content/cms/publications/ lc_trans_plan/lc_trans_plan.aspx

Heat and Energy Saving Strategy, DECC (2009), p12– : http://hes.decc.gov.uk/consultation/consultation_summary)

The Clean Air Act banned the burning of coal in urban areas and this meant that the fuels of choice became gas from the national gas mains, where available, LPG or heating oil. By the turn of the twenty-first century, mains natural gas had reached around 50 per cent of the homes in the UK, although most of these were in the major towns and cities. Rural communities relied heavily on oil, with some coal and LPG, with some use of wood where it was easily, and sometimes freely, available, and able to be transported. It soon became apparent that affordability was not the only issue involved in the burning of these fuels. They were also contributing to pollution (through particulates, smoke and the oxides of carbon, nitrogen and sulphur), and the notion that a

The Greenhouse Effect

The Greenhouse Effect produces a rise in temperature in the atmosphere because certain gases present in it, known as 'greenhouse gases' (water vapour, carbon dioxide, nitrous oxide, and methane), trap the energy from the sun. Incoming solar radiation passes almost unimpeded through the Earth's atmosphere and eventually it reaches the oceans or the Earth's surface. This radiation is absorbed and then re-radiated at longer wavelengths as heat (or infra-red radiation). However, the greenhouse gases in the atmosphere do not allow this outgoing infra-red radiation to escape; instead, the heat is trapped and absorbed and it raises the temperature of the atmosphere. The Greenhouse Effect is an entirely natural process and without these gases the heat would be lost into space, the Earth's average temperature would be about 30 degrees centigrade colder, and life as we know it would not exist.

The consensus view of the world's climate scientists (represented by the Intergovernmental Panel on Climate Change, or IPCC), is that the quantity of greenhouse gases, notably carbon dioxide, present in the atmosphere has been increasing steadily over the last 250 years and it now far exceeds the natural range of the past 650,000 years. The current level of carbon dioxide present in the atmosphere is estimated to be around 370 parts per million (or ppm). It is almost certain that this rapid increase is attributable to man – most of it as a result of increasing industrial and economic growth – and that the rising atmospheric concentration of carbon dioxide and other gases is producing an increase in temperature in the atmosphere. There is an ongoing debate about how much of an increase can be sustained before the planet reaches a tipping point – that is, the point of no return, after which positive-feedback processes are instigated, releasing even greater quantities of a variety of greenhouse gases into the atmosphere. This rise in temperature will eventually unlock methane from the permafrost layers in the Polar Regions, release vast amounts of carbon dioxide from the oceans and, eventually, melt the Polar ice sheets, with a resulting increase in sea level. There is uncertainty about the exact timing and consequences of reaching the tipping point, but there can be no doubt that, if this is a realistic scenario, then the effect on the global population will be widespread and catastrophic.

It has been suggested by the IPCC that a global rise in average temperature of 2 degrees centigrade (above the level before the Industrial Revolution of the late eighteenth century), or an increase in the carbon dioxide level in the atmosphere to around 450ppm (from the current 370ppm) will be sufficient to trigger the tipping point. The IPCC predicted a rise in global temperatures of 1.4 to 5.8 degrees centigrade between 1990 and 2100, but the estimate takes account only of global warming driven by known greenhouse gas emissions. Evidence suggests that human activity is currently contributing around 2ppm of carbon dioxide a year and rising, and that the tipping point may therefore be reached within thirty years.

Internationally agreed targets have been set to reduce the quantities of the gases being emitted. The targets cover emissions of the six main greenhouse gases:

- carbon dioxide (CO_2);
- methane (CH_4);
- nitrous oxide (N_2O);
- hydrofluorocarbons (HFCs);
- perfluorocarbons (PFC_s); and
- sulphur hexafluoride (SF_6).

In November 2007, the IPCC reported in its 'Draft Synthesis Report' that most of the observed increase in global average temperatures since the mid-twentieth century is very likely to be due to the observed increase in anthropogenic GHG concentrations. It is likely that there has been significant anthropogenic warming over the past fifty years, averaged over each continent (except Antarctica). Source: AR4, SYR 2007 Synthesis Report of the IPPC.

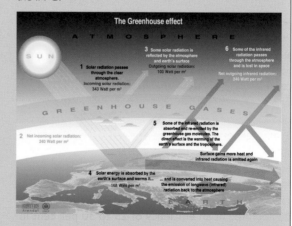

The general consensus is that human activities are causing greenhouse gas levels in the atmosphere to increase. This graphic explains how solar energy is absorbed by the Earth's surface. This radiation is re-radiated to the atmosphere as infra-red radiation, which is, in turn, trapped by the greenhouse gases. The infra-red radiation raises the temperature of the atmosphere. (Philippe Rekacewicz)

change in the climate was instigated by man became an emerging theme.

The 1990s saw the identification of a customer group within the population who struggled to pay their energy bills, the so-called 'fuel poor'. In some regions of the UK, as many as 50 per cent of households are in fuel poverty – in other words, they spend more than 10 per cent of their weekly income on providing heat and electricity for their homes. Those in this group struggle to afford the basic essentials of adequate heating for living space and hot water.

Concern for such households, combined with increased anxiety about global climate change, has led to the search for buildings that lose their heat less easily and therefore produce more afford-able energy bills. Governments in Britain, across Europe and globally have been forced to address the pressing need to reduce the amount of carbon dioxide released during the burning of fossil fuels. The importance of properly insulating homes and buildings to minimize fuel bills, save energy, increase the security of national energy supplies and reduce harmful emissions has become a central theme for those in power.

The idea of a building that could be constructed with such high levels of insulation that it would not require very much heat to be added – even during the coldest periods of the year – has led to the emergence of a concept known as the 'Zero Car-bon Home' (ZCH). The aim is to construct a dwell-ing that may be heated to an acceptable level, and provide the necessary amounts of hot water and electricity for the occupants, without the release of any carbon dioxide. The desired outcome can be reasonably well achieved in respect of the provi-sion of heat; however, electricity that is produced at low efficiencies in a conventional power station provides a much more difficult challenge. (Electricity is generated at an efficiency of 25 to 30 per cent in older power stations and this figure is perhaps as high as 55 per cent at the newer combined cycle gas turbine power stations, or CCGTs.) Renewably generated electricity produces very little or no car-bon dioxide.

One concept that has great appeal is a large heating boiler unit or pass-out turbine that pro-

A Proven Energy (provenenergy.co.uk) wind turbine can supply sufficient electricity for medium-sized loads such as a four- to six-bedroom home or a small farm. Electricity produced can benefit from the Feed-In Tariff (FIT) in GB.

vides enough heat to supply large residential areas and industrial developments at high efficiency. 'District heating systems', as they are known, are frequently standard in continental Europe, but they have proved difficult to bring forward in the British Isles. Only a limited number of schemes have been constructed and many of those have experienced some degree of technical and operational difficulty or failure.

The concept of producing both electricity and heat from a single appliance, at a much higher overall efficiency – perhaps as high as 75 per cent – is known as 'combined heat and power' (CHP). The difficulty of locating loads that can use the heat ('heat sinks') as well as the electricity generated has restricted the widespread roll-out of this technology. Domes-tic, industrial and commercial buildings, all of which require both heat and electricity, seem to present an ideal opportunity for CHP. A device that can pro-vide heat and electricity to satisfy the demands of a domestic or small building should, in theory, find a ready market. A number of these devices have appeared over the last decade and several compa-nies brought forward domestic combined heat and power units (d-CHP) as a first step. These d-CHP units burn natural gas using a Stirling engine; vari-ous adaptations use other fuels, including biomass and oil. The early versions produce sufficient heat (around 8kW) to satisfy a standard home (of around 1000m²) and they also generate around 1.5kW of electricity when operating.

LOW-CARBON BUILDING

Security of fuel supply is another important factor in the consideration of our energy future. Despite some recent finds, the on- and offshore resources of oil and gas around the British Isles are past their peak production, and the country is no longer in a position to support its energy requirements from these reserves. It continues to be necessary to import fuels and to compete on the international market for these vital commodities. The future global availability of these limited resources and the security of their supply will depend on factors outside our direct control, such as the stability of producer countries. The likely sustained increase in the costs of fossil fuels, combined with the growing uncertainties surrounding their supply, are additional reasons for pursuing a sustainable energy strategy, as part of any energy policy. The central tenets of this policy must be conservation, insulation and the use of indigenous renewable energy.

Diligent conservation, constructing new buildings with an adequate level of insulation, and the wider introduction of small-scale renewables may not initially have a large impact on national targets. However, over the course of time, these measures will significantly affect how we use (and waste) energy in our homes and help achieve the paradigm shift that delivers the low-carbon future.

The generation of electricity and heat in homes, businesses and communities, using small-scale renewable energy technologies, will help to reduce emissions of carbon dioxide. At the same time, it will also minimize the energy losses associated with the transmission of electricity from the power stations to homes and industry, which stand at between 5 and 10 per cent.

In future, it is hoped that all new buildings will be super-insulated and well ventilated, resulting in dramatically lower, almost negligible, heat requirements compared with current demands. It is considered that a significant proportion of domestic and commercial heating needs can be met from renewable

The Green House in Holywood, County Down, is super-insulated and requires no external source of heating to maintain a comfortable inside temperature all year around. Sufficient heat is supplied from the appliances, computers and inhabitants. The Green House has an air source heat pump for supplementary heating requirements.

technologies. Eventually, electricity-producing technologies such as photovoltaic (PV) panels, d-CHP and small-scale wind turbines will be integrated within a building's structure and these will fully supply the demand from lighting, cooking and entertainment appliances. Existing properties present more of a challenge – once a building has been constructed, its ability to insulate against heat loss is determined largely by the design and the materials used in its construction. The heat lost through the fabric will then remain the same over a building's lifetime, unless the insulation is upgraded, or the building fabric is improved, using DIY where possible.

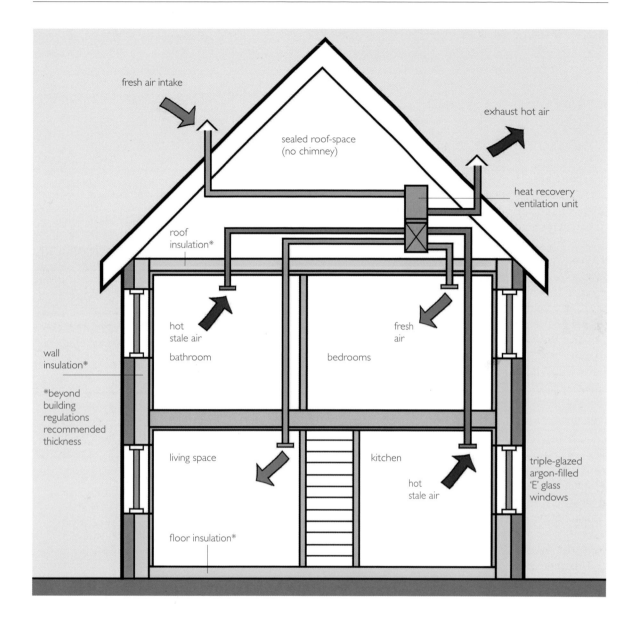

fresh air intake

exhaust hot air

sealed roof-space (no chimney)

heat recovery ventilation unit

roof insulation*

hot stale air

fresh air

bathroom

bedrooms

wall insulation*

*beyond building regulations recommended thickness

living space

kitchen

hot stale air

triple-glazed argon-filled 'E' glass windows

floor insulation*

BUILDING REGULATIONS AND ZERO-CARBON HOMES

Building Regulations are discussed in greater detail in Chapter 3. They were first introduced to the UK and Ireland in the mid-1960s and governments have set and updated the standards which are used when new buildings are constructed ever since. The regulations set down the minimum 'U-values' (for a detailed description, see Chapter 2) for the

Airtight low-energy house with super-insulation. Fresh air is drawn in through intakes at roof level. The heat-recovery ventilation unit (HRVU) uses the heat from the exhaust 'stale' hot air being removed to heat the incoming fresh air in a heat exchanger. The stale hot, damp air is removed from the bathroom and kitchen and the fresh air is introduced to the living room and bedroom areas.

components of a building's structure and fabric, and designers and architects must ensure that the standards are met. Prior to the introduction of the

DIY Activity	Task/improvement	Insulation treatments	Target improvement in insulation
Repairs to walls or new wall construction	• Repairs to render or external re-facing • Re-pointing • Room or home extensions • Replacing, repairing or removing external cladding • Internal wall re-plastering • Re-tiling bathrooms, kitchens or utility rooms	• External-wall insulation • Cavity-wall insulation (CWI) • Internal wall treatments	Solid walls with a typical value of $2.1W/m^2K$ should be insulated with 80–140mm of wet render, dry cladding or similar insulation to achieve a maximum value of $0.3W/m^2K$ Cavity walls with a typical value of $1.5W/m^2K$ should be filled with insulation to provide 0.5 to $0.6W/m^2K$
New roof or roof repairs	• Replacing roof • Repairing roof timbers or missing roof tiles • Chimney repairs • Repairing flat roof (leaks) • Room or home extensions	• Loft insulation • Pitched-roof insulation • Flat-roof insulation • Roof-space ventilation • Insulate pipes and water tanks in loft	For pitched roof, insulate lofts with 250–300mm mineral wool insulation between joists and rafters; aim for a U-value of $0.16W/m^2K$. For flat roof aim for $0.25W/m^2K$. For flat roof add 100–160mm of insulation to raise typical U-value of $1.5W/m^2K$ to $0.25W/m^2K$
New floors or floor repairs	• Replacing or repairing concrete ground floor • Replacing or covering wooden floor • Replacing tiled floor • Room or home extensions	• Timber-floor insulation • Solid-floor insulation • Ventilate floor void • Draught-proofing of floors by sealing skirting board and floorboard gaps	Insulate below concrete floor or between joists with 100–200mm insulation. Typical U-value is around $0.7W/m^2K$. Target value for floors should be in the range 0.2 to $0.25W/m^2K$
Repair or replacement windows	• Replacing or repairing old windows • Draught-proofing sash windows • Air tightness work to reduce draughts and air leakage • Fitting a ventilation system	• Draught-proofing windows • Sealing gaps around windows • Draught-proofing	Existing windows have a U-value of around $3.1W/m^2K$ and should be draught-proofed. Replacement windows should have a BFRC rating in Band C or better with integral draught-stripping. EST best-practice guidance on air leakage is for an air permeability of $5m^3/(hm^2)$ at 50Pa
Repair or replacement doors	• Replacing or repairing old doors • Draught-proofing around doors • Air tightness work to reduce draughts and air leakage	• Draught-proofing windows • Sealing gaps around windows • Draught-stripping	New or replacement doors should have a U-value of $1.0W/m^2K$. Existing doors should be draught-proofed. EST best-practice guidance on air leakage is for an air permeability of $5m^3/(hm^2)$ at 50Pa
Home heating and plumbing modifications	• Room or home extensions • Replacement hot-water cylinder * • Replacement cold-water storage tanks • Replacing an old boiler	• Insulate pipes and water tanks in loft • Floor insulation • Lofts and roof insulation • Install heating controls • Insulate hot-water cylinder*	Work should be done to Central Heating System Specification (CHeSS) — year 2005, standard HR6 or HC6. For electrical heating, systems recommendations in CE185/GPG345, *'Domestic Heating By Electricity'* should be followed
Kitchens and bathroom modifications and refurbishments	• Re-tiling • Re-plumbing • Re-plastering • Re-fitting units and appliances	• Internal wall insulation • High-performance doors and windows • Ventilation • Draught-proofing • Low-energy lighting • Insulate hot-water cylinder and pipework • Install heating controls	See targets for floors and walls above
Electrical work	• Rewiring • Electrical repairs • Fitting a new spur • Replacing lighting	• Low-energy light bulbs • LED lighting • Low-energy lighting	Use only approved bulbs carrying a certification mark

OPPOSITE:

Table 2: DIY activities with insulation opportunities. Note: The units and term 'U-values (W/m²K)' as used in this table are described in detail in Chapter 2.
* Subject to space, when replacing or upgrading an existing hot-water cylinder (of around 100 litre capacity) it is always worth considering a larger, insulated cylinder (say, 220 litres with at least 50mm of factory-fitted polystyrene insulation). It may be useful to make sure the cylinder has a second internal heating coil to anticipate the installation of a future solar water heating panel. (Source: EST CE83).

Building Regulations, there were no mandatory building standards available, although some local authorities had by-laws, which, since 1952, incorporated minimum standards for this work. The vast majority of existing buildings and homes built before that time have standards (and U-values) that are significantly lower than those detailed in today's Building Regulations; for example, they are unlikely to have insulation in the loft or in the cavity between the outer and inner walls, where such a cavity exists.

The Building Regulations and their amendments in 2000, and thereafter, include regulations that consider the conservation of fuel and power. There is software available from the Building Research Establishment (BRE), among others, which can be used to determine these values. Previously, the overall U-value for a property was calculated by totalling the individual component U-values; this summation had to be lower than a target value in order to comply with Building Regulations. This method, known as the 'calculated trade-off', has now been superseded by a new method of demonstrating compliance, known as the 'whole-building approach', or the 'whole-building method'.

Nowadays, it is simply inconceivable that a new building should be constructed without full regard for insulation. New homes should be super-insulated – that is, with levels of insulation for the building fabric, roof, floors, windows and doors that are well above those specified even in the most recent version of the Building Regulations. Insulation is cheap and simple to install at the construction stage and it provides fuel savings year on year. It is, of course, more difficult to retrofit insulation into existing properties, especially if access to the space under the floors is necessary.

Building Regulations typically call for a U-value of around 0.3W/m²K. A super-insulated new dwelling could have an overall U-value of around 0.2W/m²K and this would mean that only a small amount of heat would be required to keep the property at the desired comfort level. This implies that a smaller boiler could be installed, with a consequent offset against the cost of the extra insulation, as well as the year-on-year savings on fuel bills. Future revisions of the Building Regulations will require the inclusion of renewable energy to provide the necessary carbon dioxide reductions; more details in Chapter 2.

INSULATION OPPORTUNITIES IN THE HOME

Most people will have a go at DIY activities at some stage; see Table 2 and the picture on page 19 for the opportunities that exist to introduce energy efficiency and insulation into a whole range of DIY jobs.

Chapter 2 describes the main areas in homes and buildings that lose heat, concentrating on the building fabric. The Building Regulations are important in this work since they set the quality, best practice, legal compliance and safety standards for a range of home improvements and new construction work. Chapter 3 presents an overview of the current and proposed regulations. Chapter 4 reviews the range of materials that can be used to insulate a home or building, ranging from natural substances such as hemp and sheep's wool to mineral insulation such as glass wool and oil-derived products, including polystyrene and phenolic foam. Some products are better in certain applications than others; Chapter 4 will guide you through the maze.

Chapter 5 gets down to the nitty gritty and takes a look at the practical DIY opportunities that are available to reduce the heat loss through walls. A significant portion of a building's heat also escapes through the floors and roofs, and these are addressed in Chapters 6 and 7 respectively. Chapter 8 describes how heat is lost through draughts and ventilation and suggests some simple DIY approaches to minimize this. Energy-efficient glazing is the theme in Chapter 9 where potential savings using

DIY activity	Scope of Energy Efficiency and Insulation Works										
	Internal wall insulation	External wall insulation	Cavity-wall insulation	Draught-proofing and ventilation	Energy-efficient windows	Loft insulation	Pipe, cylinder and tank insulation	Floor insulation	Low-energy lighting	Heating controls (including 'A'-rated boiler)	Install a renewable technology
General wall repairs, including re-plastering	DIY	DIY	DIY	DIY							
Re-wiring (including lighting)									DIY		DIY
Doors and windows					DIY						
General roofing work						DIY					
Work to floors (and ceilings)						DIY	DIY	DIY	DIY		
Work on heating and plumbing systems							DIY			DIY	DIY

Table 3: Scope for DIY energy efficiency and insulation in home repairs.

double- and triple-, and gas-filled glazing units are described. It is also very important that attention is given to properly insulating pipework and water storage tanks around the home – especially in lofts or exposed areas, and Chapter 10 describes how to tackle these areas. Chapter 11 reviews the tools, special clothing, materials and techniques which are needed to get the job done safely.

Two additional chapters have been added as Appendix I and Appendix II. Appendix I reviews the literature and standards which give guidance on the specification and installation of insulation. Appendix II lists some of the relevant legislation which should be taken into account when planning work on your home or building. This book also includes a comprehensive listing of useful contacts, website links and of places to go for helpful advice, as well as a full glossary of terms.

Refurbishments, repairs or extensions all offer the opportunity to introduce better insulation into your home. Depending on the scope of the work, there may be quite a few opportunities for improvement. A range of options have been identified below and utilizing any or all of the measures (in the diagram opposite and listed in Table 2) will save money, waste less energy and reduce your carbon footprint.

The most important aspect of fitting insulation is getting the right advice before you begin and making sure it is carried through to completion. In most instances the insulation product manufacturers, the suppliers and the installers will be different people or companies. A full evaluation and inspection of the building will ensure that the most appropriate materials are selected and installed in line with the very best practice. The work can be completed either on a DIY basis, subject to competency, or, depending on the complexity of the job, using fully trained and accredited installers (for cavity-wall insulation, for example).

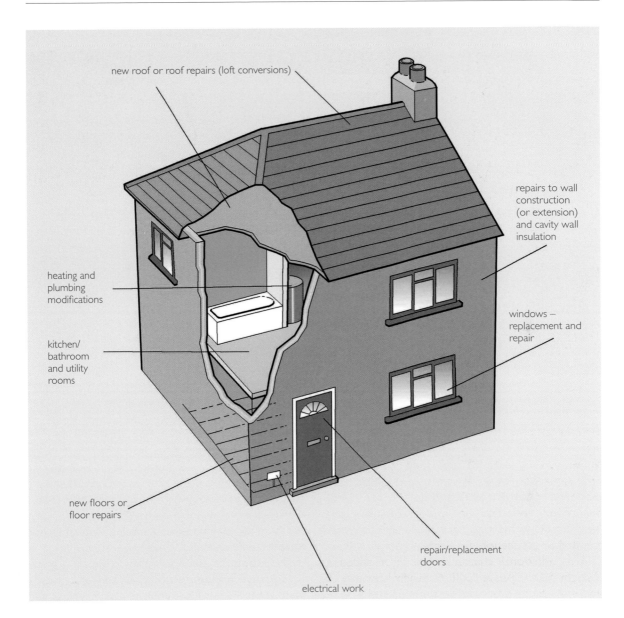

new roof or roof repairs (loft conversions)

heating and plumbing modifications

kitchen/ bathroom and utility rooms

new floors or floor repairs

electrical work

repairs to wall construction (or extension) and cavity wall insulation

windows – replacement and repair

repair/replacement doors

There is a wide range of opportunities for DIY work to introduce or enhance insulation in a property.

GRANTS FOR HOME INSULATION

Insulation is widely recognized as a way to produce lower energy bills, reduce emissions and enhance fuel security. In support of these objectives and acknowledging the fact that home insulation is beneficial because it provides jobs and supports the economy, from time to time there are grants available in the UK and RoI. Such funds may contribute to the cost of loft insulation, cavity-wall insulation and draught-proofing, all of which will save on energy bills and reduce your carbon footprint.

In Scotland, England and Wales, grants are available from utility companies as a result of the Carbon Emissions Reduction Target (CERT) programme.

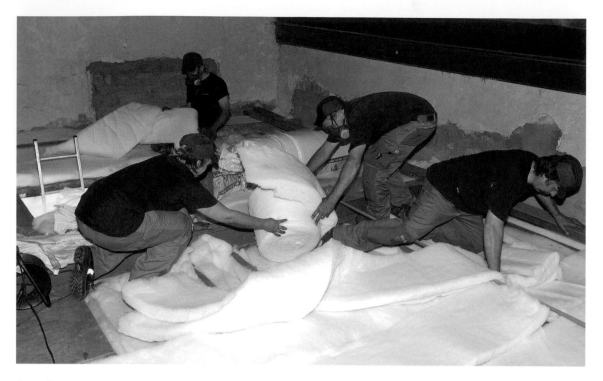

Specialist contractors installing rolls of loft insulation made mostly from recycled plastic bottles. (Homeseal Insulation Installers, Magherafelt, NI, homesealni.co.uk)

In Northern Ireland the equivalent scheme is the NI Sustainable Energy Programme (NISEP). Information on grant eligibility and how to process an application can be obtained by contacting the agencies detailed in the 'Contacts' section at the end of the book. For example, in Britain the Warm Front scheme provides grant assistance to insulate and draught-proof houses and flats; such grants may be means-tested. In the Republic of Ireland, the Sustainable Energy Authority for Ireland (SEAI) (see the 'Contacts' section) provides information relating to grants, which are available from time to time, and lists of approved contractors.

From time to time there are *ad hoc* grant or loan schemes available. For example, in Northern Ireland in July 2010, Land and Property Services (LPS), a division of the Department of Finance and Personnel (DFP), introduced two schemes that will allow home owners to benefit from a rate rebate once they have installed specific energy-efficiency measures. The scheme known as the 'Low Carbon Homes Scheme' promotes the construction of new low- and zero-carbon homes by providing an initial exemption from rates for the first two years of occupation of a new home. There are qualifying conditions around these rebates and details should be checked at Land and Property Services website, www.nidirect.gov.uk/low-carbon-homes.htm. Other similar rates relief schemes are being planned across the UK and Ireland.

To find out whether you are eligible for a grant (some grants may be means-tested) and for help with your application, call the following numbers, as appropriate to your area:

- in England or Wales, call 0800 316 2805 or 0800 028 2373;
- in Scotland, contact the Energy Assistance Package, 0800 512 012;
- in Northern Ireland, contact Warm Homes, 0800 512 012;
- in the Republic of Ireland, contact the Sustainable Energy Authority for Ireland (SEAI), 1800 250 204, or email warmerhomes@seai.ie.

CHAPTER 2

Heat Loss in Buildings

ENERGY EFFICIENCY AND HEAT LOSS

Over time, all the heat supplied to a house to raise the temperature of its rooms to a comfortable level will be lost to the surroundings. The rate of heat loss will depend on how well the materials from which the house is constructed conduct heat. All the materials used in the construction of the house act to some extent as insulation and they resist heat flow from the rooms to the surroundings. Materials such as wood or brick are reasonably good at resisting heat loss, while others such as glass or metal are poor, allowing heat to escape rapidly through them. Well-insulated houses made from materials that have good insulation performance, or those that include extra insulation as part of the construction, lose their internal heat less rapidly. Super-insulated houses that have very high levels of insulation fitted lose their room heat to the surroundings very slowly.

Most of the existing dwellings in the British Isles, especially those constructed before the 1970s, suffer from significant heat loss, having been built either with insufficient insulation or, very often, with none at all. Installing high-efficiency, or even environmentally friendly renewable energy-based heating systems will be of little value if heat is lost

from the building as soon as it has been supplied. The design standards and building fabric of British homes differ dramatically from those elsewhere in Europe, notably the Scandinavian countries, where building insulation standards are much higher.

Before any form of new or replacement heating system is contemplated, it is essential that the

A semi-detached house in the process of having external wall insulation installed to make it warmer and reduce its energy bills. (Seamus O'Loughlin Viking-House, viking-house.co.uk)

building is insulated to the highest level – exceeding the Building Regulations standards, where possible. There are two main causes of heat loss from buildings: heat conduction through the walls, windows, floor and roof, known as 'fabric heat loss'; and uncontrolled ventilation heat losses through and around draughty windows, doors and other air-flow paths. The table below shows where the heat losses of a typical two-storey dwelling arise:

Heat loss area	Approximate heat lost (%)
Walls	30 to 35
Roof	15 to 27
Ventilation and draughts	Up to 15
Doors and windows	Up to 20
Floors	8 to 15

Table 4: Sources of heat loss in a two-storey dwelling. *Note: Percentages will be highly dependent on the house design, location and age.*
(Sources: Various)

The table shows that walls represent the most significant source of heat loss; cavity-wall insulation (CWI) (*see* Chapter 5) is an excellent way to reduce this where it is feasible. In buildings with no cavities, or cavities which cannot be filled, it is usually possible to apply external or internal insulation on the outside walls. Houses in which walls are insulated on their internal surfaces will not benefit from their thermal inertia – that is, their ability to retain the sun's heat that accumulates throughout the day and which would otherwise be re-radiated into the house. New buildings can benefit from pre-fabricated, highly insulated wall panels and from Building Regulations that demand higher thermal performance standards for construction fabric and specify insulation. Best practice would suggest that insulation standards around 25 per cent above those recommended in the Building Regulations would be optimal.

The insulation of existing or refurbished properties can be improved via a number of measures, which range from low-cost DIY jobs to more expensive approaches such as the application of external or internal-wall insulation treatments, possibly using specialist contractors.

As well as the obvious economic benefit from using less fuel, there are the additional social and environmental advantages of reducing a building's energy consumption. A better-heated building will lead to improved comfort, working and living conditions and energy saved will preserve fossil fuel supplies and minimize the impact on climate change. Once a building is constructed and in operation it can be difficult to improve the fabric, but ongoing maintenance and upkeep can play a part, especially with regard to draughts.

Table 5 shows the energy (kWh) required for domestic space heating and to provide hot water for a range of property types with differing number of bedrooms and external wall construction.

Property type	No. of bedrooms	Floor area (m²)	Cavity-wall construction (kWh/yr)	Solid-wall construction (kWh/yr)
Flat	2	61	4,441	7,525
Mid-terrace house	3	79	5,262	8,914
End-terrace house	3	79	9,236	15,648
Semi-detached bungalow	2	64	6,306	10,684
Detached bungalow	2	67	7,786	13,192
Semi-detached house	3	89	9,674	16,390
Detached house	3	104	15,774	26,724

Table 5: Energy required for space heating houses for a range of property types, number of bedrooms and different types of construction. *Note: Hot-water demand is assumed to be 3,742kWh/yr for all house types. The figures assume filled cavity walls and 150mm loft insulation (where appropriate).*
(Source: DECC Consultation on Renewable Heat Incentive, February 2010)

Building Design, Construction and the Building Fabric

The illustration below shows the main areas of heat loss of a typical building. Usually around two-thirds of its heat is lost through the building fabric, with the remaining third being lost through gaps and vents, including the chimney.

The walls, ceilings, floors, windows and doors of a building are the components that make up the building fabric and their ability to transfer heat will determine how efficient the building is at retaining its heat. The building fabric must balance the requirements for ventilation and daylight, while providing thermal and moisture protection that are appropriate to the local climatic conditions. In infra-red images taken of buildings; the brighter colours indicate the areas where most heat loss is occurring (see the illustrations on page 24).

Regardless of the heating system, it is largely the fabric of a building that will determine its heat loss, so when upgrading a heating system, prioritization should be given to improving the fabric and making a building more airtight. These actions will reduce heat loss and this will, in turn, influence the size of any new heating under consideration.

The gaps and vents in a building permit warm air to leave and cold air to enter the building space. Air flow through the building can occur in an uncontrolled way through draughts, and so on, or deliberately through ventilation. Fresh cool air coming in will also be an additional source of heat loss because it, too, will need to be heated.

Improving the building's fabric will result in better temperature control, which will in turn affect the heating, cooling and ventilation characteristics. For a business, fabric improvements can lead to enhanced productivity, with occupant comfort and morale improved through draught elimination, lower solar glare, less building overheating and lower noise. A more efficient, well-insulated building needs a smaller heating and cooling system, leading to reduced capital costs. Better insulation can increase a building's value and attractiveness, with lower running and maintenance costs.

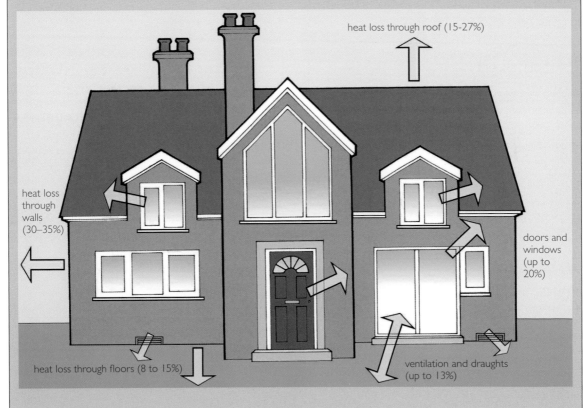

Areas of significant heat loss in a building. (Energy Saving Trust)

Thermal infra-red image of terraced houses showing areas where heat is escaping (brighter areas). The house on the right has been treated with cavity-wall insulation and appears to be radiating much less heat than the property on the left. (Horton Levi Ltd)

Thermal IR survey images identify places where heat is escaping most rapidly (bright areas). The detached house on the left is un-insulated and large amounts of heat are leaking through the upstairs window. The semi-detached house on right shows the heat leakage after cavity-wall insulation has been installed. Bright areas below windows are probably due to radiators below windows. (Horton Levi Ltd)

HEAT FLOW IN A BUILDING

Heat will flow from hot places to cooler places and this means that the heat supplied to keep a building warm inside must be continuously replenished. To say that heat is 'lost' is not really true. Heat is a form of energy and, according to the first law of thermodynamics, 'energy can neither be created or destroyed', in this case it is simply moved from one place to another. In most instances, heat moves from the hot inside of a building to the cooler outside.

Heat Transfer

Heat may be transferred in three ways – conduction, convection and radiation – and these are all active when a building heats up or cools down. Heat energy (or thermal energy) moves from one place to another, or flows, because of a difference in temperature between the two locations. The energy flow is always from the hot to the cold place.

In conduction, the heat energy is passed from atom to atom within the structure of the material. It is the most important heat-transfer mechanism in solids such as metals, bricks and wood. In a building, heat is transferred from the hot inside surface of a solid wall to the external, cooler surface by conduction – this is fabric heat loss.

In convection, heat energy is carried around by free atoms or molecules, so this is only possible in gases or liquids. In a home, heat is transferred from the hot surface of a central-heating radiator into the room through contact with the surrounding air. The air in the room is constantly in motion, with the hot air rising away from the radiator to be replaced by cooler air. One type of room heater is the assisted convection heater, which has a fan and blows the hot air away from the heated element of the appliance. Air movement through convection is a significant mechanism in ventilation heat loss.

The third heat-transfer mechanism is radiation. Radiant energy at infra-red wavelengths is given off by any hot object – a glowing coal, for example, or the sun – and this energy is absorbed on a cooler surface as heat. In a building on a bright sunny day, dark roof tiles or a south-facing wall will absorb the radiant energy from the sun. After the sun has set, the heat will be re-radiated to the cooler surrounding air, or to the inside of the building. Radiant heat travels in straight lines directly from the heat source, warming any objects in its path, without significantly heating the air through which it travels.

One good example of the way in which these heat-transfer mechanisms can be combined effectively is a solar water-heating panel using evacuated tubes. The objective of the solar collector in the panel is to retain as much of the incident radiation as possible by not re-radiating it to the air or surroundings. The incident solar radiation heats the primary circuit fluid (by radiation), which in turn heats the water. Collectors are frequently coloured black to encourage absorption of the solar radiation. Insulation is used to minimize heat loss from the collector through conduction and convective losses are prevented by evacuating the glass tube containing the collector.

From a practical point of view, it is essential to hold on to the heat before it is 'lost' to somewhere else and this is the job of insulation. When heating a house, the heat that flows from a warm living space to a colder unused part of the house is not really lost, because the cooler area benefits through a rise in temperature. Heat can be considered lost only when it moves from the living areas of the house to places where it is neither wanted nor needed.

On a cold day, it may be necessary to keep the heating system running all day, in order that the rooms in a house are maintained at constant temperature. Keeping a building hot means that it will lose heat at a higher rate; if the heating system is kept running for a prolonged period of time, the heat will continue to flow to the cooler outside surroundings for longer. Once the heating has been switched off then the temperature of the inside of the building will start to fall, eventually reducing to the same temperature as the air outside.

SOURCES OF HEAT LOSS

The amount of heat that is lost from a building will depend on a number of factors, including the type of building, its orientation, its exposure to the elements and the construction fabric.

Fabric Heat Loss

In fabric heat loss, the heat will seep out through the building fabric in exactly the same way that it leaks away through a kettle after the water inside has boiled. Some well-designed kettles use insulation to try to keep the heat inside for as long a time as possible. The same principle applies to our buildings where the heat inside will eventually make its way to the outside through the fabric unless it is insulated to prevent heat loss.

The sources of fabric and ventilation losses in a building. Ignoring the intended air flow through windows, vents, and so on, it is clear that there are a variety of air paths that are unwanted, and which can lead to significant heat loss if not addressed.

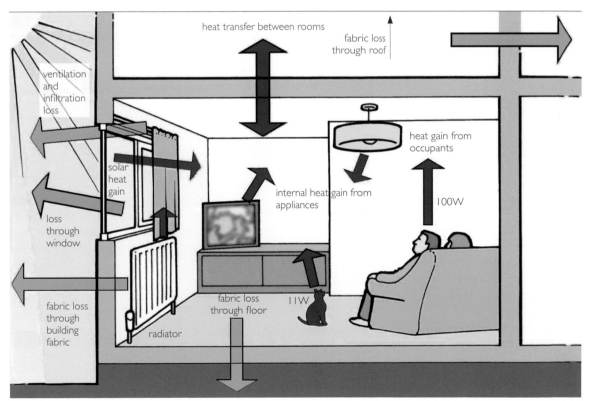

Building component	U-value (W/m²K)
Single-glazed metal-framed window	5.8
Single-glazed wooden-framed window	4.7
UPVC double-glazed window/door	2.0
Double-glazed wooden-framed window	2.0
Solid brick wall	2.1
All-brick cavity wall	1.5
Pitched roof (un-insulated) – including ceiling	2.1

Table 6: Typical U-values for building materials.

The building fabric will lose heat due to three principal factors. The first, as we have seen, is that the building materials themselves conduct the heat away; the second factor is the temperature difference between the inside and outside will drive the heat out or in, and the final factor is the size of the external area of the building, since this will determine how much surface is available for the heat to escape from. The material's ability to transmit the heat is known as its thermal conductivity. The rate at which the heat travels through the material (or heat flow rate) is dependent on the material's thickness and its thermal conductivity.

The components which make up the external parts of a house are made from a variety of different materials, of varying thicknesses. These include glass in windows, bricks, blocks, render, concrete and wood – and each of these will conduct and transmit heat at different rates. Some materials do not let the heat flow through them as readily as others and this is shown in the infra-red images. Metal window frames for example, lose heat rapidly in comparison with wooden ones. This is because metals in general are good conductors of heat and the frames are made from thin strips of metal which allow the heat to be quickly lost. Brick on the other hand is a better insulator – it is made from dried clay which is a relatively poor conductor of heat and the bricks are thick relative to window frames. Thermal blocks are even poorer at letting heat through them and they are also lighter. The standard measure which indicates how readily heat flows through materials is the U-value. The 'U' is not an abbreviation or shortened form of another word – it is simply the symbol which is used to indicate how easily heat will flow through a material. The lower the U-value the better, from the point of view of the material preventing heat loss – so in this case, small is best. Some U-values are shown for a variety of building materials in Table 6.

Temperature Difference and Building External Area

Unless the temperature outside is high, as would be the case on a hot summer day, the heat from the inside of the house normally flows to the outside surroundings. Clearly, when looking at heat loss through the fabric of the building, the greater the difference in temperature between the inside and the outside, the greater the heat flow and the greater the resulting heat loss. This temperature difference (or 'temperature gradient') is what drives the heat flow. A temperature difference of 5 degrees will always produce the same heat flow, regardless of whether it represents the gap between 10 and 15 degrees centigrade, say, or 20 and 25 degrees centigrade.

Another key factor that influences how quickly a house loses its heat is the area of its outside walls. The loss from an end-of-terrace house will be much greater than that from a house in the middle of a terrace, since its gable-end wall will represent a significant exposed exterior area through which heat can flow. (This assumes, of course, that the houses on either side of the one in the middle are occupied and heated.) The situation is similar with flats and apartments, where walls, floors and ceilings are shared with neighbouring flats and apartments. Flats that share exterior wall surfaces with corridors, stairwells, lift shafts or garages that are not heated will lose almost as much heat through those walls as if they were fully exposed to the outside air.

Houses with large areas of glazing – for example, large single-pane windows or conservatories – are particularly at risk of losing heat quickly. The installation of double-glazing will help, but glass loses heat much more quickly than other building fabrics (see U-values Table 6). Roofs are also exposed parts of the building and where the roof area is large in proportion to the rest of the house, as is the case in a bungalow, the heat loss from here can be very substantial.

If the house is rendered, cracks will encourage damp to penetrate the wall structure.

Energy labelling of houses will indicate which homes have been fitted with the highest level of insulation and which have the lowest energy running costs. (Xtratherm Insulation Limited, xtratherm.com)

Cold Bridging and Damp Exposure

When part of a house structure is exposed to both the heated interior and to the cooler external surroundings, there is a possible 'cold bridge', which will allow heat to flow directly from inside to outside.

Houses such as this, which are located in coastal or exposed locations, will benefit significantly from good insulation.

Cracked or missing render on a gable wall will result in damp penetration.

One example could be a large slab of concrete in a block of flats that is the floor for one or more flats and also forms their external balcony. The heat can flow through the concrete floor to be lost from the outside balcony.

A similar problem can arise in buildings which have become damp; for example, a damp outer wall will lose heat much more quickly than a dry section of the same wall. The damp patch of wall will also require more heat to warm it than the dry section.

Buildings in certain locations, for example, at the coast, or in places that are unprotected by surrounding buildings or trees, can be exposed to damaging climatic conditions, such as rain or the sea, and can become damp. Once a building becomes damp and if it is then subsequently subjected to a strong or persistent wind, it will cool rapidly, losing its heat.

Ventilation Heat Loss

In ventilation heat loss, the heat is carried in and out of the house via air currents, draughts or ventilation air flow – normally, this means cold air coming in and hot air escaping. Controlled ventilation involves the use of windows, grilles, airbricks and vents to provide adequate amounts of fresh air for a range of purposes required by the building and its services. Uncontrolled ventilation is the result of unwanted air infiltration through gaps and cracks around windows and doors, via floors and through holes where pipes and cables enter and leave the building. Once cold air has entered the house, it will take up heat from its surroundings and then, if it moves outside through a gap or open door, this heat will also be lost. This is known as 'heat exchange', with the heat being exchanged between the hot interior and the cooler external surroundings. The warm air that has escaped will in turn be replaced by cooler air coming in to take its place, and so the cycle continues.

Ventilation heat loss tends to be worse in older properties with open fires and wooden ground floors. An open fire has a chimney flue, which is necessary to ventilate and carry away the combustion gases from the fire, but will also allow cold air to penetrate directly into the heart of the building when the fire is not lit. The insulation and draught-proofing of ground floors (see Chapter 6) represents one of the easiest and most effective

Making Sense of the Numbers: k-values, R-values and U-values

k-value or λ-value	R-value	U-value
Thermal conductance	Thermal resistance	Thermal transmittance
W/mK	m^2K/W	W/m^2K
	R = t/k or t/λ	
	$R_t = R_1 + R_2 + R_3$	U = 1/R_t
A measure of the rate of heat flow through a material – or its resistance to heat flow	A measure of the rate of heat flow through a material, accounting for its thickness	A measure of the rate at which heat passes through the building fabric or components

Table 7: k-value, R-value and U-value and the relationship between these values.

A material's thermal conductivity or thermal conductance is known as its k-value or lambda-value (λ); these are shown for various insulating materials in the tables in Chapter 4. It is measured in units of W/mK – that is, the heat energy (in Watts) flowing through the insulating material of a given length (in metres, m), with a temperature difference of K degrees Kelvin across it. Insulation products can be compared on the basis of their lambda-values – the lower the lambda-value or thermal conductivity, the better the insulation.

Thermal resistance (the R-value) is another way to express the flow of heat through a material. This allows a comparison of insulation products of different thicknesses. The term R-value is used more in the United States than in the UK and Ireland, but it is still widely quoted in written material and in product specifications. The R-value is calculated by combining the lambda-value and the thickness of the material. R = t/λ, where t is the thickness of the insulation (0.3m for example) and λ is the thermal conductivity, as quoted by the insulation manufacturer.

In order to assess the thermal performance of a building's fabric (windows, walls, ceilings, and so on), the thermal conductance of each component (the bricks, insulation, plaster, external render, and so on) may be obtained from the manufacturers' data sheets. The thickness of each component (in metres) is then divided by the lambda-value for the material and this will give the R-value for that specific component. These individual R-values are then added together to give an overall R-value for the wall or ceiling. Units are measured in m^2K/W. The higher the R-value, the more effective the insulation.

A complete U-value calculation will take into account all the lambda-values of the various parts of the roof/wall structure, as well as the factors that determine the transfer of heat from inside the room to the roof, and from the roof to the outside air.

The R-value may also be used to calculate the U-value. The thermal transmittance, or U-value, is a measurement of the rate at which heat passes through (or is lost through) the building fabric or a component (window, door, roof, floor, and so on). In technical terms, a U-value is a measure of the rate (in Watts) at which heat will flow through one square metre of the material or fabric, assuming a temperature difference across its two sides of one degree Kelvin (or centigrade). U-values are expressed as Watts per square metre per degree Kelvin, or W/m²K, although it is not unusual to hear the U-value used without its units attached. It takes account of all the different elements in a building component and gives an overall indication of heat loss. This is a widely used term and can be found extensively referenced, for example, in the Building Regulations. Using the typical values from Table 6, the U-value for a solid wall (brick) is 2.1,

meaning that heat will flow through each square metre of the brick wall at a rate of 2.1 Watts for every degree centigrade of temperature difference between its inside and outside surfaces. So for a 5 square metre (m²) wall area with a 10K (or 10 degree centigrade) temperature difference across it, heat will be lost at the rate of 5 × 2.1 × 10 = 105 Watts.

Rate of heat loss (Watts) = temperature difference (in K or C) × area of fabric (m²) × fabric U-value

U-values can be calculated knowing the thicknesses and thermal conductances of the individual materials that make up any building component. An example is shown below.

NOTE: Example for illustration. The total U-value in this simplified calculation, is given by 1/(Rp+Rrc+Rb+Ri+Rbk+Rr).

So in this case:
the U-value = 1/Rt ; so

$$= 1/(0.032+0.04+0.25+4.28+0.12+0.035)$$
$$= 1/(4.76), so$$

Rt = 4.76m²K/W and U-value = 0.21W/m²K

This is an approximation, to show how the principle of the calculation can be applied to produce a U-value from the k-values for the various materials and their thicknesses.

The U-values of building elements should be calculated in accordance with the European standards, BS EN ISO 6946 and BS EN ISO 13370, and the GB Building Regulations, part L1, Conservation of Fuel and Power, Appendix B, sets down the more complete calculation (with examples), which require evaluation of the upper resistance limit, the lower resistance limit and the appropriate adjustments to be applied.

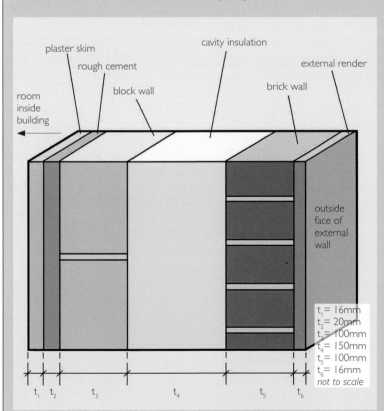

Illustrative U-values for various construction materials used in an external cavity wall of a building.

plaster skim

rough cement

block wall

cavity insulation

external render

brick wall

room inside building

outside face of external wall

t₁ = 16mm
t₂ = 20mm
t₃ = 100mm
t₄ = 150mm
t₅ = 100mm
t₆ = 16mm
not to scale

t₁ t₂ t₃ t₄ t₅ t₆

Material	k-Value (or λ) W/mK *	Thickness (t, mm)	Component R-value	R-value (t/λ) (m²K/W)
Plaster	0.5	16	Rp	0.032
Rough casting	0.5	20	Rrc	0.040
Block	0.4	100	Rb	0.250
Insulation	0.035	150	Ri	4.280
Brick	0.84	100	Rbk	0.120
Render	0.45	16	Rr	0.035
			Rt	4.76

Table 8: k- and R-values for some external wall materials. * *From insulation manufacturers' data sheets.*

As a further example, using mineral wool glass insulation of 0.2m thickness to insulate a loft, the U-value of the insulation element is 0.175W/m²K. Doubling the thickness of the insulation gives a much improved U-value of 0.0875W/m²K. A complete U-value calculation will take into account all the lambda-values of the various parts of the roof/wall structure, as well as the factors that determine the transfer of heat from inside the room to the roof, and from the roof to the outside air.

DIY opportunities to reduce ventilation heat loss.

The ventilation rate is the rate at which air flows into or out from a building, either purposefully or otherwise, and it can be assessed by an airtightness test. The air is continuously changing in a building. If there are lots of leaks and gaps, then air will change rapidly, whereas an airtight house will lose less heat through ventilation loss. The more airtight the building is, the longer it will take to cool down.

Quality of construction will influence ventilation heat loss. If the house has been poorly built, with too many gaps and badly fitting windows and doors, the house will lose its heat rapidly. As with fabric heat loss, a house in an exposed, windy location will lose heat quickly through ventilation loss because the draughts will find their way through the gaps and vents, resulting in faster air changes.

When all the air in the building has been completely replaced with fresh air from outside, this is known as an 'air change'. The ventilation rate is an indication of how many air changes take place within a specified time interval, usually one hour. As an example, in a typical house it might take two hours to completely replace all the air with fresh air from outside. This means that in one hour one half of an air change will have been completed, and the ventilation rate of the house will be 0.5 air changes

per hour (AC/h). Clearly, the ventilation rate and the number of air changes per hour will depend on a number of factors – age of the building, wooden floors, gaps around windows and doors, and so on. The higher the number of air changes per hour (the bigger the AC/h value), the higher the flow of warm air (or heat loss) from the building.

Other Sources of Heat Loss

Heat can be lost in other ways: for example, hot water flowing down the drain from a sink, bath or shower, or being carried away in the chimney gases from an open fire. Heat stored in a hot-water tank, or in hot pipes that traverse the rooms and corridors, will be lost to the surroundings, but, if this is inside the living or working space of the building, it may be acceptable. If the heat travels through an unoccupied area or to the outside or garage, this represents a loss. Similarly, washing clothes, having a bath or shower or even using warm water to wash the car will result in the loss of hot water to the environment and this is described as water heat loss. The heat carried up the chimney from open coal or gas fires and central-heating boiler flues, without heating the building, is known as flue heat loss. Acknowledging the above sources of heat loss, the most significant percentage of the heat loss from a building occurs through ventilation and fabric heat loss, and these are the main areas on which to concentrate. A number of strategies may be employed to prevent heat from escaping, such as looking at some of the building materials used to construct homes, and also considering the range of products (and their thermal properties) that can be used to insulate dwellings and other buildings.

ROOM TEMPERATURE – WHAT IS BEST?

Generally, elderly people, who may be inactive, and families with young babies are recommended to live with an indoor temperature of around 21 degrees centigrade to keep them fit and well. Body temperature is around 36.9 degrees centigrade, but in terms of the ambient conditions in which we live, 'comfortable' is generally accepted to be in the range of 15 to 20 degrees centigrade. This means that heat is flowing from our bodies to the environment around us, and humans at rest release a similar amount of heat to a 60W light bulb. Even our pets and animals are a source of heat – for example, a cat provides around 11W of heat input to a room. Occupants look for different levels of heat in a room in order to feel comfortable, but a room's temperature should be no higher than required to avoid unnecessary heat loss, and the use of a temperature controller or thermostat is recommended.

CORRECTLY SIZING A HEATING SYSTEM

The satisfactory performance of a heating system is very dependent on installing the correct size of boiler. A boiler that is too big or too small will result in an inefficient and expensive system. When installing any heating system, especially a renewable energy technology such as a heat pump or biomass boiler, it is important to perform a heat load, or 'heat loss' calculation for the building, to indicate how good the building is at holding on to its heat. The heat load for new buildings is determined according to the method set down in EN 12831 ('Heating Systems in Buildings – Method for Calculation of the Design Heat Load'). There are also a number

of other methods that allow estimates to be made, including the use of special software. Clearly, heat demand will vary from season to season and between years, and the heating requirement should be estimated on the basis of the maximum heat load.

A useful assessment can be made for existing properties from previous annual energy bills, averaged over a number of years. This will give a better indication than any calculation based on the house area. Rule-of-thumb estimates have been traditionally used by plumbers and heating engineers to give a rough estimate of the heat load, and these are summarized in Table 9.

USING HEATING SYSTEMS EFFECTIVELY

Building type	Heat load
Existing buildings	Over 75W/m^2
Existing buildings with CWI and roof-space insulation	Around 75W/m^2
New buildings	Around 50W/m^2
Low-energy buildings (super-insulated)	30W/m^2 or below

Table 9: Rule-of-thumb heat load for a range of buildings. *Note: Rule of thumb assessments as given here are simply estimates and must not be applied when installing boilers into new or existing buildings – a proper heat load calculation must be carried out.*

Insulation will help keep the heat in a building once it has been supplied, but it is worth considering how heating bills may be reduced and rooms made more comfortable by using the heating system as efficiently as possible. Some forms of heating are more controllable than others, although the objective is generally the same: to provide the required heat (and hot water) in the right space, when it is needed and at the lowest possible cost. Most residents have limited control over their heating systems as they simply inherit what is already installed in the house, so the trick is to make it work as efficiently as possible. The Building Regulations specify that, when installing new or replacement boilers, only condensing boilers can be used. A condensing boiler runs at a higher efficiency than a standard boiler.

Calculating a Building's Heat Loss

Calculating a building's heat loss in order to determine the size of the heating system that should be installed is sometimes called 'sizing'. The total heat requirement for a house can be estimated by calculating the heat loss for each room and then simply adding the heating requirements for all the rooms together. The principles can be extended to cover any sort of building.

In order to calculate the heat loss from a room, it is necessary to establish the following:

- The temperature difference across each wall, ceiling and floor. This is done by defining the required internal temperature and the anticipated outside temperature.
- The materials used in the construction of the walls, ceiling and floor, and their thickness, and from this the appropriate U-values.
- The area of each component (walls, ceiling, floor, doors, windows, and so on) of the room.

Another factor to take into account is air changes, quoted as 'the number of air changes per hour' (AC/h) (see Chapter 8). Regardless of how well a room is draught-proofed, there will be a certain amount of natural air change.

The calculation also has to consider heat loss through ventilation and through infiltration.

The *temperature difference* involves not just the difference between the inside of a property and the outside temperature, but also the differences between adjacent rooms. Typical UK room temperatures for different rooms are given in Table 10.

Typical U-values for some of the more common construction materials are given in Table 6. The *transmission heat loss* is the amount of heat that the fabric will conduct away, given in Watts and calculated using the U-values. Heat loss through the roof is taken to include a factor representing radiation losses (generally 15 per cent).

The *area of each construction component* is measured. Where a window or door is included on a wall, the area of the whole wall is measured and then the area of the window/door is subtracted. (Remember: units must be in either metric or imperial for consistency – do not be tempted to mix units and then convert.)

In the UK there are nominated typical values for *air changes* for each room (see Table 11). Where the rooms have not been draught-proofed, the number of air changes will increase. With each air change, there is a certain amount of heat carried away, so it is necessary to calculate the energy required to heat the volume of air in a room and multiply this by the temperature difference. Heating one cubic metre of air by one degree centigrade requires 0.36 Watts.

Typical room temperatures	°C	°F
Lounge	21	70
Dining room	21	70
Bedsitting room	21	70
Bedroom	18	65
Hall and landing	16	60
Bathroom	22	72
Kitchen	18	65
WC	18	65

Table 10: Typical room temperatures.

It is acceptable to take the temperature difference as being the difference between the design temperature of the room and the lowest winter outside temperature, which in the UK is taken to be an average of -1 degree centigrade. To be on the safe side, a universal figure of three air changes per hour can be used with confidence. The above calculations do not take into account thermal energy introduced within the property; the main contributions come from the people occupying the property

	Air changes per hour (AC/h)
Lounge	1
Dining room	2
Bedsitting room	1
Bedroom	0.5
Hall and landing	1.5
Bathroom	2
Kitchen	2
WC	1.5

Table 11: Typical air changes for various rooms.

and the heat generated by cooking and water heating for washing, and so on. In general, these contributions can be ignored.

So, the heat loss for each room is as follows:

(Watts) × (volume of the room) × (number of air changes) × (temperature difference)

For information online relating to the calculation of heat loss, see pages 181–2.

High-efficiency condensing natural gas boiler.

- Room thermostats switch the system on and off at a set temperature for each room. A master thermostat may be used in a hall or landing to give overall control of the heating system.
- Thermostatic radiator valves (TRVs) control the flow of hot water through individual radiators. TRVs are mechanical switches that are sensitive to air temperature, switching off the flow of hot water to the radiator once the temperature in the room has reached the desired level.
- A boiler thermostat is located in the boiler itself and switches it on or off when the water temperature in the boiler reaches a pre-set temperature.
- A hot-water cylinder thermostat is used to control the temperature of the water in the hot-water cylinder and will shut down the boiler when the water gets to a pre-set temperature.

Thermostats do not make the room heat up any more quickly but they do switch off the boiler when

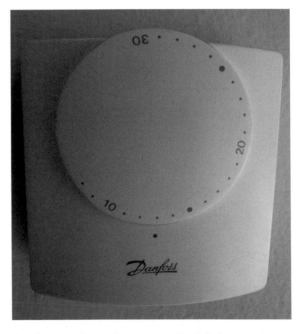

A wall-mounted room thermostat will switch the central-heating boiler on and off, depending on the temperature of the air surrounding the thermostat. If it is located in a living room, the temperature of that room will control the boiler. If it is in a hall or landing, then the temperature of the air in this space will switch the boiler on and off.

Heat wastage may be reduced by ensuring adequate insulation and installing an energy-efficient boiler, but there is another opportunity to save energy and that is through heating controls such as thermostats and time switches. These can also contribute towards substantial savings on heating bills.

There are a variety of controls available, which will provide the required room and water temperature. Those fitted to wet central-heating systems fall into a number of categories:

- Time switches or programmers switch the system on and off at predetermined times or on specified days (for example, at weekends).

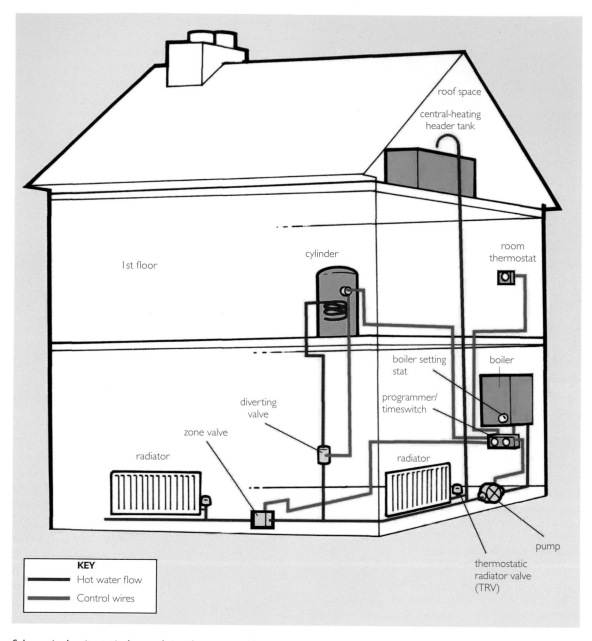

Schematic showing typical controls in a home central-heating system.

the desired temperature has been reached, thereby preventing the room overheating wastefully. They can be fitted directly to most heating devices, such as gas fires and electric heaters, or they can be mounted on room walls or in corridors, halls or landings. In most central-heating systems, the whole system is controlled from a master thermostat and the individual radiators are switched on and off with thermostatic radiator control valves (TRVs).

It is also possible to fit zone valves to control the temperature in different areas. In a house, for example, zone valves may be used to control the

Thermostatic radiator valves (TRVs) control the flow of hot water to individual radiators and so control the room temperature. They will stop the flow of hot water to the radiator when the air temperature of the room rises above the control temperature for the TRV. The desired room temperature can be manually set.

colder rooms by making sure that doors are kept shut and draught-proofed as much as possible.

It is important to understand when the heat should be switched on in order to provide acceptable comfort. This is not achieved by simply switching the heating on and off when you need it — it will take time to raise the temperature of the building and this period will depend on the temperature difference between inside and out. It will also depend on the heating system and the characteristics of the building, particularly the extent and quality of its insulation. The time the building takes to heat up and cool down is important because it will affect the average temperature. Different fabrics, furniture, wall coverings, and so on, as well as building materials demand different amounts of heat to raise their temperature by the same amount.

In a controlled system, once a heating system is switched on, it will run at full output until the control temperature is reached, at which time the master thermostat will switch the boiler off and the house will start to cool again. If individual rooms reach a comfortable temperature before the master thermostat operates, then the flow to individual radiators will

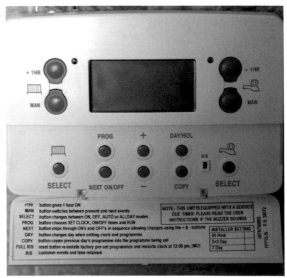

A programmable central-heating system controller will switch the heating and hot water on and off at predetermined times. In more advanced systems, a programmable timer can open and close 'zone valves' to control the flow of hot water to radiators in various parts of the house.

upstairs and downstairs heating circuits separately. A programmable controller can be used to open and close the zone valves on the heating circuit at predetermined times or temperatures.

As a general rule, only occupied rooms need to be heated, although communication spaces also need to be comfortable (albeit at a lower temperature). Some rooms may require heat to prevent condensation forming as a result of them getting too cold, but the minimum setting on TRVs will help control this. It is also worthwhile trying to keep the humid air from kitchens and bathrooms away from

be shut off by their TRVs. The thermostat will sense the temperature falling and will switch on the heating again once the pre-set value has been reached and the heating will re-start. However, there is a delay between switch-off and switch-on temperatures, known as 'hysteresis', which prevents the system switching on and off too frequently. The drop-off in temperature between switch-off and switch-on is generally insignificant in terms of the difference in temperature levels in rooms. Radiators tend to continue to give off heat for 15 to 20 minutes after the boiler has been switched off, thus reducing the rate of the room temperature fall-off.

Of course, outside temperatures vary on a daily basis and the comfort of rooms will change with this variation. On a cold day it may be necessary, therefore, to intervene manually and switch the system on earlier. Alternatively, if the room temperature gets higher than desired, the system may need to be manually switched off.

ENERGY PERFORMANCE CERTIFICATES

EPCs were originally intended to form part of the now-discontinued (except Scotland) Home Information Pack (HIP), which was to be mandatory for public sector buildings as well as homes. The requirement for an EPC will however, remain in place. In the Republic of Ireland (RoI), the Building Energy Rating (BER) is an indication of the energy performance of a dwelling (similar to the EPC). It covers energy use for space heating, water heating, ventilation and lighting, calculated on the basis of standard occupancy.

Since 1 October 2008 public buildings in the UK over 1000m² must display a Display Energy Certificate (DEC) prominently at all times. Display Energy Certificates were introduced by the British Government in response to the EU Energy Performance of Buildings Directive which all EU member states must implement by January 2009.

ENERGY EFFICIENCY AUDITS AND ENERGY RATING

In order to produce an EPC, a building energy efficiency audit or survey is carried out. This will determine how much energy is being used and identify the potential areas where it might be saved. To complete the survey, information on the house and its construction, along with the details on how and where the energy is used, are entered into a special computer programme. The programme will then process and assess the information to provide a view on how energy-efficient the building is and how good it will be at retaining (or losing) its heat. The software will identify the key areas that are losing heat and also suggest a range of possible options to reduce energy consumption using various energy-efficiency and insulation measures. It will also provide annual fuel bill estimates and payback times for the various energy saving options. Provision of this kind of information is very valuable and is often used in the planning of maintenance, repair and improvement work in local-authority and private housing stock. The software is only as good as the data that is input, so the information entered needs to be accurate to make the audit recommendations meaningful.

On completion of the audit, the building is given an energy 'rating', which will indicate how much energy it consumes and its energy running cost. There are a number of different approaches to rating a building, but the National Home Energy Rating (NHER) computer programme is accredited by the Building Research Establishment (BRE), so this makes it one of the most appropriate. Another rating process is the UK Government's Standard Assessment Procedure (SAP) energy rating, which takes into account the performance of the building's existing heating and hot-water systems as well as the building fabric when making its assessment.

Building auditing is gaining wider recognition in the UK and under the amendments to the Building Regulations, which are now in effect, all new homes are required to have an energy rating. However, other countries have led the way in this area. In the USA, for example, fuel-supply companies are obliged by law to provide a free energy rating to a customer on demand, while Denmark has insisted for many years that all houses offered for sale must have an Energy Rating Certificate. An Energy Rating Certificate provides a new owner with a statement of the home's insulation and heating standards and may also stimulate the installation of new insulation and improved heating systems.

The front page of an EPC, a five-page report rating a home's energy performance and its environmental impact. Every home offered for sale requires an EPC. A super-insulated home will have much lower energy bills than a conventional house. (Her Majesty's Stationery Office, 2010, under PSI licence)

THIS IS AN EXAMPLE REPORT AND IS NOT BASED ON AN ACTUAL PROPERTY

Section H: Energy Performance Certificate
Save money, improve comfort and help the environment

The following report is based on an inspection carried out for:

Address:	Building type: Home	Certificate number: XXXX
100 Any Street,	Whole or part of building: Whole	Date issued: XXXX
Any Town,	Assessment method: SAP	Name of inspector: XXXX
Anywhere, AB1 CD2	Date of inspection: XXXX	

This home's performance ratings

This home has been inspected and its performance rated in terms of its energy efficiency and environmental impact. This is calculated using the UK Standard Assessment Procedure (SAP) for dwellings which gives you an energy efficiency rating based on fuel cost and an environmental impact rating based on carbon dioxide (CO_2) emissions.

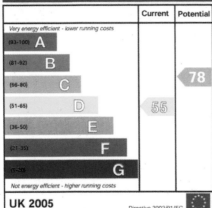

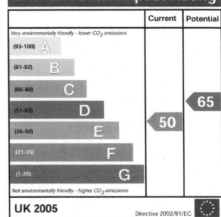

The energy efficiency rating is a measure of the overall efficiency of a home. The higher the rating the more energy efficient the home is and the lower the fuel bills will be.

The environmental impact rating is a measure of this home's impact on the environment. The higher the rating the less impact it has on the environment.

Typical fuel costs and carbon dioxide (CO_2) emissions of this home

This table provides you with an indication of how much it will cost to provide lighting, heating and hot water to this home. The fuel costs and carbon dioxide emissions are calculated based on a SAP assessment of the actual energy use that would be needed to deliver the defined level of comfort in this home, using standard occupancy assumptions, which are described on page 4. The energy use includes the energy used in producing and delivering the fuels to this home. The fuel costs only take into account the cost of fuel and not any associated service, maintenance or safety inspection costs. The costs have been provided for guidance only as it is unlikely they will match actual costs for any particular household.

	Current	Potential
Energy use	xxx kWh/m^2 per year	xxx kWh/m^2 per year
Carbon dioxide emissions	xx tonnes per year	xx tonnes per year
Lighting	£xxx per year	£xxx per year
Heating	£xxx per year	£xxx per year
Hot water	£xxx per year	£xxx per year

To see how this home's performance ratings can be improved please go to page 2

CHAPTER 3

The Building Regulations

The Building Regulations are there to help, so do not be frightened of them! The golden rule is to check with your local Building Regulations control office before you begin any work. This will ensure that the work is done safely, satisfies the law, and that it is completed in accordance with current best practice.

STAYING WITHIN THE LAW

When carrying out any type of building work – extensions, conversions or general home repairs – the work should always be completed to the highest standards and in a manner that conserves energy and reduces the emission of carbon dioxide. The Building Regulations are designed to help by ensuring that work is completed in a safe, competent manner, using best-practice techniques. Depending on what you envisage doing, when undertaking projects (including insulation work), the work that your project involves may be subject to a range of statutory requirements. These may include planning permission, fire precautions, water regulations, licensing or registration and the Party Wall etc. Act 1996. Anything other than minor jobs will almost certainly be subject to the Building Regulations.

Most properties in the UK and Ireland are covered, or, to use the more formal language of the legislation, 'controlled', by the Building Regulations. There are a number of aspects of the Regulations that cover different areas of work carried out on a building. The conservation of fuel and power is one

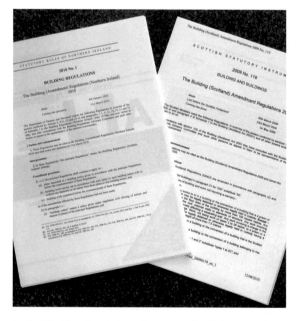

Typical Building Regulations documents for Northern Ireland and Scotland. Similar documents cover the rest of the UK and Ireland. (Her Majesty's Stationery Office, 2010, under PSI licence)

area, among others, of the Regulations that is relevant to insulation and energy-efficiency work. The Regulations discuss 'controlled items' in the context of this work. A 'controlled item' might be, for example, a new floor. The work on the floor must meet the requirements of the Building Regulations and of particular interest in this example would be the floor insulation. The table opposite lists work that

'Controlled' general work activity	Building Control required	Building Control section	Relevant chapter of this book
House conversions	Yes	All, Parts A to P	Most, but specifically 5 to 11
Building extensions or modifications	Yes	ALL, Parts A to P	Mostly 5, but other chapters relevant
Building fabric work (e.g. walls, roofs and floors)	Yes	All, Parts A to P	5, 6 and 7
Replacement openings (windows, doors, roof lights etc.)	Yes	Parts A to P, particularly Parts F, M and N	7, 8 and mostly 9
Heating system replacement and its control and pipework systems	Yes	Parts A to P, particularly Parts J and L	2, 7 and 8 and mostly 10
Other work, e.g. lighting	Generally yes, but check with local building control authority	Particularly Part P	3

Table 12: Building Control – 'controlled' activities.

will be classified as controlled work and will need to be assessed by building control.

Note: some work is not 'controlled' by building control, including emergency work such as repairs to a leaking hot water cylinder, and garden and landscape work. The table above is for illustration only and you must check with your Local Authority building control service before commencing any work. The table refers to England and Wales; although other countries will have similar, if not identical requirements.

Major work such as renovations or home extensions will require Building Regulations approval.

Complying with the Building Regulations is a separate issue from obtaining planning permission for your work; similarly, being given planning permission is not the same as complying with the Building Regulations. For information on planning requirements and procedures and links to the Building Regulations, see page 182.

The required minimum standards for building control are similar across the UK and Ireland and each region has its own set of regulations to which builders must adhere. Building Regulations across England and Wales were set down in the Building Act 1984, which has now been updated to 'The Building Regulations 2000' (as amended) and the majority of building projects are required to comply with these Regulations. In England and Wales, this is the responsibility of the Department of Communities and Local government (DCLG), which offers a series of 'approved' documents containing guidance on complying.

In Scotland the Building Regulations are set down in the Building (Scotland) Act 2003 and guidance on compliance is provided through a series of 'technical handbooks', with Section 6 dealing specifically with energy.

In Northern Ireland the Building Regulations unit of the Department of Finance and Personnel (DFP) provides guidance via a series of 'technical booklets', with 'Technical Booklet F' dealing specifically with energy.

In Ireland the relevant legislation is set down in the Building Standards, as specified in the Building

House repairs under way. Such work will require Building Regulation authorization and contact should be made with the local building control authority before work begins.

carrying out building work that is subject to the Regulations is required by law to make sure it is compliant. The Regulations specify the use of one of the two types of building control service available. The first is the building control service provided by local authorities or local councils and the second is provided by approved inspectors. There is a charge for both of these services.

The Regulations place minimum standards on building work by way of 'controlling' the various elements and fixtures and fittings which are being worked on, amended or replaced. The primary responsibility for achieving compliance with the Regulations rests with the person carrying out the work. Importantly for DIY work, if you are carrying out the work personally, the responsibility will be yours. If you are employing a builder the responsibility will usually rest with his or her company, but you should confirm this position before the work starts. You should also bear in mind that, if you are the owner of the building, it is ultimately you who may be served with an enforcement notice if the work does not comply with the Regulations. As a result, it is important to choose your builder carefully or, if the work is DIY, to have a full understanding of your obligations. Enforcement means that the work will have to be undone if it is not compliant. This situation is obviously to be avoided at all costs.

Control Act (2007). The Act is the responsibility of the Department of Environment, Heritage and Local Government (DEHLG), based in Dublin. The Irish Building Regulations have been updated to include the requirements of the Energy Performance of Buildings Directive (EPBD). Previously Part L of those Regulations required minimum performance targets (as U-values) to be reached in walls, floors, roof and glazing etc., but in May 2006 the Technical Guidance Document (TGD) or Technical Guidance Note (TGN), Part L (Conservation of Fuel and Energy – Dwellings), changed its emphasis to the goal of reducing carbon dioxide emissions.

The Regulations cover access to and the use of buildings and they exist to ensure the health and safety of people in and around all types of building (that is, domestic, commercial and industrial). They contain various sections, which deal with definitions, procedures, and what is expected in terms of the technical performance of building work. Anyone

BUILDING CONTROL SERVICES

The Local Authority building control service can be contacted through your District, Local or Borough Council. Approved inspectors are private-sector companies or practitioners who are approved for the purpose of carrying out building control service as an alternative to the Local Authority. Approved inspectors can provide a service in connection with most sorts of building project involving new buildings or work to existing buildings, including extensions or alterations to homes. For insurance reasons, most approved inspectors cannot currently deal with projects involving building new houses, flats for sale, or private renting. All approved inspectors are registered with the Construction Industry Council (CIC), which can provide a list of members (*see* pp. 181–183).

BUILDING REGULATIONS REQUIREMENTS

There are a set of 'requirements' with which building work must comply. These are contained in a schedule (Schedule 1) to the Building Regulations and are grouped under fourteen 'parts' (listed below). These deal with individual aspects of building design and construction, ranging from structural matters, fire safety and energy conservation to hygiene, sound insulation and access to and use of buildings.

These parts are also referred to as 'functional requirements' and are expressed in terms of what is 'reasonable', 'adequate' or 'appropriate'. Not all the functional requirements may apply to your building work, but all those that do apply must be adhered to as part of the overall process of complying with the Building Regulations.

Importantly for DIY enthusiasts, practical guidance on ways to comply with the functional requirements in the Building Regulations is contained in a series of 'Approved Documents', which are to be read alongside each of the fourteen 'functional requirements' set down below.

Besides containing general guidance on the performance expected of materials and building work in order to comply with each of the requirements of the Building Regulations, these documents also contain practical examples and solutions on how to achieve compliance for some of the more common building work that is undertaken. These are available from the building control website (see page 182).

The fourteen 'parts' of Schedule 1 to the Building Regulations in England and Wales are as follows:

Part A – Structural Safety
Part B – Fire Safety
Part C – Site Preparation and Reststance to Contaminants and Moisture
Part J – Heat Producing Appliances

Part L – Conservation of Fuel and Power
Part M – Access to and Use of Buildings
Part N – Glazing Safety
Part P – Electrical Safety

Part F – Ventilation

Part G – Sanitation, Hot Water Safety and Water Efficiency

Part E – Resistance to Sound

Part K – Protection from Falling

Part D – Toxic Substances

Part H – Drainage and Waste Disposal

Building control approval will be required for the areas of work to a property as identified. (E&W Building Regulations)

- A – Structural Safety
- B – Fire safety
- C – Site Preparation and Resistance to Contaminants and Moisture
- D – Toxic Substances
- E – Resistance to Sound
- F – Ventilation
- G – Sanitation, Hot Water Safety and Water Efficiency
- H – Drainage and Waste Disposal
- J – Heat Producing Appliances
- K – Protection from Falling
- L – Conservation of Fuel and Power
- M – Access to and Use of Buildings
- N – Glazing Safety
- P – Electrical Safety

(In the different regions of the UK and in Ireland, the various parts of the Regulations will not necessarily have the same designated letter; for example, Part L, which deals with the conservation of fuel and power, is designated Part F in Northern Ireland. In Ireland, TGN Part L of the Irish Building Regulations refers to 'Conservation of Fuel and Energy – Dwellings'.)

The guidance in the documents does not amount to a set of statutory requirements and does not have to be followed if you wish to design and construct your building work in some other way, providing you can show that it still complies with all the relevant requirements. Building control inspectors will check that the completed work conforms to these relevant requirements before approval is granted.

DEFINING 'BUILDING WORK'

The Building Regulations specify that the following activities amount to 'Building Work':

- The erection or extension of a building.
- The installation or extension of a service or fitting which is controlled under the Regulations.
- An alteration project involving work which will temporarily or permanently affect the ongoing compliance of the building, service or fitting with the requirements relating to structure, fire, or access to and use of buildings.
- The insertion of insulation into a cavity wall.

- The underpinning of the foundations of a building.

If whatever your project involves amounts to 'Building Work' then it must comply with the Building Regulations. This means that if you want to carry out any of the following work, then the Building Regulations will probably apply:

- putting up a new building, or extending or altering an existing one (for example, by converting a loft space into living space); or
- providing services and/or fittings in a building, such as washing and sanitary facilities (for example, WCs, showers, washbasins, kitchen sinks, and so on), hot-water cylinders, foul-water and rainwater drainage, replacement windows, fuel-burning appliances of any type (including a new or replacement boiler). (As an example, the provision of replacement double-glazing must not reduce compliance in relation to means of escape, air supply for combustion appliances and their flues, and ventilation for health.)

Generally, there is no obligation to consult with neighbours about proposed DIY building work, but it would be sensible to do so. In any event, you should be careful that your proposed building work does not interfere with neighbouring property. Any problems could lead to bad feeling and, possibly, even civil action, which could result in the removal of the work.

It is worth bearing in mind that, although the work involved in a building project may not amount to 'Building Work' as defined, and consequently may not be subject to the Building Regulations, it may be subject to other statutory regulations. Even a project that is not subject to Regulations may result in a dangerous situation, or in damage to your own or a neighbour's property, and the golden rule is always to check with your local building control authority before you start *any* work.

PROCEDURE

The correct procedure for carrying out work that is subject to Building Regulations is outlined in the flow chart below. The objective in this process is to work closely with local building control officers to ensure the smooth running of the project from inception to completion. (The flow chart is provided for guidance only, since individual building control services will have their own specific processes for applications.)

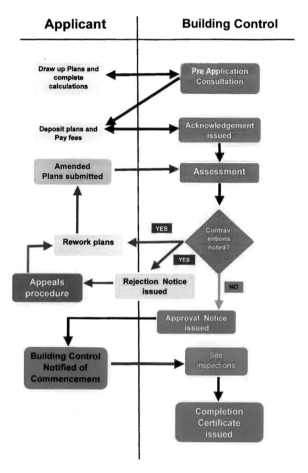

A comprehensive summary of the exemptions in the Building Regulations is listed under Appendix A of the Regulations. If you have any doubts about whether or not the work you are undertaking – DIY or otherwise – is subject to Building Regulations, you should always consult your local building control service at the earliest opportunity. Also, if you have any concerns regarding the health or safety implications of the work you intend to carry out, you should consult your building control service.

ENERGY-EFFICIENCY WORK AND THE BUILDING REGULATIONS

The following (non-exhaustive) list illustrates some common examples of the type of work which might be undertaken and explains its relevance to the Building Regulations. The examples relate to DIY work that specifically involves the installation of insulation and other energy-efficiency measures. The Building Regulations apply to the replacement and installation of windows, roof lights, roof windows, doors (with more than 50 per cent of the internal facing glazed), space heating or hot-water boilers, or a hot-water vessel.

The Building Regulations provide a range of opportunities for energy improvements. For windows, doors and roof lights on any house type, energy-efficient improvements are required where the elements are to be fully replaced. However, the requirement does not apply to repair work on parts of doors, windows or roof lights, such as replacing broken glass or sealed double-glazed units,

Points to Watch Out For

When carrying out any work on or around the house, careful planning can help prevent unnecessary disasters. There are a number of pitfalls to avoid and and points to look out for:

- work involving any form of construction close to your own home or your neighbour's boundary, which might, for example, obstruct ventilation grills to ground-floor voids, obstruct or cause the malfunctioning of boiler flues or produce boiler exhaust fumes that are a nuisance;
- in changing or replacing a central-heating boiler (which will require building control approval), particular care should be taken to make sure that the work does not adversely affect the safety of combustion devices. This might occur through altering the ventilation, damage to pipework or by excessive temperature exposure. Work should not prejudice the safe operation of gas appliances;
- in constructing a building such as a car port, conservatory or porch (all of which are exempt from the Regulations), care should still be taken to avoid any adverse effect on the safety of combustion devices.

or replacing rotten frame components. Building Regulations require all doors and windows in new-build properties to be draught-proofed. There is no similar requirement for existing properties and planning permission is not generally required for draught-proofing. If you are in any doubt, check with the local planning office.

Material Alterations

When carrying out material alterations to the building as set down below, energy improvements need to be made.

Roof insulation needs to be installed to the standard matching new homes when substantially replacing any of the major elements of a roof structure in a material alteration, or when substantially replacing any of the major elements of a roof structure. This should include improvements to airtightness. When upgrading insulation in accessible lofts where the existing insulation provides a U-value of less than $0.35W/m^2K$, additional insulation should be installed in order to achieve a U-value of $0.25W/m^2K$.

Floor insulation needs to be installed to the standard for new homes where the structure of a ground floor or exposed floor is to be substantially replaced or re-boarded. This should include improvements to airtightness.

A reasonable thickness of wall insulation, along with improvements to airtightness, should be installed when substantially replacing complete exposed walls or external renderings or cladding, or internal surface finishes.

If buildings are subject to a material 'change of use', energy improvements are required in accordance with new-build standards. Lighting needs to be provided in accordance with new-build standards.

Heating Systems and Hot Water

Currently, if a heating boiler is to be replaced in a home with a floor area of greater than $50m^2$ then the boiler needs to be provided as if for a new home. Ordinary oil or gas boilers should be replaced with a condensing boiler with an effective SEDBUK percentage rating of at least 78 for gas and 85 for oil. It will need to include appropriate zone controls, timing controls and boiler control interlocks. Back boilers should have a separate rating of

at least 3 percentage points lower than that shown above. Solid-fuel boiler efficiencies must equal the recommendation for their type as set out in the HETAS certification scheme (*see* page 182).

When replacing hot-water vessels, equipment must meet the standard set out for a new building. In normal cases this will involve 50mm factory-applied insulation, but good practice standards suggest 80mm factory-applied insulation that does not contain HCFCs. Boiler and hot-water storage controls must be included with any new installation, to include the time switch and programmer, room thermostat and hot-water vessel thermostat

Building Regulations will apply for the installation of a replacement hot-water cylinder within an unvented hot-water storage system.

and provision of a boiler interlock and fully pumped circulation. Alternatively, if work is carried out to the above elements in accordance with guidance in good practice guide GPG 155 (2001), this will be acceptable as long as the overall carbon index is achieved. GPG 155 was updated in 2003 to exceed Building Regulations requirements.

Advice and Information

Information must be provided for the operation and maintenance of heating and hot-water systems. This could take the form of easy-to-understand guidance on the specific boiler and heating system installed. It should also identify the level of routine maintenance needed for efficient operation. Heating and hot-water systems should also be inspected after installation to ensure effective operation. Responsibility for this lies with the contractor or the individual installing the system.

Examples

It is worth saying that the DIY installation of insulation must not introduce any form of danger into a construction project. Neither should it compromise the structural strength of floors or other building fabric components.

Insulation in Loft Conversions

The Building Regulations will apply when carrying out a loft conversion to a home. The appropriate requirements of the Regulations ensure that the structural strength of the proposed floor is sufficient; the stability of the structure (including the roof) is not endangered; safe escape from fire is possible; the stairs to the new floor are safely designed; and there is reasonable sound insulation between the conversion and the rooms below. In some instances, loft conversion projects may be subject to the Party Wall etc. Act 1996, under which it may be a requirement to give adjoining owners notice of the intended work (see Appendix II, 'Building Regulations').

A loft conversion, or new loft rooms, will need to be insulated in accordance with the Building Regulations, Conservation of Fuel and Power. This work includes installing insulation between the loft room ceiling and the roof. The installation of loft and roof insulation is detailed in Chapter 7.

Replacement Windows

The Building Regulations apply if you want to replace the whole of the fixed frame and opening parts of one or more windows in any type of building, with double-glazing or other windows that have a higher thermal performance. If the work is being done in your home and you employ a FENSA (Fenestration Self-Assessment Scheme) registered installer, you will not need to involve a building control service. On completion, the installer must give the Local Authority or Council a certificate that confirms that the work complies with Part L and other appropriate parts of the Building Regulations. You will also be provided with a certificate of compliance for your records (see flow chart, page 43). The installation of new window systems provides a great opportunity to improve airtightness and upgrade their thermal performance and is detailed in Chapter 9.

If the work amounts to no more than, for example, replacing broken glass, replacing fogged double-glazing units, replacing some rotten sashes (the opening parts of sliding windows) in the main window frame, replacing rotten sections of the main frame members or applying any form of draught-sealing or draught-proofing strips, then the work will not be subject to the Building Regulations.

Listed Buildings

If your building is listed nationally, or locally in some way, because of its architectural or historic interest and/or is located in a sensitive urban or rural environment (for example, a Conservation Area or an Area of Outstanding Beauty), you should note that English Heritage has produced an Interim Guidance Note on the application of Part L ('Conservation of Fuel and Power') of the Building Regulations. This Note offers advice on ways in which to balance the needs for energy conservation with those of building conservation (see page 182). Other regions of the UK and Ireland will have similar guidance.

Cavity-Wall Insulation (CWI)

The Building Regulations will apply to the installation of cavity-wall insulation, which they specifically define as 'building work'. The appropriate requirements will be applied so as to ensure that the insulation material is suitable for the wall construction,

| | Construction | U-value | \multicolumn{5}{c}{Possible insulation product solution} |
			Celotex 3000	Kingspan	Xtratherm	Thermal plasterboard	Glass or rock fibre
Solid wall (Chapter 5)	200mm thick solid wall constructed using high-performance thermal block, such as Celotex Solar or similar	0.3	–	–	–	55mm thick ThermaLine SUPER	–
Solid wall (Chapter 5)	215mm thick solid wall constructed using high-performance thermal block, such as Celotex Solar or similar	0.3	–	Thermawall TW 55 52.5mm thick		50mm thick ThermaLine SUPER	–
Solid wall (Chapter 5)	250mm thick solid wall constructed using high-performance thermal block, such as Celotex Solar or similar	0.3	–	Thermawall TW 55 47.5mm thick		50mm thick ThermaLine PLUS	–
Solid wall (Chapter 5)	265mm solid wall constructed using high-performance thermal block, such as Thermalite Turbo or similar	0.3	–	Thermawall TW 55 47.5mm thick		45mm thick ThermaLine PLUS	–
Solid wall (Chapter 5)	250mm solid wall constructed using high-performance thermal block, such as Durox 400	0.3	–	Thermawall TW 55 42.5mm thick	–	45mm thick ThermaLine PLUS	–
Cavity wall (Chapter 5)	Brick/100mm lightweight block cavity wall	0.3	50mm thick in a 75mm cavity	50mm thick Thermawall TW 50 in a 75mm cavity	50mm thick in a 75mm cavity	–	80mm cavity batt with 115mm block
Cavity wall (Chapter 5)	Block/100mm lightweight block cavity wall	0.3	35mm thick in a 75mm cavity	35mm thick Thermawall TW 50 in a 75mm cavity	35mm thick in a 75mm cavity	–	80mm cavity batt

Table 13: Typical insulation schemes which satisfy the Building regulations.

Note: All data relating to specific products has been sourced from the manufacturers at the time of writing. They are typical examples for information only and are not specifically recommended by any Building Control Office. All the listed materials must be installed in strict accordance with manufacturers' guidance and with due regard to the need to ensure continuity of insulation and a reasonable standard of airtightness.

To achieve the target U-values shown here, the product solutions listed will provide the target value if used at the suggested thickness. For example, to give a U-value of 0.3 in a 250mm thick solid wall constructed using Durox 400, 42.5mm of Kingspan rigid polyurethane board TW55 (internal insulation in studwork) or 45mm thick ThermaLine PLUS polystyrene laminate insulated plasterboard can be used (internal insulation).

Celotex Solar are thermal blocks with good insulation performance suitable for use in solid- or cavity-wall construction.

Durox Supabloc 400 is primarily used for the load-bearing inner leaf of external cavity walls. Other key applications are solid walls, load-bearing and non-load-bearing walls.

Thermalite Turbo building block offers very high thermal insulation properties and is therefore ideal for external wall applications where low U-values are required.

Kingspan Thermawall TW 50/55 is high-performance urethane insulation that can be used in timber or metal wall framing systems.

Gyproc ThermaLine Super is a laminated plasterboard with integrated vapour control and with layers of thermal insulation such as expanded polystyrene, extruded polystyrene or phenolic foam.

The products and manufacturers are listed for example only; no preference or guarantee of any specific product performance is implied.

	Construction	U-value	Possible insulation product solution				
			Celotex 3000	Kingspan	Xtratherm	Thermal plasterboard	Glass or rock fibre
Cavity wall (Chapter 5)	Brick/100mm medium-weight block cavity wall	0.3	45mm thick in a 75mm cavity	45mm thick Thermawall TW 50 in a 75mm cavity	45mm thick in a 75mm cavity	–	90mm cavity batt
Stud walls Dormers	125 × 50mm timber frame at 400mm centres with tile hanging to outside face	0.3	112mm thick between studs	70mm thick between 100 × 50mm studs 12mm across inside face	112mm thick between studs	30mm ThermaLine with 75mm Celotex between 100 × 50mm studs	N/A
Pitched roofs and sloping ceilings in loft conversions (Chapter 7)	Insulation between ceiling joists at 400mm centres	0.16	70mm across underside with 150mm fibreglass between joists	60mm TP10 underside and 150mm fibreglass between joists	60mm across underside with 150mm fibreglass between joists	N/A	100mm between and 150mm across joists
	Insulation between ceiling joists at 600mm centres	0.16	This assumes that storage is required on top of ceiling	80mm TP10 underside and 100mm fibreglass between joists		N/A	100mm between and 150mm across joists
Pitched roofs and sloping ceilings in loft conversions (Chapter 7)	Sloping ceiling in new building, extension or loft conversion with rafters at 400mm centres and 50mm airspace over	0.2	50mm between and 75mm across underside	50mm between and 70mm across underside	50mm between and 75mm across underside		N/A
	Sloping ceiling in new building, extension or loft conversion with rafters at 600mm centres and 50mm airspace over	0.2	90mm between and 40mm across underside	75mm between and 45mm across underside	50mm between and 70mm across underside		N/A
Flat roofs (Chapter 7)	Warm pitched roof with insulation on top of rafters	0.2	100mm made from a combination of thicknesses	100mm TP10 ensuring counter battens under tiles	100mm ensuring counter battens under tiles	N/A	N/A
	Warm deck flat roof	0.2	115mm TD3115	96mm TR31 with 20mm TP10 placed between joist to underside TR31		N/A	N/A
	Flat cold deck roof with joists at 400mm centres ensuring 50mm ventilated air space over insulation	0.2	100mm between with 40mm across underside	170mm cut between joists		100mm Kingspan between with 50mm ThermaLine SUPER across	
Floors (Chapter 6)	Timber ground-floor joists at 400mm centres	0.22	120mm	120mm	120mm	N/A	175mm between joists
	Solid concrete floor	0.22	75mm	75mm	75mm	N/A	125mm polystyrene
	Timber floor at 400mm centres over a garage	0.22	125mm	125mm	125mm	N/A	200mm glass or rock fibre

Building work including an extension will require building control approval. (Xtratherm Insulation Limited, xtratherm.com)

and that, in the case of some foam insulants, the risk of formaldehyde gas emission is assessed (*see* Chapter 5).

Replacement Hot-Water Cylinder

If you are installing or replacing a hot-water cylinder within an unvented hot-water storage system (in other words, a system supplied directly from the cold water mains with no open-ended pipe for venting and with a storage capacity greater than 15 litres), then the Building Regulations will apply. The requirements are for hot water to be safely stored under pressure and for the installation to be energy-efficient. The cylinder should only be installed by a person competent to do the work.

The Regulations will also apply if you are installing or replacing a hot-water cylinder within a vented hot-water storage system. The requirements are for the installation to be energy-efficient. Details of tank and pipework insulation are given in Chapter 10.

In all cases, to determine whether or not your work needs to achieve compliance with the Regulations, you must contact your Local Authority or Council building control service, or an approved inspector's building control service. Full details of where copies of the Building Regulations can be obtained are given on pp.181–183.

AMENDMENTS TO THE BUILDING REGULATIONS

To keep the Building Regulations up to date and relevant they may be amended from time to time. Following the 1997 Kyoto Agreement, international and European governments committed to reduce by 20 per cent the carbon emissions created through the burning of fossil fuels (*see* Chapter 1). The European Parliament passed laws requiring Member

States to put in place national legislation, under the Energy Performance of Building Directive (EPBD). This was to ensure that all energy usage in new and existing buildings is assessed and made known to the building owners or those renting, leasing or otherwise using the building. In the UK the Microgeneration and Sustainable Energy Act 2006 makes provision for microgeneration to be brought within the Building Regulations and increases to two years the time limit for prosecuting contraventions relating to energy use, energy conservation or carbon emissions.

In 2006 important amendments were introduced to the Building Regulations, which required energy in new and existing buildings to be measured. The scope of 'building work' was also extended to include renovation of thermal elements and energy used by space-cooling systems as well as space heating. New additional 'competent persons' schemes were proposed and authorized in respect of energy systems and energy-efficient design.

CONSERVATION OF FUEL AND POWER

One section of the Regulations specifically addresses the conservation of fuel and power (Part L in England and Wales, Part J in Scotland and Part F in Northern Ireland) and this has been amended in line with developing environmental and climate change policy. These amendments relate to energy conservation, flues and fuel storage, access to commercial buildings and consequential changes regarding glazing and stairs.

Buildings are estimated to contribute around 50 per cent of the total UK energy use and domestic homes account for approximately two-thirds of this. Amendments to the Building Regulations can help significantly to reduce this energy consumption; so far there has been a reduction in carbon emissions of some 40 to 45 per cent on 2005 levels, with a similar reduction in fuel bills. The national methodology established for calculating energy rating is set down in two software suites: for dwellings, the Standard Assessment Procedure, or SAP, and for buildings other than dwellings, the Standard Buildings Energy Model, or SBEM.

The amendments or changes aimed at cutting carbon dioxide emissions take into account the following aspects of the building:

- its type, shape and size;
- insulation levels of floors, walls, roofs and windows (U-values);
- number, size and type of windows and orientation of the building;
- boiler efficiency, fuel type and the controls for space heating and hot water;
- secondary heating efficiency and type of fuel used;
- construction – its quality and the airtightness of the building;
- efficiency and controls of fixed internal and external lighting.

They also incorporate the introduction of low- or zero-carbon technologies, such as solar panels, wind turbines and photovoltaic (PV) panels. For building designers, building control officers and architects, the changes will be far-reaching, requiring a new building to produce less carbon dioxide than a standard building.

There is a certain procedure for assessing the building, which is as follows. First, the Target Carbon Dioxide Emissions Rate (TER) is established, measured in kilograms of carbon dioxide per square metre per year (kg CO_2 /m^{2}yr), using the characteristics

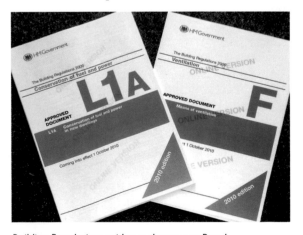

Building Regulations guidance documents Part L – conservation of fuel and power and Part F – ventilation (England and Wales). (Her Majesty's Stationery Office, 2010, under PSI licence)

of the proposed building and the SAP 2005 software package. The detailed design of the dwelling is then undertaken, using the exact figures relating to the building criteria listed above (using U-values for walls, floor, roof, windows, boiler type, and so on), to provide a Dwelling Carbon Dioxide Emissions Rate (DER), again using the SAP 2005 computer software. If the DER is less than the TER the dwelling will comply with the Building Regulations. If the DER is more than the TER, then the design needs to be revisited and measures taken to reduce the DER. This may involve the use of a more efficient boiler and heating controls, increased insulation in walls, floors or roof, windows with a lower U-value, low- or zero-energy technologies, such as a solar panel for water heating, or a combination of all these components. The approach is to look at the whole building with all its separate components (a holistic approach), to ensure the overall building complies with the Regulations.

There are limiting values set for the components of the building, such as the fabric, to prevent condensation and ensure a reasonable level of insulation. This means that, in the event of any future removal of energy-saving equipment, the building will remain reasonably energy-efficient. DIY constructors or builders will need to 'quality assure' their work (or that of their tradesmen) by making sure that specified construction details are adhered to and regularly checked. The Regulations call for air-testing of a dwelling, to check that heated air is not escaping through heat paths or leaks in the building (see Chapter 8). Heating and ventilation equipment and controls must be properly commissioned with certification by competent persons, and adequate operating and maintenance instructions should be supplied in the form of a manual, set out in language that the layman will understand. At the end of every job the energy rating of the 'as constructed' building must be calculated and a copy of the Energy Rating displayed in the building (in an Energy Performance Certificate or EPC).

Under the amended Regulations, measures should be undertaken to improve the energy rating of existing properties when thermal elements such as roofs, walls or floors are significantly altered, or controlled fittings and services such as doors, boilers, hot-water heaters, ventilation and lighting systems are replaced. The emphasis here is placed on the word 'significant' and clearly many insulation jobs, such as loft or underfloor insulation, can be completed on a DIY basis. A new energy rating calculation will always be required when any work affecting the energy efficiency is undertaken in the home.

The same situation applies with non-domestic buildings insofar as the design buildings must incorporate energy-efficient construction methods with additional energy-saving measures, to reduce carbon dioxide emissions to approximately 40 to 48 per cent below 2005 levels. Energy rating calculations will be required for new non-domestic buildings when they are constructed and when alterations or extensions, or additions or replacements of controlled fittings or services are undertaken that affect the energy efficiency. The SBEM methodology is used in the energy-efficiency calculation for buildings that are not dwellings. The basis for the calculation is the establishment of the carbon dioxide emission for a notional building of similar form to that proposed. This notional figure is then adjusted by an 'improvement factor' related to the type of services in the building and by a factor of a further 10 per cent, known as the LZC (low- or zero-carbon) factor, to encourage the use of these new technologies in commercial applications. Similar requirements will apply to a non-domestic building as to a dwelling, and these require quality assurance of construction, air-testing, commissioning of mechanical and electrical equipment, and provision of operation and maintenance instructions. Where work is being undertaken to an existing commercial building over 1000m^2, such as in the creation of an extension, the building must be brought up to the latest thermal standards, using insulation or materials with an improved thermal performance, and subject to a fifteen-year payback period.

The key point is that, regardless of whether the building is a dwelling or a business construction, when alteration or renovation is being undertaken there will be a requirement to bring particular elements of the construction up to the current thermal standards. When the construction work has been completed, an energy rating calculation will be required by building control and the details of the energy rating will have to be included in the building logbook and displayed in the building.

For your guidance and to help you and your builders to order and use the correct materials, and of course to prevent any unnecessary delays, expenditure and problems on site, Table 13 provides some suggested alternative ways of achieving the new standards.

BUILDING REGULATIONS AND ZERO-CARBON HOUSING

In December 2006, the UK Government made an important announcement, stating that by 2017 every new home constructed in the UK should be a zero-carbon home. The requirement to design for zero-carbon housing is a challenge because it implies that absolutely no carbon is released as part of the normal activities that take place in the dwelling. This raises the issue of how to provide a source for the energy for heating and for running the electrical appliances that are so much an essential part of modern life. The first part of the solution must be conservation and super-insulation. The second part requires source(s) of heat and electricity generation that have no carbon dioxide emissions. Small micro-generators integrated into buildings, spread across the country in domestic dwellings, businesses and the public estate, have the potential to meet much of the demand for heat and electricity in those buildings. This means that losses due to centralized generation, transmission and distribution can be reduced, or even virtually eliminated, which would help defer electricity grid re-enforcements and upgrades.

There are three strands to achieving the zero-carbon home objective:

- Progressive tightening of building control regulations over the next decade to improve energy efficiency of construction.
- The creation of a new Code for Sustainable Homes (CSH).
- Amendment to the planning legislation to account for carbon emissions.

The primary measurement of energy efficiency in the Building Regulations is the Dwelling Carbon Dioxide Emissions Rate (DER), an estimate of carbon dioxide emissions per m^2 of floor area described earlier. Proposed revisions to the Regulations require a 25 per cent reduction in DER. A further review in 2013 will seek a 44 per cent improvement, with zero-carbon emission from 2016. The challenge is to bring forward creative solutions such as the increased use of low-carbon technologies, for example, heat pumps. The CSH was launched in 2006 to supersede the BRE EcoHomes scheme. Initially it will apply only in England, with Scotland, Wales and Northern Ireland still applying the EcoHomes code. The CSH allocates points in nine areas: energy, potable water, surface water run-off, materials, construction site waste/household waste, pollution, health and well-being, management and ecology. Codes 5 and 6 are extremely challenging, prompting difficult questions around how zero carbon may be achieved and exactly what this means in practice. Progress towards the zero-carbon home is shown in the table.

CSH level	Percentage better than DER (on 2006 basis)	Note	Building Regulations route map timescale
1	10%	EST Good Practice	
2	18%		
3	25%	EST Best Practice	2010
4	44%	Near PassivHaus	2013
5	100%	Zero space/water heating and lighting	
6	Zero carbon home	Zero including cooking and appliances	2016

Table 14: CSH and Building Regulations energy requirements.
Note: EST is the Energy Saving Trust. The term 'PassivHaus' refers to a specific construction standard for residential buildings that have excellent comfort conditions in both winter and summer.

CHAPTER 4

Insulating Materials

The challenge is to achieve the most effective insulation performance in any given application, with the lowest environmental impact at least cost.

HOW INSULATION WORKS

Insulation works by creating small cells or pockets of static air in the walls, floors or ceilings of a building. These unmoving pockets of air do not transfer heat as effectively as an unimpeded, freely moving airstream. The air pockets are held rigidly within the insulation materials, which are required to provide a stable, lightweight structure, with an overall good resistance to heat flow across them. The job of insulation is to ensure as far as possible that the mechanisms of heat transfer (see Chapter 2) are not permitted to function.

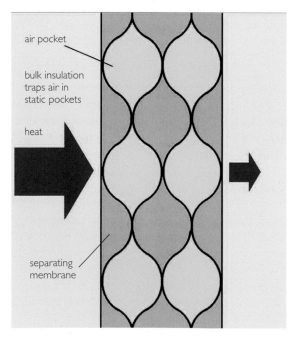

Air cells, constrained to be static, can provide insulation in a range of applications.

DIFFERENT TYPES OF INSULATION

There are a wide variety of insulating materials available to the DIY enthusiast and it can be very difficult to determine which product is most suitable for any given job. A number of very useful web-based resources – including the NGS Greenspec website, the Building Research Establishment (BRE) Green Guide website and the Energy Saving Trust's insulation materials chart (CE71) – deal with the various products in some detail, explaining how they are best suited to the range of applications, and making recommendations. Products range from the very familiar mineral wools and polystyrene, through to natural products, such as sheep's wool and hemp.

Insulation materials can be grouped in three general categories, based loosely on their origin:

1 natural insulation (derived from plants or animals);
2 mineral insulation; and
3 oil-derived insulation.

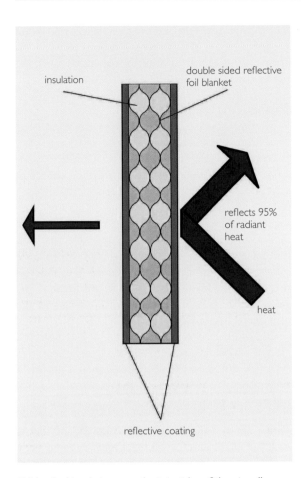

insulation

double sided reflective foil blanket

reflects 95% of radiant heat

heat

reflective coating

Foil-backed insulation uses the principles of the air cells above, but also reflects heat into the required area.

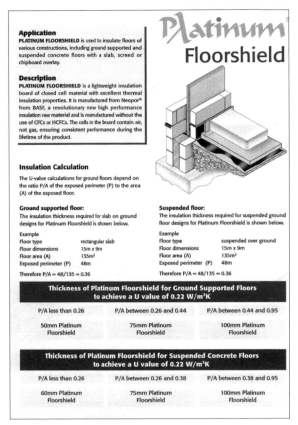

Application
PLATINUM FLOORSHIELD is used to insulate floors of various constructions, including ground supported and suspended concrete floors with a slab, screed or chipboard overlay.

Description
PLATINUM FLOORSHIELD is a lightweight insulation board of closed cell material with excellent thermal insulation properties. It is manufactured from Neopor® from BASF, a revolutionary new high performance insulation raw material and is manufactured without the use of CFCs or HCFCs. The cells in the board contain air, not gas, ensuring consistent performance during the lifetime of the product.

Insulation Calculation
The U-value calculations for ground floors depend on the ratio P/A of the exposed perimeter (P) to the area (A) of the exposed floor.

Ground supported floor:
The insulation thickness required for slab on ground designs for Platinum Floorshield is shown below.

Example
Floor type   rectangular slab
Floor dimensions   15m x 9m
Floor area (A)   135m²
Exposed perimeter (P) 48m

Therefore P/A = 48/135 = 0.36

Suspended floor:
The insulation thickness required for suspended ground floor designs for Platinum Floorshield is shown below.

Example
Floor type   suspended over ground
Floor dimensions   15m x 9m
Floor area (A)   135m²
Exposed perimeter (P) 48m

Therefore P/A = 48/135 = 0.36

Thickness of Platinum Floorshield for Ground Supported Floors to achieve a U value of 0.22 W/m²K		
P/A less than 0.26	P/A between 0.26 and 0.44	P/A between 0.44 and 0.95
50mm Platinum Floorshield	75mm Platinum Floorshield	100mm Platinum Floorshield

Thickness of Platinum Floorshield for Suspended Concrete Floors to achieve a U value of 0.22 W/m²K		
P/A less than 0.26	P/A between 0.26 and 0.38	P/A between 0.38 and 0.95
60mm Platinum Floorshield	75mm Platinum Floorshield	100mm Platinum Floorshield

Springvale 'Platinum Floorshield' data sheet showing typical product information provided by suppliers and manufacturers of insulation material. (Springvale Insulation Ltd, springvale.com)

Some insulating materials will be better suited to certain applications and it pays to do thorough planning before selecting a particular product for any given job.

CHOOSING THE RIGHT INSULATION MATERIAL

The most important aspect is the material's thermal and structural performance over the lifetime of the building. Ideally it should provide the designed-for resistance to the passage of heat throughout the building's lifetime, without settlement or sagging and with no degradation in performance or structure. A good starting point is the insulation manufacturer's published performance specification sheet, but there

are a range of additional factors associated with the actual 'in situ' performance of the material that also need to be considered as part of the process.

Ease of Installation

It is vital for an installer (either a builder or a DIY enthusiast) to be able to install the insulation materials easily. For example, there must be no gaps between adjoining insulation board slabs, or between the slabs and other construction components that form part of the overall insulation envelope, such as rafters or joists. Gaps will allow the passage of air through the insulation layer and this will result in a reduction in performance. Joints should be taped with the appropriate adhesive tape to ensure that they are airtight.

Shrinkage, Compaction, Settlement or Sag

Once installed, some materials are likely to change their shape and form over time. For most products this can be anticipated and to an extent overcome, through choosing the right material, and carrying out careful planning and proper installation. In order to minimize the impact, guidance should be sought from the manufacturer as to the anticipated shrinkage, compaction or settlement of the product. This information will be particularly important if the insulating material is new and does not have an established record of installed performance, or where the conditions under which the product will operate are likely to be onerous or close to the design specification.

Prevention of Moisture Ingress

Some insulation materials will suffer a degradation of performance when moist or wet. This can be anticipated from the manufacturer's specification for the product. Insulation can be appropriately protected from moisture at installation but, if moisture is likely to penetrate, or if the insulation will experience prolonged exposure at high relative humidity (RH over 95 per cent), then a suitably moisture-resistant material should be selected. This can be particularly important when using internal dry-lining on solid walls that are prone to damp. Great care needs to

be taken to avoid the introduction of condensation or damp into a wall system. If there are any concerns about damp or moisture ingress, a professional contractor should be consulted.

Environmental Impact

With the increasing awareness of environmental issues, concerns have been raised as to the environmental impact of the materials used in construction. This impact has become the subject of government guidance in recent years, notably with the introduction of the Code for Sustainable Housing (CSH). Making the right decision on a particular insulation material's environmental merits is difficult because there is a profusion of claims for one material over another. The challenge is to achieve the most effective insulation performance, in any given application, with the lowest environmental impact, at least cost.

One method that can be used to compare the lifetime environmental impact of different products – that is, the impact from extraction and manufacture, through operation to the eventual removal and recycling (where appropriate) – is to use a Life Cycle Assessment (LCA). This 'cradle to grave' approach, as it is known, can be undertaken for each material, enabling a fair assessment to be made. LCA is still under development, with some products already having been assessed, but the vast majority

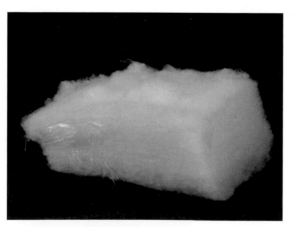

Loft insulation made from 85 per cent recycled plastic bottles. The insulation is around 250mm thick and is suitable for loft top-ups or new installations. (Homeseal Insulation Installers, Magherafelt, NI, homesealni.co.uk)

Polystyrene beads used in cavity-wall insulation. The beads are blown into the cavity and held together with a binder to prevent movement. (Homeseal Insulation Installers, Magherafelt, NI, homesealni.co.uk)

still remain to be tested. The eventual aim is to have these assessments carried out, independently if possible, for each product, on an agreed standardized basis. International standard ISO 14040 provides a method by which product life-cycle analyses may be assessed and compared. However, the conclusions of this approach cannot be compared with other LCA results.

A further, more exacting method of providing good environmental comparisons is to use the PAS 2050 standard on carbon footprints. PAS 2050 is more rigorous than ISO 14040. It is likely that, in the long term, LCAs will become more standardized, with a common approach to reporting all the variables. When attempting to compare different products on the basis of their environmental impacts, caution must be exercised to ensure that products are compared on a truly like-for-like basis.

Embodied Energy

The embodied energy of an insulation product is a measure of the energy necessary to manufacture, transport and deliver the insulation product to the point of supply. It is, however, crucially important to consider embodied energy within the wider context of the significant energy saving that will result from the installation of the product over its lifetime. Most of the energy a building consumes during its lifetime is 'operational or functional energy', that is, the energy required to provide space heating, raise the temperature of water or power appliances.

An insulation material should be considered first for its thermal performance and only subsequently for its environmental impact. If a building has been designed to be constructed using the very highest standards of insulation (that is, to a standard of 'Passivhaus' or the Code for Sustainable Homes levels 4, 5 and 6), only then can it be appropriate to consider the embodied energy as a potential environmental impact. Once that level of insulation has been achieved, the embodied energy of the insulation may be considered as a relevant factor in the overall lifetime energy expenditure of the building. Energy conserved through the appropriate installation of insulation far outweighs the energy consumed in its manufacture (the embodied energy). (Source: Greenspec, greenspec.co.uk, 2010)

50mm thick polystyrene board glued to the ceiling of a basement room will provide insulation for the living space above.

Embodied energy values can be expressed as the energy used to produce one kilogram of insulation material (kWh/kg), but for any useful comparison to be made between insulation materials, thermal performance and material density need to be included. Thus, for example, based on rough assumptions, for 1m^2 of surface to attain a U-value of 0.2W/m^{2}K, the energy required would be the thickness of the material x material density x embodied energy value.

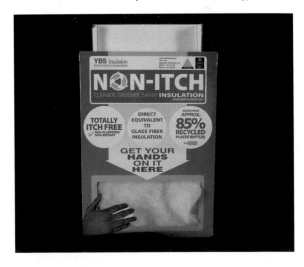

Non-itch insulation made from recycled plastic bottles (85%) is widely available and is very suitable for DIY installation. (Homeseal Insulation Installers, Magherafelt, NI, homesealni.co.uk)

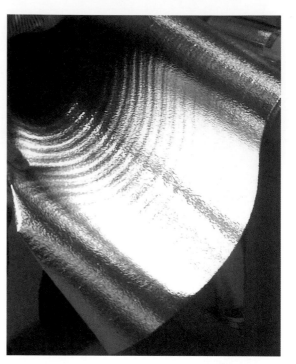

Cellulose insulation that has been blown in to the loft of a detached house. It provides a good covering over all the loft surfaces.

Reflective foil-backed insulation roll, a product that is very suitable for a range of applications and can be stapled or nailed to roof timbers or to the joists below suspended floors.

Knauf Loftroll glass mineral wool insulation suitable for loft insulation. (Homeseal Insulation Installers, Magherafelt, NI, homesealni.co.uk)

Foil-backed insulation board is suitable for use in a range of applications including solid-floor insulation.

Selecting Materials According to Environmental Suitability

To help identify materials for construction or insulation that are suitable from an environmental perspective, the Building Research Establishment (BRE) has published a set of guides (or Green Guides). The Green Guide is part of BREEAM (BRE Environmental Assessment Method), which is an accredited environmental rating scheme for buildings, and contains more than 1200 specifications used in various types of building. The Guide examines the relative environmental impacts of the construction materials commonly used in six different generic types of building, including commercial buildings such as offices, educational, health-care and retail sites, as well as residential and industrial properties.

The environmental rankings are based on Life Cycle Assessments (LCAs), using BRE's Environmental Profiles Methodology 2008.

Materials and components, including insulation, are arranged on an elemental basis so that designers and specifiers can compare and select from comparable systems, or materials. The elements covered are external walls, internal walls and partitions, roofs, ground floors, upper floors, windows, insulation, landscaping and floor finishes.

This data is set out as an A+ to E rating system, where A+ represents the best environmental performance/least environmental impact, and E the worst environmental performance/most environmental impact. BRE's Green Guide rating covers the following issues: climate

Sheep's-wool insulation, a natural product that is well suited to a range of applications including lofts.

change, water extraction, mineral resource extraction, stratospheric ozone depletion, human toxicity, ecotoxicity to freshwater, nuclear waste, ecotoxicity to land, waste disposal, fossil fuel depletion, eutrophication, photochemical ozone creation and acidification.

Hemp insulation slabs, similar to sheep's-wool insulation in that it is natural and appropriate for a range of applications, including lofts.

Through evaluating the performance of materials and building systems to protect against these specific environmental impacts, it is possible to select specifications on the basis of personal or organizational preferences or priorities. This will help make decisions based on the performance of a material selected for its particular environmental impact. Perceptions regarding best environmental practice are subject to change as understanding increases and a clear consensus develops regarding what is the most important and what is the best 'practically achievable performance'.

(Source: BRE website, bre.co.uk/greenguide/podpage. jsp?id=2126)

The NGS GreenSpec website is very comprehensive and helpful for those intending to construct or undertake DIY work. The site has a wealth of information on the mechanical and environmental properties of a vast range of construction materials. (GreenSpec, greenspec.co.uk)

The following section reviews the key environmental impacts and performance issues associated with the most important available insulation materials. When selecting any product on the basis of its environmental credentials or embodied energy, the data available within the public domain and on manufacturers' data sheets should be treated with caution. The limited amount of data available and the inconsistency of the methods used to evaluate the properties of the various insulation products mean that the basis for comparison is far from perfect.

INSULATING MATERIALS AND PRODUCTS AVAILABLE

The tables on pages 60–64 set out a variety of the commonly used insulating materials, with a summary of some of their properties and applications. The products are listed in the three categories of natural products, mineral-based products and oil-derived materials.

Most of these materials and products will be available to DIY enthusiasts and will be off-the-shelf, through the popular DIY outlet stores. Assuming the proper precautions are taken and the necessary protective clothing is worn, most materials are safe to handle and install, and they will release little in the way of gaseous emissions once in place. However, some of the products, notably those that have been derived from oil, may over time release trace amounts of unpleasant vapours, such as formaldehyde, CFCs or styrene. Polystyrene, polyurethane, polyisocyanurate, polystyrene foam and phenolic foam are the most likely offenders, although some of the mineral wools may release small quantities of fine fibre particles into the air circulating within the building. Vapours from some of the product binders, insecticides and fire retardants are also released, even from the natural products, during installation and when in situ.

The tables set out the principal features of the insulation materials, including the potential to recycle products at life-end, and their carbon dioxide friendliness, that is, whether they are net absorbers or emitters of CO_2 during their manufacture and transport to their final installation. The tables also detail the products' environmental impact in terms of embodied energy and source of origin, and their ease of installation, and note any particular issues associated with their ability to resist fire, vermin, insects, pests and moisture.

The most important aspects of these materials and products is their physical suitability within homes and buildings to their intended area of application, and to their thermal performance (thermal conductivity).

There has been an increasing awareness that natural products can now be used in place of oil- and mineral-derived products although the cost difference between the alternative products may well be an issue when making this decision.

Product Thermal Conductivity

The table on page 65 shows the thermal conductivities (W/mK) for the range of products. It also shows the environmental ratings of different types of insulation (with A being the best), which have been extracted from the assessments in BRE's 'Green Guide to Specification'. It also shows the impacts associated with extraction, manufacture, transport and disposal, referred to above as 'embodied energy' (or 'embodied impacts'). The comparison between materials is on the basis of similar thermal resistance, rather than mass or volume. (Sources: BRE 'Green Guide To Specification' and Energy Saving Trust information leaflet CE71).

Product Application Guide

The table on page 66 provides a guide to those products that may be most suitable for a range of the applications normally encountered in DIY jobs, some of which have been highlighted to indicate their most common uses. (A blank cell does not necessarily mean that this type of insulation product is not used for a particular application.) The properties of an insulation product should always be checked using the manufacturer's data sheets prior to installation.

Material	Manufacture/ Recycling	Application	Embodied energy/ Properties	Ease of installation	Issues	Typical thermal conductivity
Cellulose fibre	Made from 90% post-consumer waste (newspapers) Reusable and recyclable Made from recycled newspaper and is usually treated with a mixture of borax and boric acid to provide fire resistance as well as to repel insects and fungi	Suitable for use between rafters and joists and timber 'breathing' wall construction Excellent resistance to fire, insects and vermin. At life-end, can be recycled or used as a soil conditioner	Good CO_2 friendliness Hygroscopic — provides a degree of humidity control Some products have low embodied energy Embodied energy varies between 4.9 and 16.64MJ/kg	Easy to install Typical density of loose-fill insulation: 32kg/m³ Cellulose insulation is available in a loose format for pouring and dry or damp spraying as well as in slab format for fitting within metal or timber frames	Contains borax, so dust inhalation hazard during installation Gives rise to occasional mould problems	0.038–0.046W/mK
Vermiculite (or exfoliated vermiculite)	A naturally occurring clay-based material It is reusable and recyclable although not a renewable product It has a variety of insulation uses, notably as a refractory insulator in industrial processes	Suitable for use between rafters and joists Similar product to perlite It is used widely in a granulated form as insulation for lofts	High embodied energy Bulk density 64-160kg/m³	Easy to install Has good fire resistance and can be mixed with concrete to help increase its insulation properties	Some fears around asbestos (pre-1990) contamination in USA, which led to scares associated with its removal. Must be installed in sealed spaces	0.058–0.071W/mK depending on bulk density
Perlite	Made from volcanic glass, which is expanded through heating, with natural fire- and water-resistant qualities	Perlite is a viable alternative to expanded polystyrene for cavity-wall applications	High embodied energy Bulk density 32–400kg/m³	Easy to install Perlite is available as a loose-fill product primarily for use in lofts and cavity walls	High embodied energy The major downside is the energy required to produce it	0.04–0.06W/mK depending on bulk density
Cork	Harvested from trees in managed forests (mostly Portugal) Reusable and recyclable	Cork insulation is used on flat roofs and insulated render systems, both of which take advantage of cork's dimensional stability and resistance to compression	Naturally resistant to rodent and insect attack (except wasps) CO_2 friendly Typical embodied energy high at 26MJ/kg (Portugal source)	Easy to install (esp. flat roofs)	Avoid inhaling cork dust Natural formaldehyde emission possible Possible mould issues	0.038–0.055W/mK
Wood wool	From managed forests Reusable, recyclable and compostable Wood wool is made from forestry thinnings and sawmill residue	Wood fibre insulation is versatile Used in breathing wall construction, ventilated pitched roofs and in ceilings and floors	CO_2 friendly Typical embodied energy: 10.8MJ/kg Hygroscopic —provides a degree of humidity control	Few installation hazards Typical density: 50kg/m³	Contains polyester binding and ammonium phosphate fire retardant	0.038–0.06W/mK
Wet formed wood-fibre board	From sawmill trimmings Reusable, recyclable and compostable Wet formed wood-fibre board is made from largely pre-consumer waste wood from sawmills	Wood-fibre board insulation is typically used in breathing wall construction as well as in roofs as insulated sarking The wood is reduced to chips and then soaked in water before being pressed and dried without additional bonding agents	CO_2 friendly but high embodied energy of 13MJ/kg Hygroscopic — provides a degree of humidity control	Easy to install Typical density: 160–240kg/m³	Few installation hazards High embodied energy	0.038–0.05W/mK

Material	Manufacture/ Recycling	Application	Embodied energy/ Properties	Ease of installation	Issues	Typical thermal conductivity
Hemp	Widely grown crop Reusable, recyclable and compostable Hemp is a renewable material Hemp insulation slabs are made from hemp or hemp mixed with either recycled cotton fibres or wood fibres, bound with a polyester binder and treated for fire resistance	Hemp insulation is used in breathing wall construction, ventilated pitched roofs and in ceilings and floors	CO_2 friendly and hygroscopic, so provides a degree of humidity control High embodied energy between 10.5 and 33MJ/kg	Easy to install Typical density: 40kg/m^3	Contains borate and ammonium phosphate fire retardant	0.038–0.040W/mK
Hempcrete	Hemp (crop) is mixed with concrete Hemp is a renewable material Hempcrete was first developed in France and is now manufactured by Lime Technology Ltd as Tradical products in the UK	Hempcrete insulation is used in breathing wall construction, ventilated pitched roofs and in ceilings and floors It is a precast, in situ cast or sprayed mixture of lime, cement and hemp insulation	Hemp is CO_2 friendly Embodied energy estimates low in the region of 2–5MJ/kg Hygroscopic — provides a degree of humidity control	Typical density: 220–330kg/m3	Lime and cement production contribute to global warming Needs care when installing	0.070W/mK
Flax	Widely grown crop Reusable, recyclable and compostable Flax is a renewable material Flax insulation slabs are made from flax with a polyester binder and treated for fire resistance	Flax insulation is used in breathing wall construction, ventilated pitched roofs and in ceilings and floors	Flax is CO_2 friendly Hygroscopic — provides a degree of humidity control Embodied energy: various figures between 11 and 30MJ/kg	Straightforward to install Typical density: 30–35kg/m^3	Contains boron-based flame retardant and biocide	0.038–0.040W/mK
Sheep's wool	Organic product Reusable, recyclable Sheep's wool has excellent hygroscopic properties that help to moderate temperatures throughout the seasons	Wool is suitable for use as insulation between rafters, joists and timber studs in timber breathing wall construction	CO_2 friendly Hygroscopic — provides a degree of humidity control Embodied energy between 12–36.8MJ/kg	Easy to install Typical density: 25kg/m3 Sheep's wool, although a fibre-based material, is non-irritant and does not require special clothing or protective masks and goggles	Contains boron-based flame retardant and biocide Also contains binder Slabs and rolls are made from wool with a polyester binder and treated for fire and insect resistance	0.034–0.055W/mK

Table 15: Insulation products made from natural materials.
(Principal Sources: NGS Greenspec, Energy Saving Trust, 2010, perlite.net, schundler.com)

Material	Manufacture/ Recycling	Application	Embodied energy/ Properties	Ease of installation	Issues	Typical thermal conductivity
Expanded polystyrene insulation (EPS)	Recyclable, re-usable A rigid board available in various thicknesses. Made from small beads of polystyrene mixed with pentane as the blowing agent	EPS boarding is used in cavity walls, pitched roofs and floors Polystyrene beads are frequently used as cavity fill in masonry walls 'Grey' type has slightly better properties due to a graphite barrier	Typical embodied energy: 108MJ/kg. Water impermeable and resistant to rot and vermin High compressive strength Heating expands the beads. EPS boards are produced by putting the beads into moulds and heating further to fuse the beads together	Easy to manage and install (especially as a cavity filler) Typical density: 15–35kg/m³	Derived from petrochemicals May outgas hazardous substances such as styrene	0.032–0.045W/ mK
Extruded polystyrene (XPS)	Recyclable and reusable Extruded polystyrene is made by mixing polystyrene with a blowing agent under pressure and the resulting fluid forced through a die. As it emerges from the die it expands into a foam, is shaped, cooled and trimmed to the necessary shape	XPS is slightly stronger than EPS, and it is used in many of the same applications. It is particularly suitable for use below ground or where extra loading and/or impacts might be anticipated 'Styrofoam' has better thermal performance and moisture resistance than EPS	Typical embodied energy: 95MJ/kg Water impermeable, rot- and vermin-resistant High compressive strength High embodied energy	Easy to manage and install Typical density: 30kg/m³	Derived from petrochemicals Contains halogens, which are environmentally unacceptable May outgas hazardous substances	0.025–0.038W/ mK Good thermal performance
Rigid polyurethane	Made from volcanic glass, which is expanded through heating, with natural fire- and water-resistant qualities	Perlite is a viable alternative to expanded polystyrene for cavity-wall applications	High embodied energy Bulk density 32–400kg/m3	Easy to install Perlite is available as a loose-fill product primarily for use in lofts and cavity walls	High embodied energy The major downside is the energy required to produce it	0.04–0.06W/ mK depending on bulk density

Table 16: Insulation products made from oil-derived materials.
(Principal Sources: NGS GreenSpec, Energy Saving Trust)

Material	Manufacture/ Recycling	Application	Embodied energy/ Properties	Ease of installation	Issues	Typical thermal conductivity
Polyisocyanurate (PUR/PIR)	Recyclable and reusable Good insulation properties, sometimes backed with foil to enhance moisture and insulation quality. Drawback is expense, although it is useful in situations where performance is important. Rigid polyurethane (PUR), a closed-cell plastic, is formed by reacting two monomers in the presence of a blowing agent catalyst (polymerization)	Wall, floor and roof insulation Polyurethane is also popular in laminate form in SIPS and as an insulation backing to rigid boarding such as plasterboard. Polyisocyanurate foam (PIR) is essentially an improvement on polyurethane where there is a slight difference in the constituents and where the reaction is conducted at higher temperatures	Typical estimated embodied energy: 101MJ/kg Water impermeable, rot- and vermin-resistant High compressive strength High embodied energy.	Easy to manage and install Typical density: 30–40kg/m^3 Suffers performance degradation over early years	Derived from petrochemicals May outgas hazardous substances Prone to shrinkage, causing gaps Also available as foil-faced	0.022–0.03W/mK Good thermal performance PIR is more fire-resistant and has a slightly higher R value
Phenolic foam insulation	Reusable if intact but not easily recyclable Phenolic foam insulation is made by combining phenol-formaldehyde resin with a foaming agent. When hardener is added to the mix and rapidly stirred, the exothermic reaction of the resin, together with the action of the foaming agent, causes foaming of the resin. This is followed by rapid setting of the foamed material	Usually employed in building services applications Phenolic foam panels are also suitable as insulation for roofs, walls and floors It is also popular in laminate form as an insulation backing to rigid boarding such as plasterboard	High compressive strength and flame-retardant properties Moisture resistant Embodied energy estimated to be in the region of 70MJ/kg	A versatile and easy to install product Typical density: 40–50kg/m^3	Made from phenol formaldehyde, a toxic petrochemical derivative Prone to shrinkage, causing gaps Also available as foil-faced phenolic foam	Good thermal performance 0.022–0.025W/mK

Material	Manufacture/ Recycling	Application	Embodied energy/ Properties	Ease of installation	Issues	Typical thermal conductivity
Rock mineral wool	Some brands include recycled mineral wool and secondary industrial waste Recyclable Rock mineral wool is made from quarried rock and recycled steel slag	Masonry cavity walls, timber-frame walls, roof rafter insulation, loft and suspended floor insulation	Typical embodied energy from 15.7 to 22.4MJ/kg Good resistance to fire and rot The insulation is produced in a variety of densities according to application Varying densities result in differing levels of thermal conductivity	Simple to install Typical density of loose-fill insulation: 24–40kg/m³	Can be a skin irritant Some products release formaldehyde Insulation performance decreases when compacted or damp	0.031– 0.044W/mK
Glass mineral wool	Includes secondary industrial waste, re-usable and recyclable Glass wool insulation is manufactured in a similar way to rock wool, though the raw materials are different as well as is the melting process. Glass wool is made from silica sand, recycled glass, limestone and soda ash	Masonry cavity walls, timber-frame walls, roof rafter insulation, loft and suspended floor insulation Glass fibre, mineral or rock wool provides flexible blankets of insulation	Typical embodied energy 49.6MJ/kg (for glass wool mat) Good resistance to fire and rot	Simple to install Typical density: 16–24kg/m³ The insulation is produced in a variety of densities according to format and function Varying densities result in varying levels of thermal conductivity	Can be skin irritant Sometimes contains boron as a moisture retardant Insulation performance decreases when compacted or damp Fitting and handling requires special clothing and protective masks and goggles	0.031– 0.040W/mK
Cellular or foamed glass	Contains around 60% post-consumer glass waste Reusable and recyclable Foamed glass insulation is made from crushed glass that is mixed with carbon and heated to 1000°C. The heat causes the carbon to oxidize to form the characteristic bubbles	Foamed glass has a relatively high compressive strength, which, combined with its water and vapour resistance, makes the insulation slab suitable for flat roofing in high-load situations such as retaining walls, car parks and green roofs	Typical embodied energy of 26MJ/kg Good resistance to fire and rot Other applications include thermal breaks, wall and floor insulation	Typical density: 100–120kg/m³	Uses bitumen in installation	0.037– 0.055W/mK
Aerogel	Aerogel is a lightweight, low-density material made from silica and air The panels are distinguished by their outstanding insulation properties Reusable if intact	Aerogel blankets are beginning to appear as a component in laminate panels bonded to boards including plasterboard, wood-fibre reinforced gypsum board, plywood and chipboard	Good resistance to fire and rot Water impermeable High compressive strength	Appears as a component of insulation boards — easy to install Typical density: 180kg/ m³	Relatively new on the market so as yet largely untried in the DIY markets Expensive	0.013 W/mK Excellent thermal performance

Table 17: Mineral-derived insulation products.
(Principal Sources: NGS GreenSpec, Energy Saving Trust)

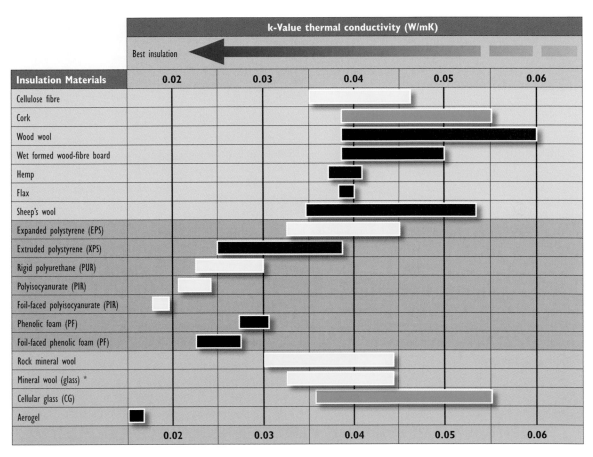

k-Value thermal conductivity (W/mK)					
Insulation Materials	0.02	0.03	0.04	0.05	0.06
Cellulose fibre					
Cork					
Wood wool					
Wet formed wood-fibre board					
Hemp					
Flax					
Sheep's wool					
Expanded polystyrene (EPS)					
Extruded polystyrene (XPS)					
Rigid polyurethane (PUR)					
Polyisocyanurate (PIR)					
Foil-faced polyisocyanurate (PIR)					
Phenolic foam (PF)					
Foil-faced phenolic foam (PF)					
Rock mineral wool					
Mineral wool (glass) *					
Cellular glass (CG)					
Aerogel					
	0.02	0.03	0.04	0.05	0.06

Table 18: Insulation product thermal conductivities.

The values and products in the table are for illustration only and actual product details should be checked with the manufacturers' data sheets. (Sources: EST C41 Data Sheet, NGC Greenspec and BRE Green Product guide etc.)
*Variation due to product density may occur.
Key to environmental ratings of insulation materials (no products tested with a 'C' rating).
'A' rating   'B' rating   'C' rating   'Not yet assessed'

	DIY Activity												
	Roofs			Walls							Floors		
Insulation materials	Loft insulation	Insulation on pitched roof	Flat roof	Internal insulation	External insulation	Cavity (full-fill)	Cavity (partial-fill)	Timber frame	Steel frame	Panel	Solid concrete	Suspended beam and block	Suspended timber
Natural materials													
Cellulose fibre	■							■					
Cork			■		■								
Wood wool								■				■	
Wet formed wood-fibre board		■						■					
Hemp		■						■					
Flax		■						■					
Sheep's wool	■	■						■					■
Oil-based products													
Expanded polystyrene (EPS)	■			■	■	■	■	■	■	■	■	■	
Extruded polystyrene (XPS)				■	■		■	■	■	■	■		
Rigid polyurethane (PUR)				■	■	■	■	■	■	■	■		
Polyisocyanurate (PIR)				■	■	■	■	■	■	■	■		
Foil-faced polyisocyanurate (PIR)		■		■			■	■	■	■			
Phenolic foam (PF)	■	■		■			■	■		■			
Foil-faced phenolic foam (PF)		■		■			■	■		■			
Mineral Based													
Rock mineral wool	■	■		■		■		■	■			■	■
Mineral wool (glass)	■	■		■		■		■	■				■
Cellular glass (CG)				■	■		■				■		
Aerogel				■	■			■					

Table 19: Applications for insulation products in DIY activities.
The applications shown for the various products in the table are for illustration only and actual product details should be checked with the manufacturers' data sheets.

CHAPTER 5

Reducing Heat Loss through External Walls

The walls are a key part of any house: they support the floors and roof; they provide protection from the wind and rain, and they keep the noise out (and sometimes in). In cold weather, the external walls retain the heat indoors and, during the hotter days of summer, they help keep rooms cooler. Some types of wall lose heat much more quickly than others.

From an insulation perspective, the areas of interest are the inside and outside surfaces of solid external walls, or the airspace cavity in the case of cavity walls. Internal, adjoining and party walls gain as much heat as they lose, so there is no benefit in insulating them.

HEAT LOSS THROUGH WALLS

The outer walls of a building can lose between 35 and 40 per cent of the heat supplied to keep it warm internally. Older properties, particularly those constructed before the 1930s, are likely to be of solid-wall construction, with no airspace cavity in the external walls. Examples of solid-wall construction homes are shown below.

It is estimated that the UK has approximately 24.5 million dwellings and around 35 per cent of these do not have cavity walls. The 35 per cent without cavities have been constructed using solid brick, solid stone or pre-1944 timber frame and some have been built using non-traditional construction methods, such as pre-cast concrete slabs.

In buildings where the brickwork is visible, the brick pattern indicates whether or not the wall has

Example of an external solid brick skin wall with no cavity.

Example of an external brick skin wall with block inner wall and air-spaced cavity.

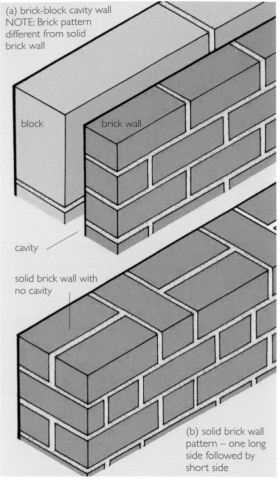

(a) brick-block cavity wall
NOTE: Brick pattern different from solid brick wall

block

brick wall

cavity

solid brick wall with no cavity

(b) solid brick wall pattern – one long side followed by short side

Solid-wall and cavity-wall construction detail showing brick arrangement on both designs.

a cavity. In solid brick-built walls, the brick pattern reveals that every brick is laid at right-angles to the previous one, so one brick will show its long side, and the next will show its short side. Some older properties or perhaps those in rural areas may not be built from bricks at all. Walls in these properties may be constructed from rough stones or they may have walls made from irregular blocks, sometimes up to a metre thick.

There is huge potential for the retrofit treatment of a solid-wall property, which can dramatically improve its thermal performance in a cost-effective way. Since they have no insulating airspace, solid walls lose even more heat than cavity walls and the only way to reduce this heat loss is to insulate them on their inside or outside surface, or both, as necessary and affordable. Wall insulation will also help to prevent condensation on the walls and ceilings. Solid-wall treatments can be expensive, although the benefits will be apparent as savings on heating bills. Insulation has the added environmental bonus that it will reduce harmful carbon dioxide (CO_2) emissions.

Solid-wall insulation is more expensive than cavity-wall insulation, but it could save between £300 and £400 a year on energy bills. According to the Energy Saving Trust, it could pay for itself in around

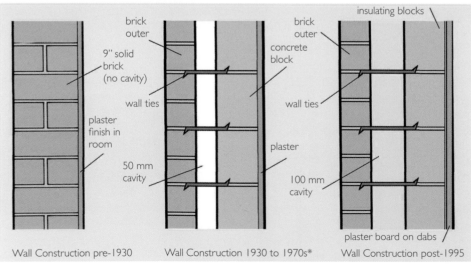

brick outer

9" solid brick (no cavity)

wall ties

plaster finish in room

50 mm cavity

Wall Construction pre-1930

brick outer

concrete block

wall ties

plaster

100 mm cavity

Wall Construction 1930 to 1970s*

insulating blocks

brick outer

wall ties

plaster board on dabs

Wall Construction post-1995

External wall construction from the early 1900s to the present day.

*NOTE: at the end of the 1970's insulating block replaced the inner concrete block

The external walls are exposed and lose heat in a variety of ways. This building has cracks, allowing damp to penetrate its gable wall.

For buildings that require periodic re-rendering, such as no-fines concrete, or where extensive remedial action is necessary due to rain ingress, the additional cost of insulation is easily justified. External insulation can also improve the appearance of a home and may add to its value.

It is possible significantly to improve the thermal performance of a building's walls and Table 20 indicates the standard of achievement that can be reached using best-practice insulation techniques. Insulating the outside or inside surface of a building's external walls will require a large area of insulation coverage, typically 80m² to 120m².

Table 21 gives examples of some insulation products that can be applied to the outer surfaces of external walls, or as a filler for cavity walls, or, alternatively, as internal dry-lining insulation which can be applied to the inside surfaces of external walls.

ten or eleven years, without a grant. As well as the financial savings resulting from installing insulation, a typical three-bedroom semi-detached house could produce around 2.5 tonnes less carbon dioxide every year.

Type of wall	Untreated U-value (W/m²K)	U-value with best-practice insulation (W/m²K)
Solid (no cavity)	2.9–2.1 *	0.4–0.3* (external or internal insulation fitted)
Cavity wall	1.5	0.5–0.6 (CWI)

Table 20: Best-practice U-values for walls.
* Based on a 220mm thick wall with internal plaster. The nature of the internal or external treatment will influence the final U-value. (Source: Energy-Efficient Refurbishment of Housing (CE83, EST))

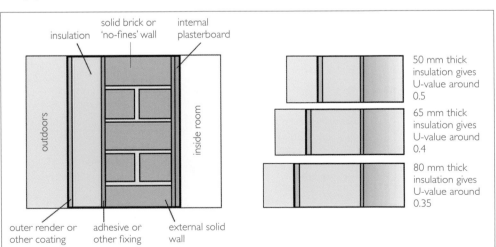

External-wall insulation thickness and U-values. There are a variety of products on the market that would be suitable for this external wall insulation.

Manufacturer	Product	Type	Application
Termex	Termex	Loose cellulose for timber-frame construction.	CWI
Excel	Warmcell 500	Loose cellulose for timber-frame construction.	Cavity walls and timber-frame filler
Plant Fibre Technology	Isonat	Hemp and cotton slab	Cavity walls and timber-frame filler
Isovlas	Isovlas	Flax slabs	Cavity walls and timber-frame wall filler
Black Mountain	Sheep's wool	Wool rolls	Timber-frame wall filling
Second Nature	Thermafleece	Wool rolls	Timber-frame wall filling
YBS	Non-itch	Polyester slab for timber-frame construction	Timber-frame wall filling
Pavatex	Timber-frame Pavaclad system	External wood-fibre board insulation system for timber-frame construction with cladding	Insulating external walls
	Timber-frame Diffutherm system	External wood-fibre board insulation system for timber-frame construction with render	Insulating external walls
	Steel Frame Pavaclad System	External wood-fibre board insulation system for steel-frame construction with cladding	Insulating external walls
Pavatex NBT	Pavatherm	Wood-fibre board for timber-frame construction	Insulating external walls (timber frame)
	Isolair	Wood-fibre board, water resistant, for ventilated facades	Insulating external walls
	Pavatherm Plus	Wood-fibre board, interlocking, waterproof, for ventilated facades	Insulating external walls
Saint-Gobain Isover	Isowool-CWS	Glass fibre for full- or partial-fill cavity walls	CWI
	Isowool-Hi-Cav 32	Glass fibre	CWI
	Isowool-Hi Therm	Glass fibre	Partial-fill cavity or party walls
	Isowool-Walltherm	Blown glass fibre	CWI
	Timber-frame roll and batt	Glass-fibre roll and batt	Timber-frame wall filling
InstaFibre	Yellow wool	Blown glass fibre	CWI
	White wool	Blown glass fibre	CWI
Rockwool	Cavity	Mineral wool slab	Full-fill cavity walls
	High-performance partial fill	Mineral wool slab	Partial-fill cavity walls
	Energysaver	Blown mineral wool	CWI
	Flexi	Mineral wool slabs	Timber-frame wall filling
	Rockliner	Mineral wool slabs	Dry-lining internal wall insulation
	Cladding Roll	Mineral wool	Industrial frame building wall filling
Pittsburgh Corning Foamglas	Wallboard	Foamglas board	CWI and external wall insulation
	Wallboard/Readyboard	Foamglas board	Underground walls insulation
	P&R Board and T4 Slab	Foamglas board	For internal walls as plaster, plasterboard, tiling, etc. finishes
InstaFibre	Rockwool	Blown mineral wool	CWI
	Instabead	Blown polystyrene beads	CWI
Springvale	Platinum Wallshield	Polystyrene board	Partial/full-fill CWI
	Platinum Fulfil	Polystyrene board	Full-fill CWI
Steico-NBT	Canaflex hemp batts	Hemp-fibre slab	Ventilated facades
Durisol	Durisol	Recycled wood and mineral wool	Permanent formwork

Table 21: Insulation products suitable for external walls. *Green shading means product has recycled content. (Source: NGS GreenSpec)*

A contractor blowing insulation into a cavity wall. (Homeseal Insulation Installers, Magherafelt, NI, homesealni.co.uk)

SOLID-WALL INSULATION AND DIY

The fitting of external insulation systems is generally considered to be a major undertaking, involving working at heights, the erection of scaffolding and the handling of specialist insulating materials. It is not generally considered to be DIY work, so it is advisable to employ a specialist builder or contractor who has experience of fitting external insulation. Contractors hired to carry out this type of work should be registered with the appropriate body, for example, CIBA, the BBA or the National Insulation Association (see page 182 for contact details). Members of these bodies carry insurance, which will protect you should anything get damaged, or in case the job is not up to an accepted standard.

It is vitally important that damp, structural problems and associated issues, such as failed or cracked rendering or plastering, are all fixed be-

Equipment for Wall Insulation

Tools: electric drill (with masonry bits), hammer, bolster chisel, cold chisel, screwdriver, wood saw, wall plugs, electric circular saw, screw nails, nails, square, measuring tape, steps and ladders of various heights.
Special tools: dedicated masonry power drill, special insulation saw (specially designed for cutting PIR insulation, reduces dust), scaffolding.
Protective clothing: overalls, safety goggles, safety helmet, protective boots, strong gloves, ear protection.

Safety Tips

- Before attempting any work from a ladder, make sure that you feel comfortable at heights. The feet of the ladder must be resting on a sound and level surface, and the ladder base should be set at an angle such that, if you lean backwards at the top, the ladder will not topple. If the angle is incorrect, the ladder can also be unstable and slip. For safety, there should always be someone with a foot on the bottom rung. For more on ladder safety, see Chapter 11, which should be read in conjunction with this paragraph.
- It is advisable to use a contractor to supply and erect scaffolding. If you do decide to build it yourself, you must ensure that it is assembled in accordance with the supplier's instructions.
- When using drills or electric tools outside always ensure that a residual current device (RCD) is used. Never use tools outdoors that require mains voltage when it is raining or the ground is wet.
- Make sure that at all times there is no possibility of dropping tools or materials on to people working or passing below. Use safety nets if possible to catch falling render, materials or tools.
- Wear tool straps when working at height.
- Use a fine-tooth saw to cut PIR insulation, to minimize dust. Special cutting saws are available.
- Wear the correct protective clothing, including face mask and goggles when carrying out the work. If dust particles get in the eyes, wash out with liberal quantities of water. (Chapter 11 covers some basic first aid).
- Aluminium foil edges on foil-backed insulation board may be sharp. Always wear strong gloves when handling these materials and avoid sliding un-gloved hands along board edges.

fore any insulation or cladding material is attached. If in any doubt, seek specialist expert advice. If this advice recommends that treatments are required, then this work must be carried out by specialist contractors.

If an installer plans to use a combustible insulation material, then the product approvals certificate should be consulted to make sure the necessary precautions are taken. When considering the finished appearance, it is essential for the wall insulation to interface properly with the roof eaves, windows and sills, door openings and other external features of the building.

Once properly installed, an external insulation system will create a waterproof barrier around the building, ensuring that rain penetration is not a problem. It is important to make sure that there is no risk of interstitial condensation occurring in the wall when the insulation system is introduced.

If you feel that you can tackle putting up plasterboard, fixing wooden battens to the wall and working on large areas at a time, applying insulation to the internal surfaces of the outside walls of your property should be a fairly straightforward process.

Note: Insulating External Walls

Always check with your local building control office to determine whether or not the work requires a building control service.

Before the outside appearance of a building is modified by the installation of external insulation, always check with the local planning authority, as planning permission may be necessary.

INSULATING SOLID WALLS USING EXTERNAL INSULATION

The best time to consider external-wall insulation is when the building is difficult or impossible to heat, or when the exterior of the building requires repair work. In these circumstances, the marginal cost of external solid-wall insulation will be lower than the full cost of dedicated insulation on its own. External-wall insulation has the advantage that most systems can be installed whilst the building is still occupied, with disruption to the internal functioning therefore being avoided.

To insulate a wall on its outside surface, a layer of insulation board is first fixed to the wall and then it is covered with a protective, weatherproof cladding material. This is often referred to as 'thermal cladding'. Insulating the external surface of a solid wall that is 220mm thick and plastered on its internal surface could provide savings of around £300 on annual heating bills. Applying best-practice insulation with an R-value of $2.1m^2K/W$ will improve the wall's U-value to $0.3W/m^2K$. Insulation thickness of between 40mm and 100mm will need to be applied, depending on the thermal conductivity of the wall.

Savings Achieved

Table 22 below approximate costs and savings for external solid-wall insulation; however, the typical cost listed does not allow for loans or grants. Governments, energy suppliers, councils and local authorities may provide grants or offers to help with the installation of energy-saving measures such as CWI, loft insulation and energy-efficient appliances. In some instances, grants (usually means-tested) are available for the insulation of solid-wall properties, although they are not generally available when the measures are to be installed using DIY. For more

Treatment	Annual saving per year (£)	Installation cost (£)	CO_2 saving per year (tonnes)	Payback (years)
External cladding/ render	450	4,500	2.5	10

Table 22: Approximate savings and costs for external wall insulation.
Note: The savings for internal wall treatments and cavity-wall insulation are given in the sections below.
(Source EST)

information, or to search for energy-saving grants and offers, see pages 181–183.

External Insulation Options

Once attached to the outside walls, the insulation is covered with a protective render or finish material, such as timber panels, decorative boards, stone or clay tiles, brick slips or aluminium panels. The insulating materials should be as thick as practicality and finances allow, and they include expanded polystyrene boards, extruded polystyrene boards, polyisocyanurate, polyurethane foam slabs, phenolic foam slabs, mineral fibre rockwool batts, glass rigid slabs and foamed glass slabs. For details on suitable insulation materials, see Tables 13, 15, 16, 17 and 21.

Some areas of the external cladding need impact and weather protection, and rainwater fittings and sills may need additional attention. External insulation systems largely avoid the problems associated with thermal bridging, except where projections arise, as in the case of a balcony in a flat (see Chapter 2). Although the insulation materials involved are robust, they are vulnerable to impact damage and care should be taken during installation.

External insulation systems are available in two main designs – wet-render systems and dry-cladding systems – with the thermal performance of either system depending on the thickness of the insulation used.

Wet-Render Systems

In wet-render systems the basic components are the insulation, the fixing elements and the render itself. The quality and thickness of the render and the insulation will be the main determinants of thermal performance. Typical traditional finishes include heavyweight, medium-weight and lightweight render or pebbledash finish. Some renders are reinforced with mineral fibre mesh, polypropylene mesh for medium-/lightweight renders, and galvanized mild steel mesh and stainless-steel mesh for heavyweight render systems.

The insulation slabs are attached to the wall using adhesive dabs or special fixing plugs. A reinforced render is then added as an outer coating and this is finished off with a thin, decorative weatherproof render. The range of render finishes available is wide, including dry-dash aggregate chips on coloured polymer (pebbledash), scratch plaster, roughcast render, simulated brick/stone, smooth and painted, and textured render.

Insulation for a solid external wall – Fasroll (Rockwool) mineral wool batts being installed. (Seamus O'Loughlin Viking-House, Dublin, viking-house.co.uk)

Dry-Cladding Systems

Due to their high cost, dry-cladding systems are rarely used on low-rise buildings such as houses or bungalows. They are more common on flats and commercial buildings.

External wall insulation batts in place on a single storey dwelling. (Seamus O'Loughlin Viking-House, Dublin, viking-house.co.uk)

60mm thick mineral wool insulation being applied to a pebble-dash finished solid-wall house. Render is applied as a finish coat on the outside surface of the insulation. (Seamus O'Loughlin Viking-House, Dublin, viking-house.co.uk)

A protective render finish is applied over the external solid wall-insulation. (Seamus O'Loughlin Viking-House, Dublin, viking-house.co.uk)

Dry cladding is usually fixed to the wall by means of timber battens or metal frames. The insulation is installed between the battens and the dry-cladding finishes are then fixed to the battens. The insulation boards are attached to the wall surface using fixing plugs. The dry cladding outer protective skin finish can be a windproof breather membrane below a weatherboard, tile or concrete outer slab.

The range of dry-cladding finishes includes cedar timber boards, vertical clay or concrete tiles, hanging terracotta tiles, aggregate finished cementitious boards, PVC, ship-lap boarding timber, and painted aluminium profiled claddings. Dry cladding is particularly suitable where regular building inspection or maintenance checks are necessary, since it can be easily removed and re-fitted.

Sometimes it is difficult to preserve the character of an existing building if the outside walls are covered in insulated cladding, since it can dramatically alter the appearance. However, the range of designs and materials now available should mean that this is not the case. Care should be taken to ensure the building's external finish is in line with its neighbouring properties, as far as possible.

SOLID WALL – INTERNAL INSULATION

An alternative to external-wall insulation on solid walls is to apply insulation to the internal surfaces of the building's outside walls. Traditionally, wall surfaces are covered with wet sand and cement render or plaster. One approach to internal insulation is to fix insulation to the wall surface and apply a wet-plaster finish over it. Dry-lining, or 'drywall' as it is called in the USA, is the term used to describe the process of covering a building with a dry material that is attached to the walls. In the UK, 'dry-lining' refers mainly to covering internal walls with insulation and plasterboard laminate. The insulation and plasterboard laminate is either stuck directly on the walls or fixed to timber studwork, or to a steel frame that is infilled with insulation and attached to the walls. Dry-lining has several advantages over the wet finish in that it can be installed much more quickly, especially in the case where it is stuck to the walls using a mix of plaster as adhesive. This method is called 'dot and dab'. Dry-lining results in a lighter finished construction and, furthermore, means that less moisture is introduced into the building structure.

Potential Savings

For an average home, installing internal-wall insulation could lead to energy bill savings of around £400 a year, and a typical three-bedroom semi-detached house could reduce its carbon dioxide emissions by around 2.4 tonnes of CO_2 a year. However, unless the inside wall is in need of replacement or needs re-plastering, or if refurbishment work is already planned (of which the cost of insulation will be a minor component), then internal insulation is difficult to justify on the basis of financial savings alone. Table 23 gives approximate costs and savings for internal solid-wall insulation.

Benefits and Drawbacks

Internal insulation is relatively simple to install, with a minimum of wall preparation necessary, and falls into the category of being a DIY activity. Installing new plumbing, fitting a replacement heating system or re-wiring all present the ideal opportunity to apply internal insulation at the same time. It is cost-effective and convenient to include internal insulation as part of a building's modernization or refurbishment. Internal insulation has a number of benefits: the external wall appearance remains unchanged, the internal wall surface will warm up more quickly, and it is cheaper, easier to install and to maintain than external insulation.

Internal insulation also has a number of drawbacks: it can leave cold thermal bridges and care

Internal-wall insulation can be installed using a wooden studwork frame or the 'dot and dab' technique to glue insulation directly in place on the wall.

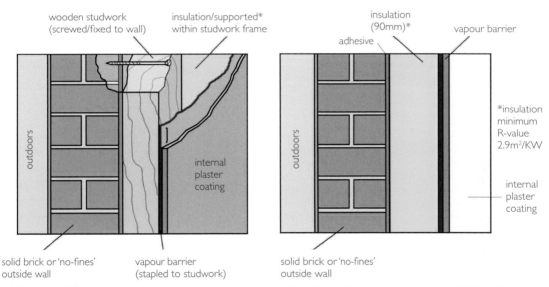

(a) insulation retained in studwork

(b) Insulation glued to wall using 'dot and dab' technique

Internal wall insulation	Annual saving per year (£)	Installed cost (£/m²)	CO₂ saving per year (tonnes)	Payback (years)
Flexible thermal lining	400	45	2.4	10
Rigid thermal board	400	50	2.4	10

Table 23: Approximate savings and costs for internal wall insulation. *(Source: EST, 2009))*
Note: As an example, for an average home of 100m² floor area, the wall area is assumed to be around 100m² and this infers a cost of £4,500 to £5,000.

Installing internal insulation using the 'dot and dab' direct-bonding technique. Adhesive is applied directly to the block wall (or suitably level brickwork). (Xtratherm Insulation Limited, xtratherm.com)

needs to be taken when hanging heavy items, such as large mirrors, on the internal walls. Shelving or cupboards can present a problem, the room size is reduced and there are disruptions to the skirting boards, window frames and door frames. It will also be necessary in most cases to have the electrical outlets repositioned. The installation of internal insulation can be a disruptive process – every aspect of the room will be disturbed until the job is completed. Some insulation materials present an increased fire risk and this must be taken into consideration. A vapour barrier needs to be installed with the internal insulation and it is most important

that this is not broken or torn, since it could introduce the risk of interstitial condensation.

Dry-lining negates the benefit of the thermal storage of the outside wall, which accumulates heat through solar gain. Solar gain is when a sun-facing wall is subjected to solar exposure over a number of hours and the sun's heat is absorbed and stored in the wall material. Later, after the sun has set, the heat is re-radiated from the wall back into its surroundings, which includes the room.

Internal Insulation Materials

The materials and equipment used to insulate interior walls can include: pre-insulated plasterboard laminate sheets, rigid thermal insulation board (possibly foil-backed), mineral wool insulation blankets or batts, flexible thermal lining rolls (typically 1 x 12.5m), wooden battens (to make a studwork frame), continuous ribbons (these are fastenings used to secure the panels), wall plaster, appropriate adhesive, mechanical fixings to secure the insulation board, and rolls of joint sealing tape. Mineral wool blanket insulation and batts up to a total thickness of 90mm can be supported in wooden studwork.

Alternatively, PVC internal cladding systems are available, and PVC sheet panels (sizes are typically 2440 x 1220mm or 3050 x 1220mm), silicon mastic, joining strips and 'J' clips will be required.

Internal insulation usually consists of dry-lining in the form of flexible thermal linings that are directly applied to the walls; laminated insulating plasterboard (known as thermal board), which can also be directly applied to the walls; or mineral wool blankets or batts held in place using a batten studwork frame. In all these approaches the number of penetrations through the insulation into the wall should be kept to a minimum, to eliminate air leakage. Extremely high thermal efficiencies can be achieved using flexible thermal linings and with most brands of insulation board. This makes it possible to achieve good thermal performance using relatively thin insulation, which is of great importance when treating a small room. Each treatment is considered in more detail below.

Dry-Lining Using Flexible Thermal Linings
Flexible thermal linings are simply rolls of insulation that are specifically for use in solid-wall homes,

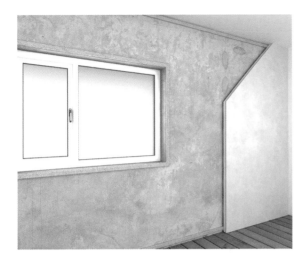

View of internal insulation glued to the wall using the 'dot and dab' technique applied to internal plastered wall surface. (Xtratherm Insulation Limited, xtratherm.com)

In the wooden batten method, the battens are fixed to the wall, spaced to suit the width of the insulation, and ensuring that they are vertically plumb. (Xtratherm Insulation Limited, xtratherm. com)

Installing internal wall insulation using studwork and plasterboard.

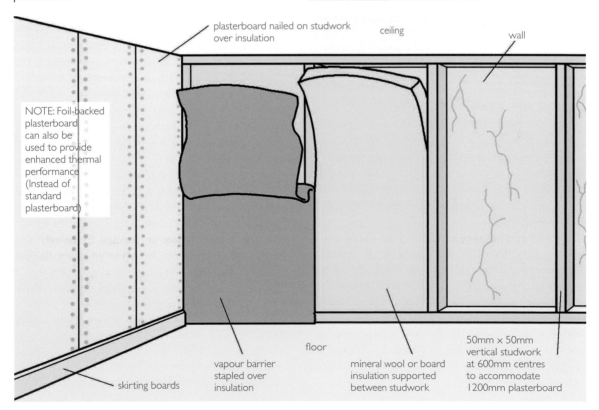

plasterboard nailed on studwork over insulation

ceiling

wall

NOTE: Foil-backed plasterboard can also be used to provide enhanced thermal performance (Instead of standard plasterboard)

floor

skirting boards

vapour barrier stapled over insulation

mineral wool or board insulation supported between studwork

50mm x 50mm vertical studwork at 600mm centres to accommodate 1200mm plasterboard

mansard roofs and dormer ceilings. Typically, the lining is 10mm thick and supplied in rolls of 1 x 12.5m. Some dry-lining products are made from a double layer of polythene bubble sheet, faced on each side with coated aluminium foil. The material can also be made from natural products such as latex. Lining generally has an outer face that can be decorated with paint, wallpaper or tiles.

Laminated Rigid Thermal Boards

Thermal boarding is a composite board made of plasterboard with a backing of insulation. The insulation backing can be specified in a variety of thicknesses. Insulation in excess of 60mm will typically be required to achieve best-practice thermal performance. Thermal boards are fixed to the internal wall surface using continuous ribbons, mechanical fixings or dabs of adhesive. Installation of the thermal boards is very straightforward since the boards are designed for direct fitting on to the inside surface of the wall. The thicker the board the better the insulation, but clearly, as the thickness of the insulation increases, this will impinge into the room space, reducing the floor area. Care needs to be taken around windows to ensure that insulation gaps or 'cold spots' are not created where insulation is difficult to apply.

Insulation Retained Within Wooden Studwork

In the third type of internal-wall treatment, wooden battens are attached to the wall to make a studwork frame and the spaces between are filled with insulation. The wooden framework containing the insulation is then covered with a plasterboard finish, which can be papered, painted or otherwise decorated.

A variation of this treatment uses studwork in combination with thermal board, which replaces standard plasterboard. Wooden battens are advantageous where the internal wall face is uneven because no time is wasted in preparing the internal wall surface. These preparations typically include re-plastering and making sure the inside surface of the wall is reasonably flat and level. A combination of thermal board and studwork can also help to reduce thermal bridging.

Internal PVC Cladding

PVC cladding can be fitted to internal walls as a DIY project. A typical cladding system consists of smooth PVC panels and there are a number of systems on the market. Each PVC sheet is joined to the next sheet by a 'joining strip' and finished with a 'J'- shaped edge trim that covers the top and bottom edges. Edges and joints are secured by drilling through and screwing their wider back sections directly to the wall. A bead of silicone is applied as the PVC sheets are slid into place, so that each sheet is secured and sealed on all four edges, at the same time concealing the fixing screws. The body of the sheets can be further secured to the wall either with drive rivets or with the appropriate adhesive. From a maintenance point of view PVC is easily cleaned with a simple soap-based solution.

Installing Dry-Lining

When fitting insulation board or insulated plasterboard laminate, the correct procedure should be followed:

1 Remove all wall coverings and inspect the wall for cracks and damp. Repair any minor cracks using appropriate filler. If more major treatment is required to remedy structural cracking or damp, get professional advice and make sure it is carried out before proceeding.
2 If necessary, use a proprietary plaster skim, to ensure the wall surface is reasonably even and level along its length.
3 Measure the wall and create studwork to cover the face of the wall using 50 x 70mm battens. The battens should be screwed securely to the wall along its length, providing a rigid and sturdy structure. The spacing of the studwork should anticipate the size of the plasterboard sheets that will eventually be nailed to it.
4 Care should be taken to finish the studwork correctly around windows and doors, to ensure that a good fit is obtained and that there are no gaps.
5 Cut the insulation material to suit the spaces in the studwork frame. The insulation should fit snugly within the framework and there should be no gaps.

6 The studwork should be covered with a suitable polythene vapour barrier.
7 Insulated or foil-backed plasterboard or PVC sheeting should then be nailed to the studwork, making sure there are no gaps between the sheets. The joints between the boards should then be sealed with joint tape or scrim cloth. A plaster skim can be applied, if necessary.

Internal-wall insulation showing studwork and insulation. In many instances, older walls are not suitable for the 'dot and dab' application because they present an uneven surface. In these situations the application of thermal liners on to mechanically fixed systems such as wooden battens or metal furring frame can provide a final-finish level wall surface. (Xtratherm Insulation Limited, xtratherm.com)

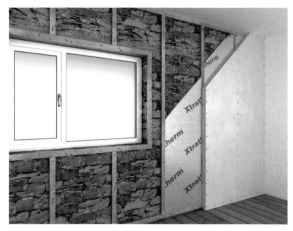

Rough finished internal wall surfaces can be insulated and effectively levelled out using a wooden batten studwork frame. (Xtratherm Insulation Limited, xtratherm.com)

Party Walls and the Party Wall etc. Act 1996

The Party Wall etc. Act 1996 ('the Act') may affect someone who either wishes to carry out work covered by the Act (the 'Building Owner') or receives notification under the Act of proposed adjacent work (the 'Adjoining Owner'). Under the Act, the word 'Owner' includes the persons or body holding the freehold title, or holding a leasehold title for a period exceeding one year, or under contract to purchase such a title, or entitled to receive rents from the property.

There may, therefore, be more than one set of 'Owners' of a single property.

It is worth noting that the Act is separate from planning laws or Building Regulations and you must remember that reaching agreement with the Adjoining Owner or Owners under the Act does not remove the need to apply for planning permission where appropriate, or to comply with Building Regulations procedures. Conversely, gaining planning permission or complying with the Building Regulations does not remove the need to comply with the Act, where it is applicable.

If you intend to carry out building work that involves one of the following Categories, you must find out whether that work falls within the Act. If it does, you must notify all Adjoining Owners:

- Work on an existing wall or structure shared with another property (section 2 of the Act).
- Building a free-standing wall or a wall of a building up to or astride the boundary with a neighbouring property (section 1 of the Act).
- Excavating near a neighbouring building (section 6 of the Act).

(Source: Communities and Local Government: 'The Party Wall etc. Act 1996: Explanatory Booklet'). Although this Act refers explicitly to England and Wales, similar legislation may well exist in your area, and it is best to consult with your Local Authority or Council before commencing work of this nature.

8 The plasterboard or PVC outer surface will now be ready to accept the final decorative finish, which can be wallpaper, paint, and so on.

Seal and finish all dry-lining joints and seams with mastic sealant. (Xtratherm Insulation Limited, xtratherm.com)

CAVITY-WALL INSULATION (CWI)

Homes built after the 1930s are likely to have been constructed with an air-spaced gap or cavity between double-skinned brick, or brick and block external walls. This gap was possibly introduced to provide a barrier to the passage of heat from inside the building to the external surroundings. Cavity-wall insulation is a technique whereby the gap between the two wall skins is filled with an insulating material and this can provide a range of benefits, such as saving energy and money through reduced fuel bills. In some cases, cavity-wall insulation can help to reduce condensation inside the building, particularly where this is a problem on external walls.

Generally speaking, a home will be suitable for cavity-wall insulation if the following apply:

- its external walls are unfilled cavity walls;
- the masonry and brickwork of the property are in good condition;
- the cavity is at least 50mm wide.

For a home that was built within the last ten years, it is likely that the cavity is already insulated. In some circumstances, walls exposed to driving rain may be unsuitable for cavity-wall insulation. It is always best to check with a registered specialist contractor who will assess a home's suitability for CWI.

The good news is that CWI is one of the most cost-effective energy-efficiency measures that can be installed in the home. An average grant-aided cavity-wall installation will cost around £300 (after grant), and should typically provide savings on heating bills of between £100 and £120 each year. The installation should pay for itself in around three years.

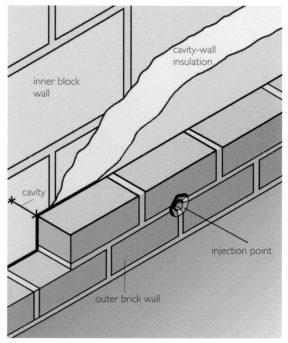

Cavity-wall section showing block inner wall, brick outer skin and insulation in 50mm cavity.

Treatment	Cost of treatment*	Annual saving (£)	Approximate payback*	Annual CO$_2$ saving
Cavity Wall Insulation (CWI)	Approximately £300	£120	Approximately 2.5 years	Around 610kg

Table 24: Typical costs and savings of cavity-wall insulation.
These are estimated figures based on insulating a gas-heated, semi-detached home with three bedrooms. The installed cost includes the grant available from the major energy suppliers under the Carbon Emissions Reduction Target (CERT) or similar offer; the typical unsubsidized installed cost is around £500. It is worth checking if there are any grant offers available in your area. For grant details, see pages 19–20.

Cavity-spaced walls are 'tied' together using wall ties, usually made from galvanized steel. The ties prevent the walls bulging or cracking. The exact reason for introducing cavity walls is unknown, but it is possible that it was simply a cheaper option than building twin-skinned brick walls to keep the elements out. Another theory is that it was introduced to prevent damp and rain from penetrating to the interior of the building. However, there is an ongoing debate as to whether or not a cavity should be filled with an insulating material, such as mineral wool or polystyrene balls.

There have been reports that filling cavity walls has led to various problems, but these issues affect a very small number of properties and the benefits of CWI strongly outweigh any perceived disadvan-

Thermal Looping:
Occurs when an air gap between insulation boards and the inner leaf allow air circulation, thus drawing heat from the inner leaf. This gap is a result of mortar and other debris falling between the insulation and the inner leaf.

Cold Bridges:
1. via Cavity Closer
2. via Window Head
3. via Window Jamb
4. via Window Cill
5. via Wall/Foundation

Thermal Looping's affect on the U-value of an insulated cavity wall construction:

Gap = 0mm   U-value = 0.34
Gap = 3mm   U-value reduced to 0.54 = 159% decrease in performance
Gap = 10mm U-value reduced to 0.65 = 193% decrease in performance

Proper attention to filling the cavity is needed to avoid setting up circulation currents (thermal looping) within the air space. (Homeseal Insulation Installers, Magherafelt, NI, homesealni.co.uk)

tages. It is the UK Government's view that cavities should be filled where they exist, and where the building is suitable for CWI installation.

It is very important when considering the installation of CWI to ensure that the walls are free from damp and that there is an appropriate source of ventilation to allow air movement within the walls. This means checking that the damp-proof course is intact all around the house, to prevent rising damp attacking the insulation, and the brickwork should be re-pointed, where necessary.

If the air is not able to circulate properly within the cavity walls, then the installation of CWI can lead to increased levels of moisture within the building, which may, over time, result in problems with damp. It is imperative that all essential ventilation openings, such as those providing combustion air or underfloor ventilation, and all flues and airbricks in the cavity wall, are clear. CWI should not proceed until these openings have been sleeved or otherwise modified to prevent blockage by the insulation material.

Cavity-Wall Insulation Materials

There are a variety of different insulating materials to choose from (see Table 21), however, they all operate on the same principle: they combine with the still, captive air between the outer and inner external wall skins to form an effective barrier to heat loss.

The preferred materials for CWI in existing buildings are mineral wool, urea formaldehyde (UF) foam, and expanded polystyrene (EPS) beads. These materials are resistant to water penetration – they will not transmit water across the cavity nor will they allow water to transfer from below the damp-proof course by capillary action. They allow moisture to disperse into the atmosphere, providing the wall has been properly ventilated. The materials are fire-retardant and are also resistant to rot, fungi and vermin. Each insulant has reasonably equivalent thermal insulation properties and should be produced under strict quality control, to ensure compliance with the Building Regulations and industry standards.

On existing properties the insulation material is normally applied from the outside of the wall through small holes that are drilled through the outer skin. The holes are drilled in a pattern that will optimize the insertion of the insulation material to avoid voids forming, thereby creating cold spots. In homes with CWI already installed, drilling patterns (repaired insertion holes) are sometimes noticeable around windows and other openings in the external walls. If possible, the installer will drill the holes in the mortar between the brick courses to avoid spoiling the external appearance of the building. The insulation material is injected through the wall to fill the cavity. Once the job has been finished the holes are filled in to make as perfect a match as possible to the existing brickwork or render.

Getting the Best CWI Job

Due to the special handling requirements of the products involved in cavity-wall insulation and the technical nature of the installation, you may not want to attempt this job yourself. Most people employ a specialist contractor to install the cavity-wall insulation for them, as a contractor will provide all the experience and equipment. CWI contractors should be registered with one of the associations listed on page 84, which provide insurance cover should any damage occur during the installation.

Installation Procedure
Whether the CWI is to be completed by a specialist contractor or installed as a DIY project, the correct installation procedure should be followed:

1 An installation survey should be carried out to check the suitability of the property to accept CWI. This may involve an examination of the cavity using a boroscope (or bore viewer/inspection mirror). Inspection using bore viewers, fitted with magnifying lenses and lamps, will determine whether or not the property has already been treated. It will also help determine whether there is debris between the inner and outer wall skins. Debris could lead to cold bridging and the installation of CWI may be detrimental to the building.

2 If a semi-detached or terraced property is to be treated, the insulation should be constrained to

Holes being drilled to accept CWI injection nozzles. (Homeseal Insulation Installers, Magherafelt, NI, homesealni. co.uk)

CWI injection holes being 'made good' after the insulation has been installed. (Homeseal Insulation Installers, Magherafelt, NI, homesealni.co.uk)

Cavity inspection using a borescope.

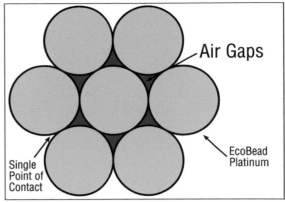

CWI beads showing the spacing and air-gap pattern. (Homeseal Insulation Installers, Magherafelt, NI, homesealni. co.uk)

the relevant property by inserting a cavity barrier at the division between the properties.

3 Injection holes of around 25mm diameter are drilled using a predetermined pattern (depending on the individual BBA certificate) (see page 85 for a typical drilling pattern).

4 The insulation material is blown into the cavity through a flexible hose fitted with an injection nozzle connected to an approved blowing machine.

5 The installation proceeds from the bottom to the top of the wall and from one end of the wall to the other. This will minimize the formation of voids in the insulation during injection.

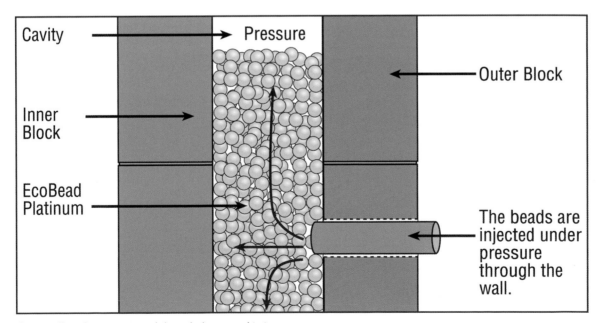

Cavity-wall insulation is injected through the outer skin into the cavity under pressure. (Homeseal Insulation Installers, Magherafelt, NI, homesealni.co.uk)

6 On completion, the injection holes are made good to match the existing finish as closely as possible.

7 Post-installation, all air vents are checked, especially those providing underfloor ventilation and combustion air. In all cases, flues must be carefully checked on completion of the installation using an appropriate test to ensure they are not obstructed by the insulation.

Selecting a CWI Installer

Registered installers of cavity-wall insulation should be members of any one or more of the following organizations:

- National Insulation Association (NIA);
- Cavity Insulation Guarantee Agency (CIGA);
- British Board of Agrément (BBA).

There are two key things to look out for when considering an installer: they must have signed up to a code of professional practice similar to those provided by the NIA; and the installation must be guaranteed for 25 years by CIGA.

A registered installer should complete the job professionally, with little or no mess. Typically, a house can be insulated in a few hours, depending on its size and the accessibility of the external cavity walls. Further advice on grant availability and local registered CWI installers is available from the Energy Saving Trust advice centre on Freephone 0800 512 012. This advice is free, impartial, and given on a one-to-one basis by advisors. They can explain any practical issues and can put you in touch with local approved installers.

DIY Cavity-Wall Insulation – Foam Injection

Most people opt to use an approved CWI contractor, who will use mineral wool, foam or polystyrene beads insulation. However, there are also foam-injection kits available to DIY enthusiasts, if you decide to undertake the job yourself. The following steps are a useful guide to the DIY installation of cavity-wall insulation foam; this is not definitive, and is included for illustration purposes only.

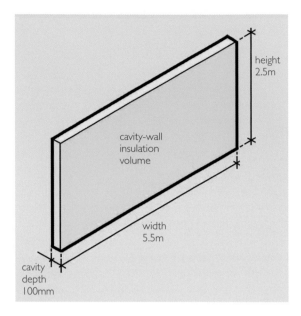

Estimating the quantity of cavity-wall insulation required. For example, for a wall 2.5 x 5.5m with a cavity gap of 100mm, multiply the height of the wall by the width of the wall by the cavity gap: 2.5m x 5.5m x 0.100m = 1.375m³. Typically, one large foam kit, with a capacity of 1.42m³, would be sufficient to fill the cavity gap in this wall. Unless the door and window areas make up a significant portion of the outside wall structure, they can be ignored.

1 Evaluate the size of the cavity you are proposing to fill (see diagram above) and estimate how much foam insulation is required.

2 Drill a hole in the external wall and use a stick or rod to measure the depth of the cavity.

3 Drill holes wide enough (at least 10mm) in the outer brick skin of the exterior wall and check that the injector supplied will fit neatly through the hole.

4 Make certain that there are enough holes drilled to ensure the even distribution of the foam through the wall.

5 The holes should be approximately 50cm apart and 50cm from the bottom of the wall (see diagrams on pages 85 and 86 for typical drilling patterns).

6 Fit a length of vinyl tubing on the end of the spray nozzle to inject the foam through the holes in the wall. Tubing is available in rolls at a cost of approximately £12 per roll.

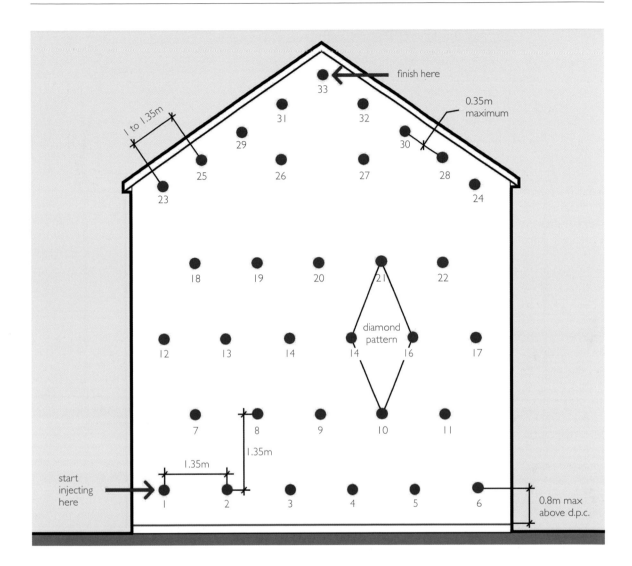

7 Referring to the suggested drilling pattern, start with hole number one and inject foam for 15 seconds. Let the foam rise. If it starts coming out of the hole, plug it with a rag (the foam will continue to rise up the cavity). After 90 seconds the foam will have expanded fully.

8 Move on to hole two and repeat the step above.

9 Proceed along the numbered holes in sequence, following the same process at each hole.

10 If after plugging a hole you find that foam starts to come out of another hole, skip that hole and move along to the next numbered hole. The foam will have expanded sufficiently to fill the

CWI injection holes should be drilled in a diamond pattern with approximately 1.35m between centres. The topmost holes should not be more than 350mm below the upper edge of the cavity and holes should be spaced no more than 1.0m apart. The bottom row of holes should start approximately 800mm above the damp-proof course (DPC). Additional holes may be required to ensure that the cavity is completely filled around windows, doors, along the tops of walls and under gables. The topmost holes should not be more than 1.0m apart under the horizontal features (windows, fascia boards, and so on) and 1.35m apart under the sloping eaves at the top of the gable end. Filling should follow the number sequence shown on the diagram, moving along the elevation and rising to the next layer of holes when one layer has been completed. (Figures are for illustration only.)

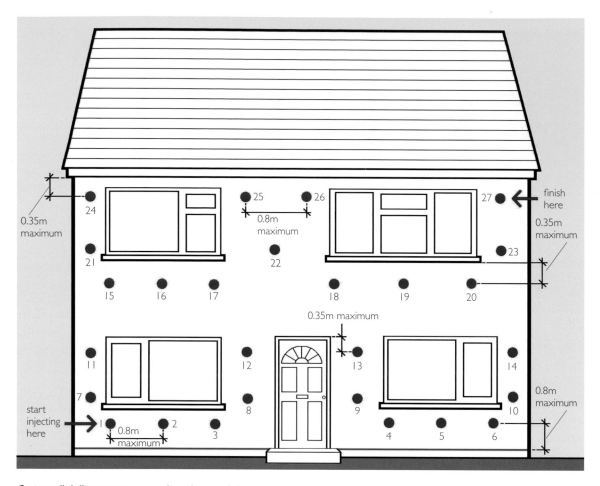

Cavity-wall drilling pattern around windows and doors.

cavity to that point. This applies to the entire wall. If foam comes out of other holes, it means that the foam has spread to that area.

11 When filling around windows and doors, it is useful to drill a pattern of holes below the windows and around doors, to ensure that the foam completes a good fill in the cavity in these areas.

12 The injected foam will eventually rise up the wall to roof level and a careful check should be made to ensure that the foam does not fill the wall and then spill wastefully into the loft or obstruct vents. The fill should be right up to the top of the wall cavity all around the house.

13 When the foam has completely filled the cavity, the injection holes can be filled with external-grade filler, or sand and cement, to be sanded down and painted as necessary to match the external finish.

Guidance on the CWI standards and drilling patterns to complete this work is given in Appendix I.

CHAPTER 6

Reducing Heat Loss through Floors

Floor insulation is cheap and easy to install and, no matter what the cost, the capital investment will always be recovered over time through savings on energy bills. The added bonus is, of course, the benefit of increased comfort.

SAVINGS MADE THROUGH FLOOR INSULATION

The heat loss from rooms through the floors can be significant, accounting for as much as 8 to 15 per cent of the total for a building. Insulating the floors will reduce this loss significantly, leading to savings in energy bills and higher comfort levels. Insulating underneath the floorboards on the ground floor will cost around £90 and save approximately £50 a year. Based on Energy Saving Trust data (2009), filling floorboard gaps and the space between the floorboards and the skirting boards with sealant could save a further £25 a year on heating bills, depending on how bad the gaps are. The materials required to complete the work are available from

Enjoying a warm, draught-free floor.

	Annual saving per year (£)	DIY cost (£)	DIY payback (years)	CO$_2$ saving per year (kg)
Suspended floor insulation	45–50	90	From 2 years	250
Filling gaps between floor and skirting board	20–25	20	Around 1 year	130
Solid-floor insulation	45–50	100	From 2 years	250

Table 25: Approximate annual savings/costs associated with insulating floors.
(Source: Energy Saving Trust)

a range of DIY stores. Filling the gaps costs about £20 if you do it yourself. About 400kg of carbon dioxide (CO_2) a year can be saved by combining both these measures in an average semi-detached three-bedroom house.

Although insulating an existing solid floor can save on energy bills, as a general rule it is not practical, nor is it an economic proposition, to lift such a floor purely to insulate it.

The amount of heat lost through floors depends on a number of factors, including the size (area and depth), the type of floor and the thermal conductivity of the ground below the floor. The shape of the floor is also important since the heat loss is greatest around the edges. Location of the building is a significant factor – for example, heat lost through the floor in a mid-terrace house will be less than that lost through the floor of an end-terrace. Improved floor insulation should achieve a U-value of between 0.2 and 0.25W/m²K, as shown in Table 26.

Using insulation to reduce the heat loss through a floor by 60 per cent to achieve the U-value above will provide a saving of £45–50 per annum on energy bills. In some properties, the floors will be a mixture of solid and suspended floors, the latter with an air space or 'void' beneath them. This void, or 'solum' as it is also known, ensures that there is an air flow below the floors to keep the timbers free from rot. It is important that the vents which supply the fresh air to the void are not blocked or constrained. Most floors can be insulated effectively and the job can be considered a relatively straightforward DIY activity.

Type of floor	Untreated U-value (W/m²K)	U-value with best-practice insulation (W/m²K)
Timber suspended floor	1.0	0.2–0.25
Solid floor	0.7	0.2–0.25

Table 26: Improvements to floor U-value using best-practice insulation.
(Source: Energy-Efficient Refurbishment of Housing (CE83, EST))

Tools and Protective Clothing

Tools

Claw hammer, wooden mallet, screwdriver, wide-bladed cold chisel, wood chisels, padsaw, tenon saw, wood saw, mastic knife, mastic dispensing (caulking) gun, electric circular saw, inspection lamp(s) on wandering lead (plus extension coil), torch, electric jig saw, electric circular saw, electric power drill, wood plane, staple gun including suitable staples, filling knife, nail punch, and a prizing bar or 'jemmy'.

Special Tools

A floorboard saw can be bought or hired – this has a curved profile and teeth on top of the blade as well as along its length. They are particularly useful when floorboards need to be lifted or cut close to the skirting. Other specialist equipment includes electronic cable and pipe detector, a power trowel, and a power sander is useful for floor dressing.

Clothing

Overalls, disposable one-piece coveralls, head covering, gloves, eye protection (safety goggles). Safety shoes with strong soles would also be helpful to protect against floorboard nails, but, for getting in and out of the floor trap and working beneath the floorboards, a light pair of trainers may be more suitable.

PLANNING AND BUILDING REGULATIONS CONSIDERATIONS

Any modification to a floor that involves a structural change, extension or building alteration, particularly to concrete floors, which might impact foundations, may require planning permission. Laying new floors will require building control approval (see page 45, on building regulations). It is good advice always to check with the local planning authority and the building control office before commencing work on floors.

FLOOR INSULATION MATERIALS

There are three main types of underfloor insulation in common use: fibre-based mineral wools, polystyrene blocks and insulation boards, and foil rolls.

Roll of mineral wool blanket suitable for underfloor insulation.

For suspended floors, the materials include mineral wool blanket (20m rolls) or batts, 60mm insulation board, plastic heavy-duty garden netting, screw nails, floorboard nails, wooden battens, mastic, wood glue, and wallpaper paste.

For solid floors, materials include solid polystyrene or XPS insulating boards, polyethylene vapour barrier and damp-proof membrane, wooden battens (50 x 50mm), and water-resistant tape.

Fibre-Based Mineral Wools (Fibreglass or Polyester)

Fibreglass-based mineral wools are commonly used to insulate floors. They are relatively cheap and not flammable, although they can melt at high temperatures. However, fibreglass is not environmentally friendly as it is not renewable, and it also has associated health concerns, with the fibres causing irritation to skin, eyes and the respiratory tract. This is especially important during installation and necessitates protective clothing, gloves, breathing mask and eye protection. Mineral wool for floor insulation is available as blanket rolls or as pre-cut slabs known as batts. Recycled blanket insulation rolls, which are made from plastic cups for example, are also very suitable for underfloor insulation, and this material does not carry the same health concerns.

There are no risks to health with polyester, but it is also a non-renewable material and its insulation value is not as good as fibreglass. Polyester is slightly more flammable, burns very slowly and releases dense smoke.

Large 60mm thick polystyrene and XPS boards suitable for solid-floor insulation.

Polystyrene Blocks and Insulation Boards

Polystyrene is a common insulation product, which is used in a wide range of applications and is suitable for fitting between floor joists. The boards can be installed as a tight fit against the floor, or they can be positioned with an air cavity immediately below the floor surface to act as additional insulation. Denser, load-bearing polystyrene slabs are often used under concrete floors, as are hollow polystyrene blocks strengthened with reinforced concrete. Although it is relatively inexpensive, polystyrene is not environmentally friendly since it is produced as a petrochemical derivative and when it burns it gives off toxic fumes. Once installed it is inert and degrades very slowly.

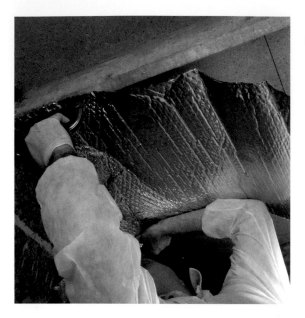

Stapling aluminized reflective foil to floor joists from below the floor.

Manufacturer	Product name	Insulation type and application
Plant Fibre Technology	Isonat	Hemp and cotton slab for between floor joists
Isovlas	Isovlas	Flax slab for between floor joists
Pavatex NBT	Pavatherm Floor NK	Interlocking wood-fibre board for floors
Saint-Gobain Isover	Isowool - Spacesaver	Glass-fibre roll for between floor joists
Rockwool	Roll	Mineral fibre rolls for between floor joists
Pittsburgh Corning Foamglas	T4, S3 and F system	Foamglas board for raised access floors
Steico-NBT	Canaflex Hemp Batts	Hemp-fibre slab, for between floor joists

Table 27: Some available insulation products suitable for suspended ground floors.
Green shading means product has recycled content.
(Source: NGS GreenSpec)

As an environmentally friendly alternative, pumice is a good choice for insulation under concrete floors, as it is a renewable, natural material and can be economical if it is available locally.

Foil Rolls

Insulation foil is made of aluminium-coated paper or plastic and fibreglass. It works by reflecting heat that escapes down through the floor back into the house and also acts as a barrier against cold air entering from below. It is an effective insulator and generally an economical choice for underfloor insulation. Foil-based products are convenient to fix to the floor joists using staples or nails and typically come in rolls 1000mm wide by 50m long. Foil products are not recommended where dampness is a problem, since they are impermeable to moisture and water vapour.

FLOOR TYPES

The nature of ground floors has evolved over the last 100 years or so. Some properties might have a combination of solid and suspended floors, especially where the building is located on a sloping site.

Manufacturer	Product name	Insulation type and application
Rockwool	Rockfloor	Glass-fibre board
Rockwool	Perinsul SL	Foamglas board for structural floors/rafts
Pittsburgh Corning Foamglas	Floorboard and Floorboard F system	
	Foamglas board for structural floors/rafts	
Pittsburgh Corning Foamglas	Jabfloor 70	Polystyrene slab for structural floors/rafts
Vencel Resil	Platinum Floorshield	Polystyrene slab for structural floors/rafts
Springvale	Floorshield	Polystyrene slab for structural floors/rafts
Springvale	Beamshield	Moulded polystyrene for suspended concrete ground beams

Table 28: Some available insulation products suitable for solid ground floors.
Green shading means product has recycled content.
(Source: NGS GreenSpec)

Ground Floors

An uninsulated solid floor will lose its heat rapidly to cooler surroundings, in this case the ground beneath it. It is a similar story with suspended floors, which lose heat through the floorboards to the air space below, by draughts through the gaps between floorboards and along the edges of the floor at the skirting boards. Early floorboarding in suspended floors used simple butt joints and over time the gaps at these joints can open, allowing cold air to be drawn up into the warm room from the void below. The air in the underfloor void is designed to circulate with the outside air, which is drawn in through the floor vents on the external walls, so it will be at the outside air temperature. Once the use of tongue and groove floorboards became more widespread, the gaps occurred less often and there were fewer associated draughts. However, heat can still be lost through uninsulated or damaged tongue and groove floorboards and along the skirtings.

Cellars and Basements

Some terraces and early properties have full-height cellars beneath the floor and these rooms usually have a solid ground floor and a wooden suspended floor above their ceiling. If the suspended floor is not boarded-in from underneath there will be good access to install insulation below it, and rigid insulation board, mineral wool blankets or wool batts can be inserted between the supporting joists. The space between the ceiling joists can also be completely boarded-in from below once insulation has been fitted in place.

Suspended Floors

In the case of suspended timber floors with a crawl space and a sleeper wall construction, the floor can be insulated between the joists by completely lifting the floorboards, or by working from the underfloor void after gaining access through a floor trap.

Solid Floors

The third commonly available type of floor is an uninsulated, concrete solid version. In most cases an existing solid floor can be insulated and finished with a concrete skim or with chipboard flooring boards.

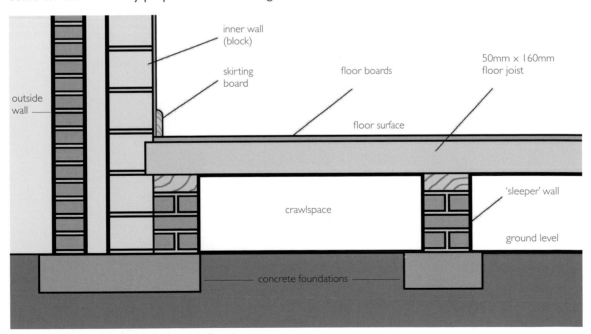

Suspended floor detail showing the sleeper wall and underfloor void or solum.

INSULATING SUSPENDED TIMBER FLOORS

Problems

Suspended floors can be draughty and cold and the conventional solution is to use heavy underlay and fitted carpets. This combination is quite effective at improving comfort, although it can also hide an attractive wooden floor. In a damp environment, the use of rubber underlay and rubber-backed carpets can trap moisture, causing decay in the floorboards.

Wooden floorboards can become warped and may develop gaps over the years. Sometimes, carpets and rugs can be seen to move when gusts of wind surge through the underfloor vents. Draughts will find their way through the gaps and the precious heat energy in the room will seep away wastefully. In more modern floors, which use uninsulated chipboard flooring, the thermal performance of the materials will depend completely on its thickness and thermal resistance.

Underfloor ventilation is usually provided by airbricks set low on the outside walls on all sides of the building. Over the years, airbrick vents may have become blocked inadvertently by flowerbeds or paths, or they may have been deliberately sealed to prevent draughts. Damp soils beneath the house and limited ventilation can present the ideal conditions for the development of fungal decay and timber rot. A common form of rot is caused by the fungus *serpula lacrymans*; see photograph below for a rampant example. Such decay can grow undetected over many years and can eventually lead to the complete destruction of the floor timbers if it is not detected and treated.

Installing Suspended-Floor Insulation Using DIY

Installing insulation below wooden suspended floors is relatively straightforward. Carpets, room furniture and floor coverings need to be shifted or removed and floorboards may need to be lifted. In most cases, however, if you are prepared to tackle clearing the room, underfloor insulation can be installed at a reasonable cost using DIY. A good time to consider underfloor insulation is during room

redecoration when a new floor covering is being introduced, house refurbishment, re-wiring or when a new heating system is being installed.

Partially blocked underfloor vent.

Dry rot fungus – serpula lacrymans – one of the fungi that are responsible for dry rot, which can destroy house timbers. (Property Repair Systems, timber-repair.co.uk/strength.htm)

General view of the void beneath a floor, showing suspended floor arrangement, joists and floorboards from below.

Work to improve the insulation quality of suspended timber floors will usually require access to the space under the floor. Unless there is a cellar beneath, or an existing floor trap, some floorboards may need to be lifted to cut a new trapdoor. It will need to be large enough to pass the insulation materials through and to let a person climb under the floor. (When entering the crawl space below the floor, wear strong overalls, gloves and a breathing mask, since underfloor voids are places which a variety of creatures and insects often inhabit especially in older buildings.)

If the crawl space under the floor is too shallow to allow working from below, then most, if not all of the floorboards, may need to be lifted. Installing the insulation is easier if access to the flooring joists is available from above. This is possible if the floorboards or chipboard flooring slabs have been completely lifted. Floorboards need to be lifted carefully as they are not easy to lever up in one piece – there is always a risk that the boards will splinter and crack. If access to the space between the flooring joists is available, then suitable insulation of the correct width (and of a suitable depth) to fill the gap between the joists should be installed.

Floors constructed using floorboards or chipboard can be insulated in at least three ways:

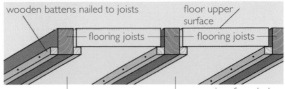

Insulating a suspended floor from below. Battens are nailed to the sides of the joists to support the insulation boards in the space between joists.

1 wooden battens (25 x 25mm) are fitted to the sides of the flooring joists to support insulation board that has been cut to fit neatly in the gap between the joists;
2 mineral wool quilt or batts are cut to fit the gap between the joists. The mineral wool can be held in place using strong plastic netting, which is stapled or tacked to the underside of the joists to prevent it falling down or sagging; or

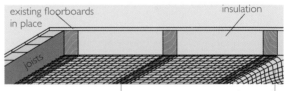

Insulating a suspended floor from below. Netting is strung across the lower surface of the joists and stapled or tacked in place to support the insulation blankets or batts between the joists.

Entering a floor void through a floor trap. Note the DIY equipment, lamps and insulation that also need to pass through the trap.

Polystyrene insulation board fitted between the joists below a chipboard floor. The board is supported by wooden battens nailed to the side of the joist.

3 reflective insulation foil is stapled or tacked to the underside of the joists (*see the illustration on page 90*).

Once access to the floor void is available, it is worth inspecting and, where necessary, carrying out repairs to the floor structure. This is especially important for older floors, which may have been weakened over the years through the inappropriate cutting of

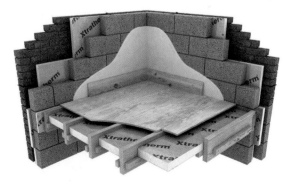

Cutaway drawing showing Xtratherm insulation board fitted between floor joists supported by battens. (Xtratherm Insulation Limited, xtratherm.com)

Handy Hints when Working Beneath the Floor

- Always leave the tools you require within easy reach of the floor trap to save you having to make your way back out again to retrieve something.
- Where possible, have an assistant to pass material back and forward beneath the floor, especially when space is restricted.
- It is a good idea to spread a tarpaulin or plastic cover sheet on the ground beneath the flooring to allow the underfloor work to proceed more comfortably.
- Always ensure that any lamps, electric tools etc. which are plugged into a wandering lead plug block are connected to the mains through a residual current device (RCD) when working below floors, and have a torch to hand in case the lead gets pulled out or the bulb blows.

Safety Tips
- When removing floorboards take care to avoid splinter injury to hands and eyes; always wear gloves and eye protection.
- Do not go under the floor without letting someone know where you are.
- Do not leave open floor traps unattended as they are a hazard.
- When a floor trap is open, ensure that family pets do not climb under the floor.
- Make sure any protruding nails are hammered back into the floorboard, or removed, to prevent a painful injury if stepped upon.
- Caution! Always check the exact location of pipework and electric cabling before commencing any work. Saws can slice through cabling and pipes and this could result in a fatal electric shock, gas leakage or flooding.

holes and notching of joists for central heating or other service pipes and cables. If this is severe, the floor may require strengthening. This is also a good opportunity for checking the sub-floor ventilation. The air vents should be clear and unobstructed and there should be a good air flow. Any work completed, including new insulation, should not restrict the air flow beneath the floor. Chicken wire or wire mesh can be placed across the inside of the vents to prevent small creatures or insects getting through.

It is important to remember that the ventilation of the ground-floor rooms may have been provided partly by draughts passing through the floorboards. If, for whatever reason, this air path is removed, alternative ventilation will be required. Occasionally, suspended ground floors have been constructed without air vents having been fitted. If this is the case, it is recommended that a specialist survey is carried out to make an assessment of the environmental conditions in the sub-floor void and to determine whether or not a new system of ventilation is required.

Completely Removing Floorboards

In some instances, it may be necessary to remove the floorboards completely, especially if they have become warped or damaged. If the flooring has been completely removed insulation can be inserted between the joists from above and strong plastic netting can be laid over the joist upper surfaces and stapled or tacked in place to support the insulation. Once the insulation has been fitted, the flooring can be reinstated. If the boards are in good condition they can simply be replaced. If a small number are damaged, the bad sections can be removed. Replacement boarding can be purchased and planed to fit in with the original flooring and the repairs made good. Most timber suppliers will provide matching, or similar timber. If the flooring is to be used as a finished surface in the room, then the boards can be sanded, stained and varnished, as desired.

In cases where the original flooring is unusable – where it has become warped or damaged through damp or rot – it can be replaced with appropriate flooring plywood, or pressure-treated tongue and groove flooring chipboard. The new flooring boards should be screwed down to facilitate easy lifting in

future. The final board butting at a wall can be positioned by removing the lower section of its groove so that it can be set in place and screwed down without engaging the tongues of the neighbouring boards.

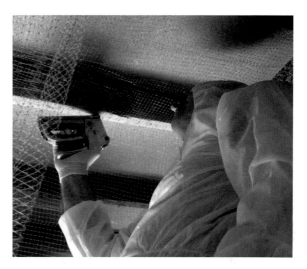

Plastic netting is stapled to the underside of the floor joists to support the 60mm mineral wool blanket insulation.

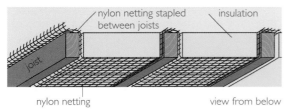

Insulating a suspended floor from above, once the floorboards have been removed. Netting is strung across the upper surface of the joists and stapled or tacked in place to support the insulation blankets, batts or boards.

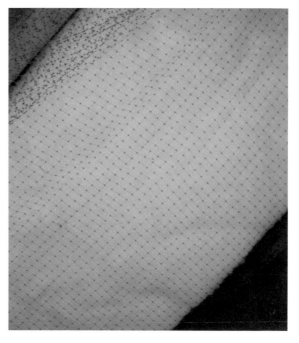

Mineral wool supported between the underfloor joists using plastic netting stapled to the joists.

When floors are laid, the floorboards are nailed to the joists before the skirting boards are fitted to the walls and as a consequence the ends of the floorboards will be trapped beneath the skirting. This means that it can be particularly difficult to take up a continuous floorboard. When a floorboard end is trapped below a skirting board, it can be freed by lifting the other end as high as possible until the board is almost vertical. It can then be pulled up and away from the gap between the skirting board and the last joist nearest the wall.

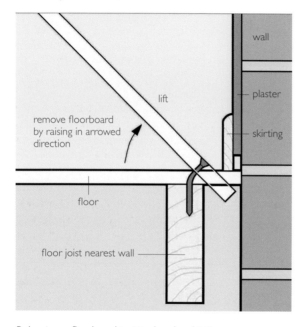

Releasing a floorboard trapped under skirting.

If a floorboard has a partition wall built on top of it, the board will need to be cut across its width close to the wall. This can be done by drilling a series of pilot holes and then cutting across the board. When replacing the board, a wooden fillet (50 x 37mm) will need to be attached to the joist to ensure that it is securely supported.

Once the underfloor insulation is installed and the flooring is back in place, then the draughts through the floor will have been eliminated. However, there is still the possibility of gaps along the edges, at the skirting boards and around the heating pipes where they rise through the floorboards. These gaps should be sealed with suitable mastic.

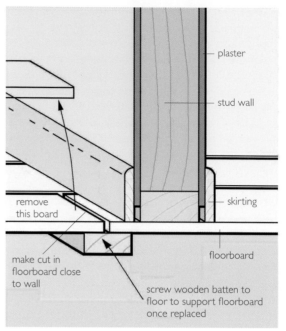

Releasing a trapped floorboard at a partition or stud wall.

Creating a Floor Trap in Square-Edge Floorboards

In some cases floor traps will already exist, for example, if the building has been re-wired or a central-heating system has been installed. If a new trap needs to be created, then generally only three or four board sections need to be lifted. In most cases, a floor trap 0.5m long by three boards wide will allow a person to crawl through.

In practice, floorboards run between joists to suit the lengths of board available when the floor is laid. This means that there may be shorter boards and these are a good place to start taking up the floor to create the trap. These boards may even have been lifted previously and this can make the job a lot simpler. Square-edged floorboards do not have tongue and groove edges so they can be lifted more easily.

A floor trap can be created by removing a section of floorboard between two joists in the following steps:

1 Begin by marking the position of the proposed floor trap on the floorboards using pencil or chalk. Use the nails in the floorboards as a guide to the centre line of the joists.

Square-edged floorboards (no tongue and groove).

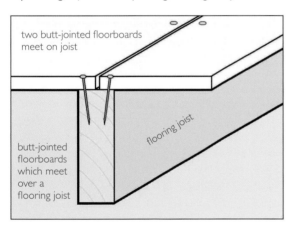

Floor joist and floorboard detail showing how two square-edged floorboards butt on the joist.

2 Select the floorboards that will be cut out to make the floor trap. Align two sides of the floor trap with the centre lines of the joists on either side. Cuts will be made along the centre lines of the joists.

3 Take great care at this stage to ensure that there are no service cables or pipes alongside the joist or below the floor which could be cut with the saw. This can be checked with an electronic detector or sometimes the route of the cables or pipes will have been marked on the floor. If there are nearby cables or pipes, then the floor trap should be moved to another position.

4 Use the pencil line along the centre line of the joist as a guide to drill a row of 3mm holes across the first floorboard section to be lifted. Drill another row of holes along the same floorboard on the other joist. The floorboard section will be lifted between the two lines of holes on the joists.

5 Make sure the holes are as close to each other as possible, being careful to avoid the nails in the joist. Remove obstructing nails as necessary using a sharp instrument such as a screwdriver and claw hammer, or use a punch to hammer the nail through the board into the joist.

6 Use a fine wood chisel or saw to cut the floorboard right through to the joist across its width on both sides of the floor trap. A tenon saw and a craft knife might help cut down to the joist to free the board. Floorboard saws are also available, with a curved blade with teeth all along its length, and these are particularly useful for this job.

7 Once the two sides of the first floorboard section have been cut, then the square-edged board is only held by the floorboard nails and it can be levered up and away from the joist using a flat-bladed chisel.

8 The chisel should be placed in the cuts at the joist and the board can be raised with the floorboard nails intact. The nails should be removed to prevent injury.

9 Once the first board is free from the joist, this will allow a cut with a tenon saw (or floorboard saw) to be made along the pencil line crossing the other boards on the joist, again avoiding the nails. The required number of floorboard sections can be removed to provide access.

10 Wooden fillets (50 x 37mm) of sufficient length can be cut and inserted along the joists to provide additional support along the edges of the completed trap.

11 When re-fitting the floor trap, the boards should be screwed in place on to the joists.

Creating a Floor Trap in Tongue and Groove Floorboards

1 Mark the position of the proposed floor trap on the floorboards using pencil or chalk. Use the nails in the floorboards as a guide to the centre line of the joists.

2 Select the floorboards that will be cut out to make the floor trap. Align two sides of the floor trap with the centre lines of the joists on either side.

3 Take great care at this stage to make sure that there are no service cables or pipes alongside the joist or below the floor, which could be cut with the saw. This can be checked with an electronic detector or sometimes the route of the cables or pipes is marked on the floor. If there are cables or pipes nearby then the floor trap should be moved to another position. This is particularly important when cutting through the tongues of the floorboard sections.

4 Use the pencil line along the centre line of the joist as a guide to drill a row of 3mm holes across the first floorboard section to be lifted. Drill another row of holes along the same floorboard on the other joist. The floorboard section will be lifted between the two lines of holes on the joists.

5 Make sure the holes are as close to each other as possible, being careful to avoid the nails in the joist. Remove obstructing nails as necessary using a sharp instrument such as a screwdriver and claw hammer.

Edge-on view of tongue and groove floorboards.

6 Use a fine wood chisel or saw to cut the floor-board right through to the joist across its width on both sides of the floor trap. A tenon saw and a craft knife might help cut down to the joist to free the board, or use a floorboard saw.

7 Now, cut through the tongue and groove joint along both sides of the first floorboard section. Use the joint as a guide to drill a row of joined-up 3mm diameter holes approximately 3cm long. Insert a pad saw through the resulting slot to cut through the tongue of the floorboard section along its length between the joists.

8 It will be difficult to cut the tongue right up to where it meets the joist; again, a floorboard or tenon saw will be useful to finish the cut. A tool with a sharp blade, such as an old scraper or strong, sharp craft knife, may also be helpful to make sure the cut is made up to the pencil line.

9 Once the four sides of the first floorboard section (two along the joists and down each tongue and groove edge) have been cut, then the board is only held by the floorboard nails and it can be

levered up and away from the joist using a flat-bladed chisel.

10 The chisel should be placed in the cuts at the joist and the board can be raised. Remove the nails.

11 Once the first board is free from the joist, this will allow a cut with a tenon saw (or floorboard saw) to be made along the pencil line crossing the other boards on the joist (again avoiding the nails). Once the other floorboards have been cut at the joist, it should not be necessary to cut through their tongues and the boards can be removed by pulling them away from the tongue and groove joint. If this does not work, the procedure for cutting through the tongues along the boards should be repeated until an adequate number of boards have been removed to make the floor trap.

12 Wooden fillets (50 x 37mm) can be cut and inserted along the joists to provide additional support along the edges of the completed trap.

13 When re-fitting the floor trap, the boards should be screwed in place on to the joists.

Drill a series of pilot holes in the gap between the two floorboards. The holes should join up to create sufficient space to allow the saw blade to fit between the boards. This will allow the saw to cut through the tongue along both sides of the board.

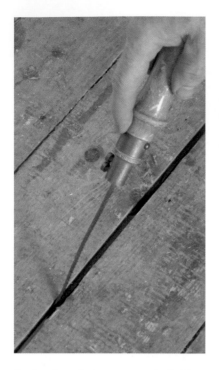

Cutting through the tongue on both sides of the floorboard using a pad saw.

Lifting the floorboard after both ends of the cut have been made.

Sawing through the floorboards to create a trap in tongue and groove flooring.

The trap should be large enough to allow comfortable entry to the underfloor void (shown in tongue and groove flooring).

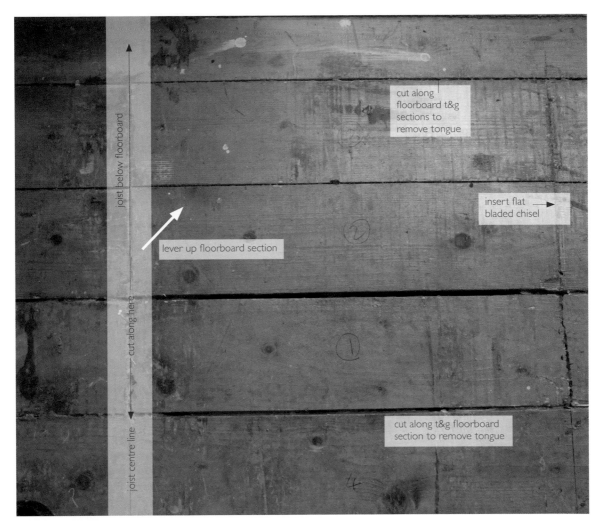

Completed floorboard inspection trap in place.

Creating a Floor Trap in Chipboard Flooring

Because they are more recent, most chipboard floors will already have a floor trap, but it is a very straightforward DIY job to cut a new one.

Chipboard flooring slabs will normally be laid on the floor joists, tongue and groove fitted to each other and screwed down to the joists. A floor trap of the required size should be drawn on the flooring, making sure there is sufficient overlap on the joists to support the edges of the floor trap (25mm will be sufficient). A floor trap can then be created by removing a section of chipboard between two joists. The procedure is outlined in the following steps:

1 Locate the chipboard slab that has been laid closest to the wall, as it will not be tongue and groove fitted (the tongue, or the lower part of the groove will have been removed to permit it to be set in place). The screws that hold it to the joists should be removed to allow the chipboard slab to be lifted clear.

2 As with the other types of flooring, it is essential to take care at this stage to make sure that there are no service cables or pipes alongside the joist or below the floor, which could be cut with the saw. This can be checked with an electronic detector or sometimes the route of the cables or pipes is marked on the floor. If there are cables or pipes nearby, then the floor trap should be moved to another position. This is particularly important if a new trap is to be cut in the chipboard.

3 Once this slab has been lifted, there may be access to the underfloor void, but if this is not the case, then a new trap will need to be cut by lifting the next chipboard slab out from the wall. Before doing this, mark the centre-line positions of the supporting joists on it. These may be evident from the line of screws securing the chipboard.

4 When lifting the flooring chipboard make sure that all the screws are removed and the board can then be withdrawn by pulling it from the direction of the gap in the floor.

5 New wooden fillets (50 x 37mm) will need to be cut to sufficient length and inserted between the joists to support the other two edges of the floor trap, so that it is completely supported along all four edges.

Filling Gaps in the Floor

Gaps between floorboards can be unsightly and ruin an otherwise attractive floor. They will also allow draughts to penetrate into the living space. There are a number of ways to plug the gaps including using papier-mâché, filling with wood strips and using mastic or wood filler. If the gaps are small, a stiff mix of papier-mâché can be made up from newspaper and wallpaper paste. The mix can be coloured to achieve a closer colour match to the flooring and then pressed into the gaps and smoothed off with a filling knife. If there are large gaps between the floorboards then a thin wooden lath can be trimmed to shape and hammered into place. A small quantity of wood glue can be applied to the lath to hold it securely. The lath should be tapped to floor surface level with a mallet and then planed to give a good finish. Mastic or wood filler of the correct colour match can also be used to fill the spaces around the floor edges at the skirting boards.

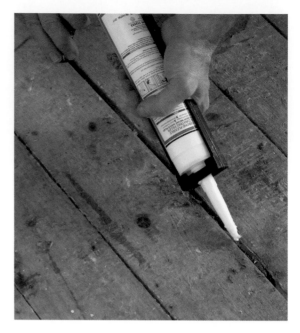

Filling cracks in flooring using mastic. A variety of materials can be used including papier-mâché, mastic and wood filler.

The gap between the flooring and the skirting board can be filled with mastic. Flexible mastic will allow the floor to expand and contract.

INSULATING SOLID FLOORS

A concrete solid floor is a cold surface that may also be load-bearing. As a general rule it is not practical, nor is it an economic proposition, to lift a solid floor purely to insulate it. If the floor is being re-laid or replaced, however, then it should be insulated as a matter of course. Floor insulation is a mandatory Building Regulation requirement for all new buildings. Concrete solid floors laid since the early 1990s should have been put down with the appropriate amount of insulation and damp-proof membrane in place.

One option is to lay insulation on the upper surface of the existing floor. However, this will result in a raised floor level and care will need to be taken, particularly at stairs and door thresholds. These problems can be avoided if the floor is being completely replaced and the original floor level can be maintained.

If insulation is placed above an existing concrete floor, then the room will warm up more rapidly when the heating is on. Where a new floor is in a warm south-facing room, then, where practical, insulation should be placed below the concrete slab. In this case, the concrete above the insulation helps absorb and retain heat and limits room overheating.

If a solid floor is being laid to replace a rotted timber floor, then all the old timbers, including the architraves, skirting boards and door, should be removed and disposed of in a fire. It would be prudent to treat the earth base below the floor and any exposed brickwork with a proprietary fungicide. Repair and fill any lost brickwork, or areas disturbed when the old timbers were removed, with replacement bricks and mortar.

Insulating an Existing Concrete Floor

A good DIY approach to insulating an existing concrete slab solid floor (which may be tiled), is to place a layer of insulation on top of the floor and then to form the new floor surface with tongue and groove chipboard. This is known as a floating chipboard floor. Before starting the job, it is wise to consult with the local building control service to

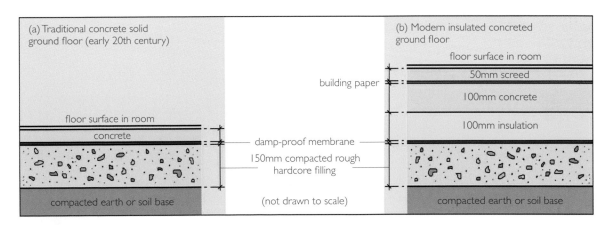

Sectional illustrations of a traditional solid ground floor and a modern insulated solid floor.

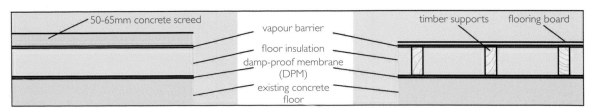

An existing or new floor can be insulated and finished with a concrete screed or a floating chipboard floor.

concrete floor

DPM

insulation board

channel for heating pipes

check that ventilation of the existing floors will not be affected and that the correct insulation is being used. Solid floors laid before the 1990s, when Building Regulations (England and Wales) changed, can be insulated by covering with thick solid polystyrene

Foil-backed solid-floor insulation in place above existing solid floor and damp-proof membrane (DPM) before final-finish floor skim is applied.

or polyisocyanurate foam insulating boards. These boards are waterproof and have sufficient compressive strength to support floor loads.

An existing solid floor that is to be retained can be insulated using the following steps:

1 Begin by removing the skirting boards since installing insulation will raise the floor level.
2 The floor levels should be marked using a long spirit level on the retaining walls to indicate where the upper surface of the new floor will be.
3 The existing floor should be overlaid with a continuous layer of thick polythene which acts as a damp-proof membrane (DPM). This is available in 4 x 3m rolls of 1000-gauge polythene, 250 micron thick.
4 In some instances pressure-treated wooden battens (50 x 50mm) can be placed across the existing concrete floor to the depth of the insulation. This will provide additional support if a floating chipboard floor is to be used (see the illustration on page 106). Insulation can then be inserted between the battens.
5 The raised floor level will reduce the height of the ceiling and clearances may become an issue, especially at door openings, where the door lintel will be at a lower height above the new floor. As a result, there must be a happy medium to this work. The depth (and benefit) of the insulation installed must be balanced against the loss in room height, which, in some cases, may be restrictive. Typically, 25mm of polystyrene will improve the insulation value (U-Value) to $0.45W/m^2K$, while 40mm of polyisocyanurate foam will give an improvement to $0.31W/m^2K$.
6 Joints between the insulation boards should be taped with water-resistant tape to prevent concrete or moisture ingress.
7 The insulation should then be covered with a layer of polythene to act as a vapour barrier (available in 2.5 x 20m rolls, 125 micron thick).
8 The floor can then be topped off with flooring-grade tongue and groove chipboard (or with a concrete screed), which is applied directly on top of the vapour barrier. Flooring-grade chipboard should be glued edge to edge to ensure that it

will remain in place.
9 A gap needs to be left along the edge of the chipboard or concrete screed where it meets the wall. This will allow the floor to expand as the temperature and moisture content changes (see the illustration on page 103).
10 If a concrete finish is selected, the gap around the edge should be filled with insulation to prevent cold bridging. A strip of insulation, the same depth as the concrete, at least 25mm thick with an R-value of $75m^2K/W$, should be placed around the periphery of the floor.
11 If the finish is concrete, the surface of the concrete slab should be very level and smooth, to a tolerance of 5mm in 3m. A power trowel can be used to achieve this.
12 Repositioned skirting boards should be attached

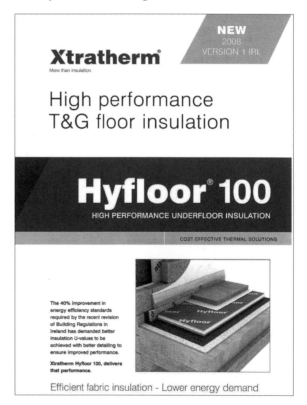

Product brochure for Xtratherm rigid polyisocyanurate tongue and groove underfloor insulation. Note the insulation at the periphery of the floor, which will prevent cold bridging and allows for expansion and contraction of the floor. (Xtratherm Insulation Limited, xtratherm.com)

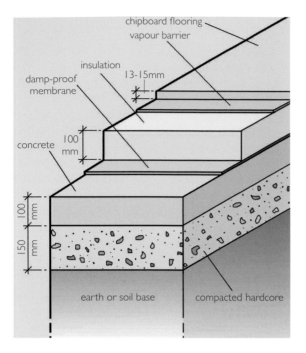

chipboard flooring
vapour barrier
insulation
damp-proof
membrane
13-15mm
concrete
100 mm
100 mm
150 mm
earth or soil base
compacted hardcore

One option is to use a chipboard floating floor with the insulation and new floor laid on top of an existing concrete solid floor.

to the wall and not the floor, to allow for floor expansion and contraction.

13 If the floor level has been raised, then the room doors will need to be trimmed as appropriate, and steps between rooms and halls may need to be addressed.

Pipes and Cables in Solid Floors

When lifting or replacing solid floors, always be aware of service cables and pipes. If there is a chance that the existing electricity or gas supply to the building crosses or comes near to the floor, it is essential to check its route with the relevant utility. Re-routed cables and wires can be laid in channels in the new floor; their position should be recorded accurately and marked on the floor for future reference. Pipes and cables can be laid in plastic duct boxes set in the floor. Pipework can be insulated inside the duct boxes to prevent freezing.

This arrangement also permits easy access should servicing be required.

FLOOR COVERINGS

A floor covering can provide insulation as well as being a useful means of draught prevention and decoration. Carpets remain one of the most popular floor coverings but, in recent years, increasing numbers of alternative fabric floor coverings have become available, including materials such as jute, sisal, coir, seagrass and wool. Natural floor covering materials are usually backed with latex, which is a natural rubber product, rather than PVC or plastic, and these will have a very similar insulation quality to conventional carpets. Rubber underlay beneath the carpet or floor covering is also an excellent heat insulator and sound attenuator, as well as being a means of preventing draughts and protecting the floor surface below the covering.

Wooden floor coverings have become more fashionable, with a huge variety of finishes available. Some of these wooden boards are laminates or engineered boards, where a real wood veneer or a plastic wood grain material is used on top of a wood composite or medium-density fibreboard (MDF). Wooden floor coverings act as a good source of insulation and are very draught-resistant, especially if the gap around the walls is sealed using mastic covered by a matching wooden trim. Cork is a particularly useful floor covering because it is an excellent insulator and can be obtained from sustainable sources. Cork is recovered from trees every nine years as it re-grows to replace material that has been stripped previously. Bamboo is an increasingly popular floor covering, with strong environmental credentials and good thermal insulation properties.

Another source of floor covering that has been in use for some time is linoleum (or lino). Some types are too thin to offer much insulation benefit, but lino can be an effective means of removing draughts. Linoleum has been used particularly in kitchens and bathrooms since it is waterproof and easy to clean. Tiled floors, as well as being extremely durable and easy to clean, provide very good draught-proofing characteristics.

CHAPTER 7

Insulating Lofts and Roofs

Heat rises and without loft insulation much of the valuable, expensive energy used to heat a home will be lost through the roof.

LOFT INSULATION COSTS, GRANTS AND SAVINGS

Insulating the loft, or topping up any insulation that is already there, is a straightforward and effective way to reduce heating bills and a job that can be done at a reasonable cost. Most homes have a loft or roof-space that can be insulated by fitting insulation between the ceiling joists. If the loft has been converted to create a new room or attic, then insulation can be applied to the rafters to prevent the heat from escaping. Loft insulation acts as a blanket, trapping heat which rises up through a building to stop it from escaping. Even if the building already has some insulation, adding more to create the recommended 270mm depth can give further savings.

From a DIY perspective, this is an ideal place to start because around a quarter of an uninsulated building's heat loss is through its roof. According to the Energy Saving Trust (EST), the warmth lost from all the uninsulated homes in the UK is enough to heat more than 1.6 million homes for a year, and if everyone in the UK installed the recommended depth of loft insulation that could save around £520 million. It would also save approximately 3 million tonnes of carbon dioxide every year, which is enough to fill Wembley Stadium nearly 380 times.

Before carrying out any loft insulation work, check whether an energy-efficiency improvement grant, cashback or special offer is available to help cover the costs. In the UK and Ireland, energy-efficiency grants that cover loft insulation can be available through a range of organizations, including gas and electricity suppliers, the EST and the Sustainable Energy Authority for Ireland (SEAI in the Republic of Ireland), as well as local authorities and councils. Depending on your personal circumstances, energy-

	Loft insulation (installing 270mm in an uninsulated loft)	Top-up loft insulation (installing sufficient insulation from 50mm to bring it up to 270mm)
Annual saving per year (£)	150	45
Installed cost (£)	250	200
Installed payback (years)	2	5
DIY cost (£)	250–350	200–300
DIY payback (years)	2–3	5–7
CO2 saving per year (kg)	800	230

Table 29: Loft insulation showing the approximate costs and payback.
Note: The figures are based on insulating a gas-heated, semi-detached home with three bedrooms. Loft insulation is effective for at least 40 years, so, as the payback using DIY is around 2 to 5 years, it will pay for itself over and over again. (Source: Energy Saving Trust, 2010 prices)

Loft insulation top-up using 270mm insulation. The space between the ceiling joists has been filled with insulation, which has settled to a depth of about 100mm.

Loft insulated with mineral wool insulation to a depth of 270mm, using two perpendicular layers of insulation.

efficiency grants can cover part or all of the cost of installing energy-saving measures such as loft insulation. The EST and SEAI will help find contact details for local schemes; for contact details, *see* page 181.

Table 29 shows that the cost of loft insulation for a typical three-bedroom semi-detached house with gas central-heating starts at around £200, and it also shows that it will take no longer than seven years to pay for itself through the savings made on heating bills. As the table indicates, sometimes getting a professional installer to fit the loft insulation can be cheaper than doing the work yourself, depending on the insulation offers and grants available.

When approaching loft insulation, it is very important to consider how the loft is ventilated. There are also issues associated with condensation that need to be taken into consideration. Careful planning and the appropriate use of vapour barriers and suitable ventilation can help avoid difficulties. Best practice suggests that the U-value of an insulated loft should be $0.16 \text{W/m}^2\text{K}$, although much higher values are achievable. Table 30 shows the thermal performance of different thicknesses of typical insulation materials between and over ceiling joists.

Equipment Required

Tools and Protective Clothing
Insulating roof-spaces is a straightforward activity and requires few tools; however, some of the insulation materials available can be irritant and their fibres and dust should not be inhaled. Skin contact with some materials can cause itching, so protective clothing, gloves, goggles and a breathing mask should be worn.

Tools
Craft knife, straight-edge ruler (1m), inspection lamp(s) on wandering lead, extension cable, torch, strong scissors (to cut insulation blankets), hacksaw, claw hammer, jemmy bar (to lift boards laid in loft), long measuring tape, steps and loft access ladder.

Special Tools
Staple gun with staples. A jemmy or prizing bar is also useful for levering up boards laid in the loft for storage or walkways, which will need to be lifted to permit the insulation to be fitted. When installing the insulation materials, temporary boards will need to be laid securely to stand or kneel on, to roll out or otherwise install the insulation. For blown-in fibre insulation a blowing machine can be hired (available from local rental stores)

Between joists (mm)	Over joists (mm)	U-value W/m²K
Sheep's wool between and over*		
100	140	0.16
100	200	0.12
100	250	0.11
Mineral wool between and over**		
100	150	0.17
100	200	0.15
100	300	0.11
Cellulose loose fill between and over***		
Total depth of fill (mm)		
250	0.18	
300	0.15	
400	0.10	

Table 30: Typical U-values for loft insulation between and over loft joists.
(Sources: *Second Nature; **Knauf; ***Excel, NGS Greenspec)

200mm thick insulation quilt made from recycled plastic bottles. Two layers laid at right-angles will provide an excellent thickness of loft insulation.

Insulation	Material	Ease of installation/DIY	Advantages	Disadvantages
Batt or blanket loft insulation	This insulation is available in rolls of rock, glass or mineral fibre and is the most common form of loft insulation Blanket is also available as foil-backed for even better thermal performance, although it costs more	Straightforward to install and well suited to DIY	Easy to install Some brands use recycled glass or sheep's wool (which is non-irritant and non-toxic) Good for insulating accessible spaces such as lofts	Some materials such as glass-fibre and rock wool can irritate the skin, so proper protection from the fibres is required The more environmentally friendly options are usually more expensive
Loose-fill insulation	Loose-fill insulation is made from a variety of granular or lightweight materials such as cork granules, exfoliated vermiculite, mineral wool or cellulose fibre Environmentally friendly loose-fill insulation includes recycled newspaper	Easy to install Available in bags for DIY application All gaps and holes in the ceilings need to be sealed off to prevent the insulation falling through If the cavity is not filled then the ends of the space between the joists will need to be blocked off with plywood to prevent the insulation falling into the cavity	Fits easily between irregularly spaced joists or around obstructions Useful for topping up existing insulation in lofts	Can come loose in draughty lofts Protective clothing and equipment needed during installation
Sheet or board insulation Some insulation boards are foil backed for enhanced thermal performance	Sheet or board insulation is a good choice for loft conversions. Sheet insulation is designed for insulating the sloping sides of the roof and is often made from polystyrene, polyurethane or polyisocyanurate boards Some sheet insulation boards are available with a fire-resistant, moisture-resistant or decorative covering Sheet insulation can also be ordered pre-cut to specific sizes for an additional cost	Easy to install	Environmentally friendly insulation options include cork, straw and wood board Excellent for insulating loft conversions Can be covered with plasterboard for an attractive finish High insulating value per unit thickness Some boards come with their own system of attachment	Synthetic board insulation materials use large amounts of energy during production Can be more expensive than other insulation types
Blown-fibre insulation	You will normally use a professional contractor to install blown-fibre insulation — the insulation is blown into the gaps between joists	Usually professionally installed, although DIY possible.	Fits easily between irregularly spaced joists or around obstructions Useful for topping up existing insulation in lofts and where loft space is cramped or heavily obstructed	Can come loose in draughty lofts Requires professional installation
Plastic foil rolls	Made from layers of aluminium and plastic foil, wadding and air bubbles and the material also reflects radiant heat	Easy and rapid to fit using a staple gun Seams require to be sealed for maximum effectiveness	Can be stapled directly to rafters across the full length of the roof-space	More expensive than the alternatives Cheaper versions are less effective
Spray foam insulation		Most suited for old or infirm roofs		

Table 31: Some commonly used loft insulation materials.
(Source: NRG GreenSpec)

LOFT AND ROOF-SPACE INSULATION MATERIALS

There are several different types of loft insulation to choose from and a variety of materials available (see Tables 31 and 32), each of which has factors for and against. Loft insulation ranges from fibreglass and mineral wool quilting to environmentally friendly recycled paper and plastic, sheep's wool and hemp. Environmentally friendly insulation materials can be more expensive but they may be from renewable sources, and most require less energy to produce.

Traditional materials, such as fibreglass blanket, reduce heat transfer by trapping air in the mass of the blanket, but this does not reduce radiant heat transfer. Foil insulation, on the other hand, does reduce radiant heat transfer very effectively. This can produce better results with less material than is the case with fibreglass rolls. Foil insulation reduces vapour and moisture condensation, which can be a problem in some installations. As with all products, there are variations in the quality of foil insulation and it is also important to check that the material

Hemp insulation slabs are environmentally sound and well suited for insulating lofts. (Homeseal Insulation Installers, Magherafelt, NI, homesealni.co.uk)

Plastic-foil insulation sheeting (from a roll) can be stapled directly to the roof rafters in situations where it is difficult or impossible to lay insulation blankets or insulation boards on top of the ceiling joists.

Insulation board is available from most DIY outlets and is ideal for supporting moderate-weight storage in the roof-space when placed on top of the ceiling joists. It can be fitted over the top of loft blanket or loose-fill insulation. The board shown is Knauf XPS Spaceboard.

meets the requirements of the Building Regulations (Chapter 3).

Table 32 details a range of insulation materials (with their product names) available to insulate roofs and lofts. The materials shaded in green are regarded as environmentally friendly.

Other materials needed include draught strip (for sealing the roof-space trap door) and screw nails to secure access boards or walkways on joists. It is better to screw boards down than nail them in place as hammering may crack the ceilings beneath.

Manufacturer	Product	Insulation type and application
Pavatex NBT	Pavaroof pitched	Pitched roof loft insulation system
Termex	Termex	Loose cellulose for lofts
Excel	Warmcell 500	Loose cellulose for lofts
Excel	Warmcell 300	Loose cellulose for lofts
Excel	Warmcell 100	Loose cellulose for retrofit/lofts
Plant Fibre Technology	Isonat	Hemp and cotton slab for between rafters/joists in lofts
Isovlas	Isovlas	Flax slab for between rafters/joists
Black Mountain	Sheep's wool	Wool rolls for between rafters/joists
Second Nature	Thermafleece	Wool rolls for between rafters/joists
YBS	Non-itch	Polyester slab or roll for between rafters/joists
Pavatex NBT	Pavatherm	Wood-fibre board for under/over rafters
Pavatex NBT	Isolair	Wood-fibre sarking board
Saint-Gobain Isover	Isowool - Spacesaver	Glass-fibre roll for between rafters/joists
Rockwool	Blown Loft Insulation	Blown mineral fibre for lofts
Rockwool	Rockfall Systems	Mineral fibre rolls for between rafters/joists
Rockwool	Flexi	Mineral wool slab for between rafters/joists
Rockwool	Cladding Roll	Mineral wool rolls for industrial framed buildings
Pittsburgh Corning Foamglas	Wallboard & Readyboard	Foamglas board for under/over rafters
Steico-NBT	Canaflex Hemp Batts	Hemp-fibre slab, for between Steico-NBT rafters/joists

Table 32: Insulation products suitable for pitched-roof lofts.
Green shading means product has recycled content. (Source: NGS GreenSpec)

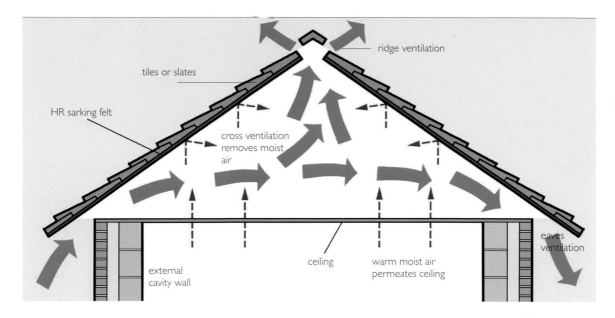

Ventilated roof-space design using HR sarking (roofing felt).

ROOF-SPACE VENTILATION

It is extremely important to avoid introducing condensation when carrying out loft or roof insulation work. Condensation occurs when warm, moist air comes into contact with a cold surface. The warm, moist air in a house rises through the ceilings from the rooms below – bathrooms and kitchens are key sources. The build-up of condensation can lead to major problems within the building fabric and the presence of damp can potentially lead to the decay of timber roof-frame components. Guidance on the control of condensation in pitched roofs is set down in British Standard, BS 5250: 2002.

Ventilated (or Cold) Roof-space or Loft

The vast majority of the existing UK housing stock has been constructed with traditional 'cold roof' or 'loft' spaces. In this design, hot moist air inside the building diffuses up through the ceilings into the roof space. From here, cross ventilation air flows are introduced to remove the moist air to the outside through ventilators fitted to the eaves or soffit boards. Cold outside air moves in to the loft to take the place of the removed hot moist air. This means

that a ventilation path is required, at least 30mm wide, between the loft insulation and the underside of the sarking felt, along the full length of the loft. Holes and gaps in the ceiling should be sealed to restrict the amount of moist air entering the roof-space. For roofs over 35-degree pitch, or over 10m span, ridge ventilation is required, equivalent to a continuous 5mm gap along the ridge. This can be provided using ridge ventilation tiles.

Unventilated or Breathing Roof-space or Loft

Modern designs handle moisture removal from lofts in a different way. In a breathing roof-space, hot moist air attempting to diffuse up through the ceiling from the rooms below is prevented by an airtight vapour control layer (VCL). The roof sarking felt will allow any residual, small amounts of moisture to diffuse through to the space between the tiles or slates and the sarking. This moisture is then dispersed by ventilation through the slates or tiles to the outside air.

Sarking Felt

The main difference between traditional ventilated roofs and modern 'breathing roofs' lies in the way

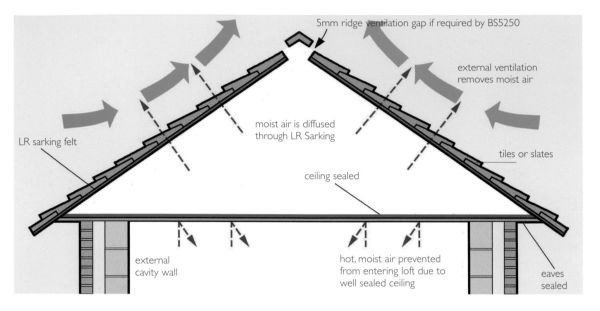

5mm ridge ventilation gap if required by BS5250

external ventilation
removes moist air

moist air is diffused
through LR Sarking

LR sarking felt

tiles or slates

ceiling sealed

external
cavity wall

hot, moist air prevented
from entering loft due to
well sealed ceiling

eaves
sealed

Unventilated roof-space design using LR sarking (roofing felt).

Roof-space ventilation can be provided through roof-mounted vents.

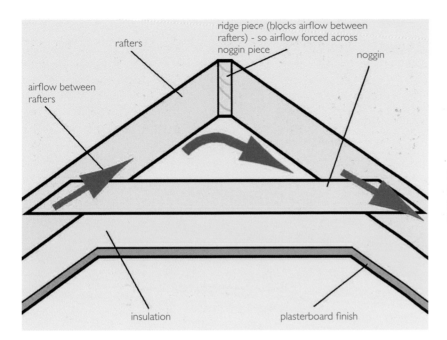

rafters

ridge piece (blocks airflow between rafters) - so airflow forced across noggin piece

noggin

airflow between rafters

insulation

plasterboard finish

Roof apex showing flattened top, which allows cross-flow ventilation above the ceiling below the roof.

in which the sarking felt operates. The sarking felt is the layer of material between the tiles or slates and the roof timbers.

Traditional cold or ventilated lofts use sarking felt that is bitumen-based and highly impermeable to air and water. Any moist air on the loft side of the felt will not be able to permeate to the outside, so it must be removed by providing adequate ventilation through the roof-space. In ventilated roofs the sarking is known as 'high water vapour-resistant' (HR) sarking.

Modern breathing or sealed roofs use breathable or 'low water vapour-resistant' (LR) sarking, which allows the transfer of moist air through the sarking membrane from the loft space to the outside, whilst inhibiting the passage of water in the opposite direction. British Standard BS 5250:2002 recommends that only LR sarking with third-party certification (for example, BBA) should be used without roof-space ventilation.

If a completely sealed ceiling cannot be achieved, then it is recommended that a 5mm ventilation slot is included at high level, along the ridge tiles. In this case, the insulation should be installed to butt firmly against the sarking at the eaves to close a potential ventilation path. Also, to prevent thermal bridging,

loft insulation should be in contact with the wall insulation (cavity, internal or external) at the eaves.

INSULATING THE LOFT OR ROOF-SPACE

Generally speaking, a home with an accessible loft and no damp or condensation problems offers a perfect opportunity for loft insulation. When installing the insulation, ensure that it is laid to the required thickness between and over the ceiling joists. To achieve the desired thickness, it may be necessary to lay two or more layers of insulation on top of each other. If the first layer is between the joists, then a second layer can be laid across the first, but at right-angles to the ceiling joist. Rigid insulation boarding with integral vapour control properties can also be used.

For roof-spaces with difficult-to-access areas or lots of nooks and crannies, loose-fill or blown insulation may be an alternative approach (see Table 32). Loose-fill loft insulation can be installed from bags or can be blown in; this generally needs to be done by a professional, although blowing machines can be rented from some hire stores. An installer will typically take just a few hours and may use

specialist equipment to blow in loose, fire-retardant insulation material. The insulation will be inserted between joists and over the full area of the loft to the required depth.

Where a new room has been created in the loft, to be used for living space, you need to consider insulating the roof of the loft room instead. This is usually done by insulating between the roof rafters. Where space and head height allow, insulation between the rafters should be supplemented with insulation below the rafters. Insulation batts and rigid insulation board can be used between the rafters. Insulation board, some types with foil backing, can also be fitted on the room side (below) the rafters.

Preparation

DIY installers should always refer to the manufacturer's instructions to ensure that the product

Installing mineral wool quilt roof-space insulation. Notice protective clothing, eye protection, knee pads and breathing mask. Note the use of a wooden board support across the ceiling joists for kneeling on. (Energy Saving Trust, energysavingtrust.org.uk)

selected is being properly installed. Whatever type of insulation is chosen, it is essential to do some preparation before starting.

Clearing the Loft

Most people have something stored in the loft, and it is essential to clear everything from the space, and to lift any boarding, even if the loft is being professionally insulated. The loft should be as clear as possible before the work commences. Most professional installers will remove loose items from the loft, but they will charge for the service.

Wiring

Wiring needs to be dealt with safely. Wires should be kept above the insulation but not stretched if they do not comfortably reach. An electrician may be required to re-route any problematic wiring. Every effort should be made not to disturb cabling or connections made from the loft to switches or light fittings.

Pipes and Tanks

Once the floor of the loft has been insulated, cold air will be trapped above it. It is, therefore, important that exposed pipework and tanks in the loft should also be insulated as less heat will be entering the loft, and the insulation will be needed to protect the pipes from freezing. This is further discussed in Chapter 10.

Safety Tips

- When working in lofts, always be aware of the dangers of working at height.
- Ladders should be securely fastened when climbing in and out of lofts and roof-spaces.
- Tools and equipment should be located away from the loft opening to ensure that they cannot be accidentally knocked down on to people below.
- Ceilings are not load bearing and will collapse if weight is applied between the joists. Always use temporary walkways or strong boarding to ensure that work can take place without damage to the ceilings.
- It is useful to have an assistant working with you to pass items and materials back and forward, in and out of the roof-space.
- Loft insulation materials may release fine fibres

Blowing loose-fill cellulose insulation into a loft. This can be blown to a suitable depth as a DIY job using a hired blower.

Access to loft storage and water tanks can be achieved using pre-insulated chipboard slabs laid on ceiling joists. The walkway boards are available with insulation attached to the lower surface. The boards also form a stable, load-bearing platform for storage, although this should not be excessively heavy. (Xtratherm Insulation Limited, xtratherm.com)

into the air, so protective clothing, especially goggles, gloves and breathing masks should be worn. Some materials are irritants.
• When working in the loft it is a good idea to close the trap door to prevent tools and materials falling from the roof-space.

Guide to Installing Loft Insulation

Insulation must be installed following the manufacturer's instructions to achieve the full benefit and to avoid problems associated with ventilation. If you intend to DIY insulate the roof-space but are unsure about any aspect of the work, you should contact a professional insulation company before

going any further. If grants are available (see page 181), then a professional job may be even cheaper than the DIY route.

Fitting Blanket Insulation

Mineral wool insulation sold in rolls is the most common type of insulation. It is laid down between and across the ceiling joists in the loft.

1 Begin by measuring the gap between the ceiling joists. Rolls of mineral wool are generally sold as 370mm wide, to suit this standard gap between joists. Ideally, the insulation should fit neatly between the joists. For wider joist spacing, perforated loft roll is available, which can be cut to suit.
2 To calculate the amount of insulation required, and hence the number of rolls required, count how many spaces there are between the joists and then measure the length of the loft. Do not stretch or tear blanket insulation; use sharp scissors to cut to the required length.

3 Unroll the insulation blanket and lay it flat between loft joists.

4 Leave a minimum gap of around 30mm between the end of the insulation and the inside surface of the sarking felt at the eaves, to permit the

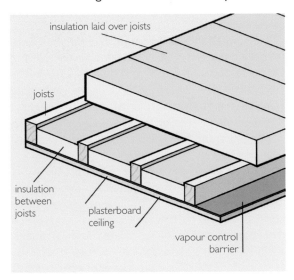

Insulation in lofts may be laid between the ceiling joists with a second layer then laid across the joists, at right-angles to the first.

Handy Tips

- Ensure that all penetrations, holes and gaps in the ceiling are sealed.
- Cold water tanks and pipes should be insulated as described in Chapter 10, although the loft area below the cold-water tank should not be insulated (see the illustration on page 155), in order to prevent the tank freezing.
- The loft trap door should be insulated to a minimum thickness of 100mm and draught-sealed. Loft trap doors should not be located, if possible, in rooms such as kitchens, utility wash rooms, shower rooms and bathrooms where high levels of moisture are present.
- Do not place insulation on or around recessed lighting fixtures. Where they exist they should be boxed in to ensure adequate ventilation and to avoid fire risk.
- In lofts with walkways or storage decks, additional battens should be fixed so as not to compress the insulation. Load-bearing insulated chipboard loft panels are available, which can be used as walkways or as platforms for storage. These should be laid down and screwed in place before work commences to avoid the need to balance on ceiling joists.

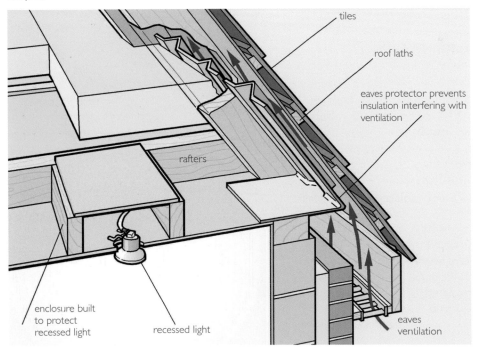

Recessed lighting should be boxed in and insulation placed over the box. Insulation should not be laid directly over the top of recessed light fittings. (Energy Saving Trust, energysavingtrust. org.uk)

necessary ventilation air flow.

5 Add a further layer of blanket insulation across both the joists and the lower layer of insulation to achieve the desired thickness of at least 270mm. Be careful not to compress the insulation. More layers of insulation should be applied to increase the depth, subject to space and cost constraints.

6 For safety and access, electrical wiring should be laid over the top of the insulation and not buried beneath it.

7 A minimum gap of 75mm should be left around recessed lighting or it should be boxed in (see the illustration on page 119), to prevent overheating.

8 If you want to use your loft for storage, you can place insulation-backed boards over the top of the insulation.

Installing Blown-Fibre Insulation

Installing blown-fibre insulation is normally a job for a professional installer since it needs to be blown into place with specialist equipment. With this type of insulation, fibres are evenly blown between and over the joists in a loft using heavy-duty fan blowers. The job can be completed quickly and this method is well suited to lofts where the use of blanket insulation is not suitable, or if the joists are obstructed in any way.

Installing Loose-Fill (Bagged) Insulation

Loose-fill loft insulation works well in hard-to-reach or awkwardly shaped sections and is a suitable top-up material if your loft has some insulation already. It is straightforward to install:

1 Begin by working out the loft space in square metres – you will need approximately 200 litres of bagged material to cover each square metre to a depth of 200mm.

2 Before laying the material, ensure the space between the joists is relatively dust-free by running over with a vacuum cleaner. The depth of the joists needs to be sufficient to hold an acceptable level of loose-fill insulation.

3 Ensure that there are no cracks or holes in the ceiling then pour the material between the joists in the roof-space.

4 Brush or rake between the joists to ensure the fill is level.

If you are not fitting boarding over the loose-fill, remember to check the level of the material during winter months as high winds can unsettle it and blow it around the roof-space.

As Table 32 shows, there are a number of loose-fill products on the market, including Termax and Warmcel 100.

Installing Rafter Insulation

Rafter insulation can be installed between the rafters, between and below the rafters, or between and over the rafters.

One of the easiest ways to install insulation between the rafters is through the use of 'squeezable' polystyrene rafter insulation boards. These boards are constructed so that they can be squeezed, and then expanded to fit the space between most standard rafters. The boards can be inserted in seconds. They are available in multi-packs with a pack of four boards giving coverage of around 0.25m². They are also available in a range of thicknesses and R-values (1.57m²K/W is typical).

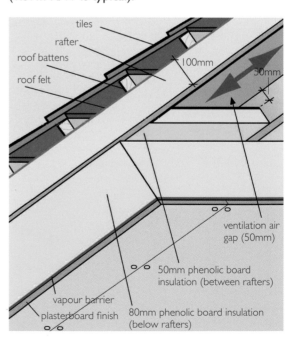

tiles
rafter
roof battens
roof felt
100mm
50mm
ventilation air gap (50mm)
50mm phenolic board insulation (between rafters)
vapour barrier
plasterboard finish
80mm phenolic board insulation (below rafters)

Roof-space insulation installed between and below rafters.

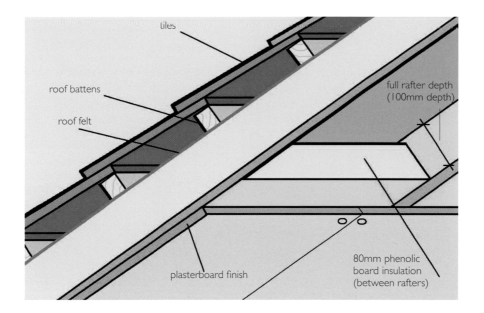

Roof-space insulation installed between rafters.

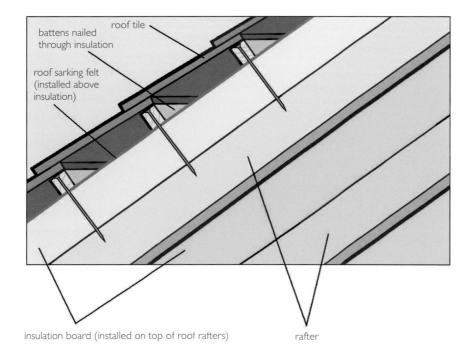

Roof insulation installed over the rafters and before re-roofing takes place with new tiles and sarking felt.

Polystyrene rafter insulation board is installed by compressing the pre-cut slabs into position between the rafters and then releasing. Slots cut in the rafter board make it flexible.

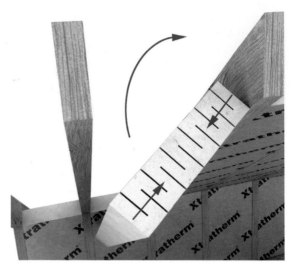

Xtratherm rafter board can be inserted between rafters in a roof-space or loft conversion. Note the foil-backed insulation also between the wall studwork. Insulated plasterboard can be fixed on top of the rafterboard on the room side of the rafters (Xtratherm Insulation Limited, xtratherm.com)

Insulation board installed between rafters on a partially removed roof. Breathable membrane for unventilated pitched roofs is being applied over the rafters before the roof is re-tiled. Note the 50mm air-circulation gap above the top of the insulation but below the sarking. (Seamus O'Loughlin Viking-House, Dublin, viking-house.co.uk)

A ventilation gap of around 50mm between the insulation and the roof sarking felt is essential. This can be achieved by fitting timber strips or by using galvanized nails to act as backstops. The gap between the rafters needs to be measured to confirm that it is within the range of the squeezable board. If the insulation boards need to be cut to fit the gap, they have pre-marked lines to suit popular rafter spacing, and they can be cut to size using a fine-toothed saw or sharp knife.

The boards need to be installed the full length of the rafters from eaves to ridge. They should be fitted together and around the various obstacles as closely as possible, and gaps should be filled with expandable foam. If the work is being completed as part of a loft conversion, then a suitable vapour barrier will need to be fitted over the insulation. The vapour barrier (minimum 100g polythene sheet) must be sealed at all joints and edges.

Fitting Sheet Insulation in a Loft Conversion

Sheet, batts or board insulation is a good choice for loft conversions and there are a number of these products identified in Table 32. If you are planning a loft conversion or already use the loft as an extra room, then insulating the sloping surfaces of the roof using sheet insulation will give good thermal performance. If flooring is already in place, placing insulation below the floor may not be the most practical option and will not retain heat in the conversion.

Before you start the work it is important to check that the roof has no leaks or gaps that could lead to damp. Any such gaps will need to be remedied. To avoid condensation problems, always leave sufficient space (50 to 60mm) between the insulation and the roof sarking felt to allow for ventilation.

Sheet or batt insulation can be fixed between the roof rafters and, like blanket insulation, it can be cut to fit. If the spaces between the roof rafters are too thin for board insulation, you could consider using foil quilt insulation instead. This can be fixed in place using a staple gun with long staples. The joints between strips of foil insulation should be overlapped by 75mm and taped to prevent draughts. Sheet (or foil) insulation can be covered with plasterboard once installed to give a range of decorative options. Insulated plasterboard is also available to improve thermal performance further. All joints and seams should be taped and sealed.

If there are loft skylight windows fitted, then care should be taken to make sure there is a well insulated and sealed joint around the area where the window is fitted into the roof.

DIY Spray Insulation

Another form of loft insulation, which can be both economic and straightforward to apply on a DIY basis, is spray-applied polyurethane. Spray foam offers benefits over other forms of insulation – it can be applied quickly and it adheres well to roofing felt and roof tiles, which can stabilize the roof structure and prevent tile slippage.

Spray foam is impervious to moisture and this means that the foam has excellent damp-proofing qualities because it seals the roof from the inside. Spray insulation can easily be applied as a DIY project, making it less costly than having the job done by a specialist contractor. The foam is simply sprayed on to the underside of the roof tiles, sarking felt or roof sheeting. The cost of the treatment (on a £/m^2 basis) is very similar to sheep's wool and it can be cheaper than conventional mineral wool blanket or phenolic foam, although it is likely to be more expensive than polystyrene or polyisocyanurate.

Traditionally, spray insulation required specialist, and potentially expensive, equipment to install and it was applied by specialist contractors. However, modern technology and improved foam chemistry has greatly simplified the process. DIY foam kits are the result of these advances, and self-contained kits require no specialist training to use and no power to operate. Spraying polyurethane foam is a straightforward process and it can be done without any previous experience. The technique employed is similar to spray painting and, with care, good results can be obtained. A few guidelines should be followed:

- Protective clothing should be worn – especially breathing masks, gloves and overalls.
- Remember that a loft is a confined space and regular 'fresh air' breaks should be taken.

- Always work with a helper, stationed below and outside the loft.
- The spray insulation tanks should be warmed to 29–30 degrees centigrade (in a bath of hot water) before commencing work.
- The insulation tanks should be shaken.
- The spray nozzle should be cleaned regularly.

Installing spray-foam insulation directly on to the inside surface of the roof will seal and insulate the roof space. Ensure that the roof-space vents are not obstructed. Protective clothing and a breathing mask should be worn. This approach may be particularly suitable for DIY applications in difficult applications or where standard loft insulation can not be used. (Spray Insulation Limited, spray-insulation.co.uk)

If these basic steps are followed, applying spray insulation to the inside surface of a roof will be very straightforward. As with all other forms of loft and roof-space insulation, it is vitally important that the roof-space ventilation is not compromised and that the eaves vents are not blocked.

INSULATING THE LOFT HATCH

The loft hatch should be insulated and draught-proofed. To insulate a loft hatch, it is possible to use blanket insulation, held in place by plastic sheet, stapled to the hatch. Alternatively, it is very straightforward and neat to use a piece of polystyrene insulation board, cut to a suitable size and glued directly to the upper face of the hatch. The lower face of the hatch can be fitted along its edges with draught-proofing strip, which will seal the gap between the hatch and the frame.

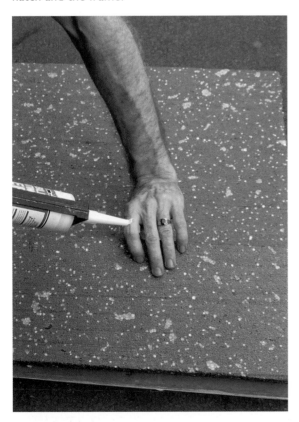

The back of the loft hatch should be insulated with mineral wool, batts or insulation board.

INSULATING FLAT ROOFS

Flat roofs can sometimes be problematical from a weatherproofing point of view, but generally they benefit significantly from the fitting of insulation. A flat roof is typically of timber or concrete slab construction and the roof structure is referred to as the roof deck. The preferred method of installing insulation is to locate the insulation above the roof deck, since it can be difficult to access the area immediately below the roof. The most suitable insulation for flat roofs is rigid insulation board and this can be installed with moderate DIY skills. Insulating flat roofs can be an expensive activity and it is best attempted when roof repair, refurbishment or re-covering is being considered.

The insulation can be installed to provide a 'warm deck' roof, where the outer weatherproof membrane is placed over the top of the insulation, or it can be installed as an 'inverted warm deck' solution, in which case the weatherproof membrane is

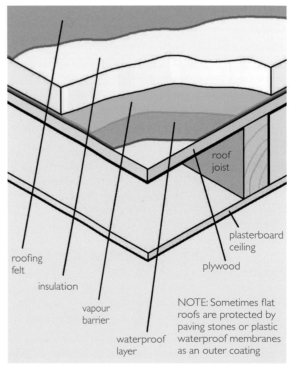

roof joist

plasterboard ceiling

roofing felt

plywood

insulation

vapour barrier

waterproof layer

NOTE: Sometimes flat roofs are protected by paving stones or plastic waterproof membranes as an outer coating

Insulation in a flat roof.

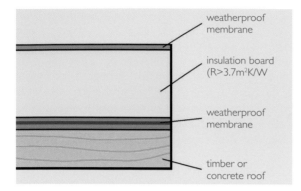

'Warm deck' insulated flat roof.

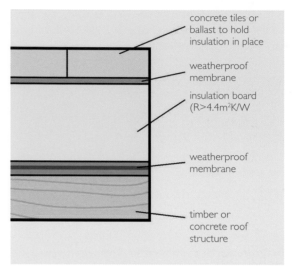

Inverted 'warm deck' insulated flat roof.

installed below the insulation board. In an inverted warm deck installation, the insulation needs to be held securely in place on the roof using weighted ballast, such as paving slabs or concrete blocks. These will increase the load on the roof, but they will also provide additional weatherproof protection and increase the insulation value of the roof covering.

Best-practice flat-roof insulation should have an R-value above 3.7m²K/W for a warm deck and provide a U-value of around 0.25W/m²K for the roof fabric. In the case of an inverted warm deck roof installation, insulation with an R-value above 4.4m²K/W should be used to provide a similar U-value for the roof.

Installing flat-roof insulation is a straightforward process:

1 Measure the roof area to be covered.
2 Select the most appropriate rigid insulation board and obtain sufficient to cover the roof area completely. The insulation material selected must be compatible with any bonding materials used in the weatherproof membrane – check this with the manufacturer if in any doubt.
3 As with pitched roofs, care needs to be taken with roof ventilation. Voids or spaces within the timber roof construction must not be vented to the outside.
4 As noted above, the roof must be capable of taking any extra weight introduced by the insulation; in the case of the inverted warm deck construction, the ballast will add significant roof load.

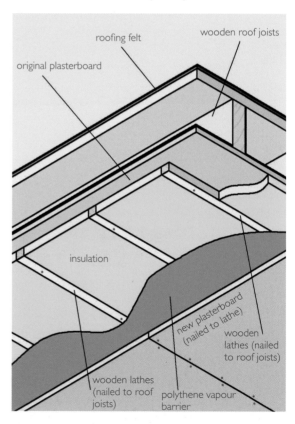

Insulating a flat roof from inside the building. If access from inside the room is available, it is a straightforward exercise to insulate the roof.

CHAPTER 8

Preventing Heat Loss by Reducing and Eliminating Draughts

Draught-proofing will reduce heat wastage and it is one of the simplest and cheapest ways to save money and improve comfort in a house.

Traditionally, homes and buildings have not been constructed to be airtight and air flows into and out of a building. This flow of air through a building should not be eliminated totally, since it is desirable to maintain a healthy environment and minimize condensation. Ventilation which provides a fresh supply of air is also essential for heating appliances to operate correctly and safely. A cold and draughty house is to be avoided if possible, however, and a few simple measures can dramatically

'P'-profile draught strip foam. It is available in brown or white rubber.

Draught-Proofing Equipment

Tools
Sharp craft or cutting knife, straight-edge ruler (1m), measuring tape, scissors (to cut flexible draught seals and sealant tape), club hammer, claw hammer, access ladder and steps, range of screwdrivers with flat blade and cross-head points, bradawl, hacksaw (to cut flexible and brush insulation strip), junior hacksaw, pencils, caulking or mastic gun, matches, candles, smoke pencil.

Draught-Proofing Materials
Draught excluder brushes, self-adhesive 'P' shaped compressed foam draught strip, crack filler, mastic - external and internal, expanding foam, door and window draught strips with shaped rubber or plastic inserts.

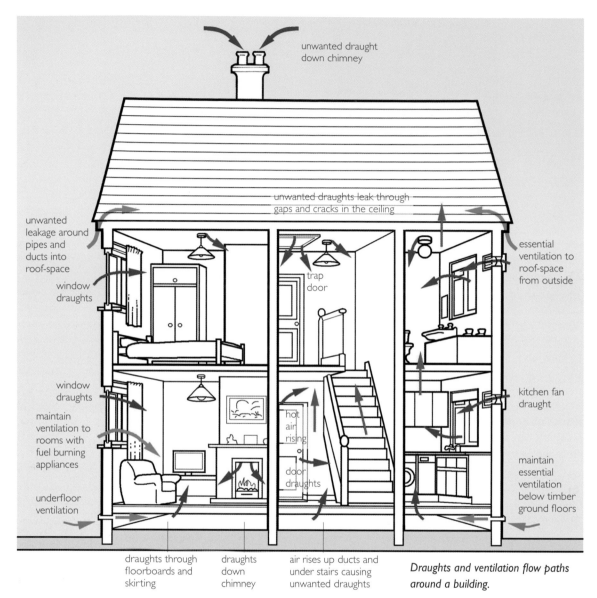

unwanted draught
down chimney

unwanted draughts leak through
gaps and cracks in the ceiling

unwanted
leakage around
pipes and
ducts into
roof-space

window
draughts

trap
door

essential
ventilation to
roof-space
from outside

window
draughts

maintain
ventilation to
rooms with
fuel burning
appliances

underfloor
ventilation

hot
air
rising

door
draughts

kitchen fan
draught

maintain
essential
ventilation
below timber
ground floors

draughts through
floorboards and
skirting

draughts
down
chimney

air rises up ducts and
under stairs causing
unwanted draughts

*Draughts and ventilation flow paths
around a building.*

*Close-up view of a brush-
strip draught excluder
fitted to an internal door.*

eliminate the heat loss and discomfort associated with draughts.

SAVINGS AND BENEFITS FROM DRAUGHT-PROOFING

Draught-proofing is one of the easiest DIY jobs and also one of the least expensive, but it can be one of the most effective energy-efficiency measures for the home. Only one-quarter of the 22 million dwellings in the United Kingdom are adequately draught-proofed. Table 33 indicates the costs and savings associated with household draught-proofing. Obviously, draught-proofing is also relevant to commercial and industrial buildings, where

Measure	Annual saving (£/year)	Installed whole-house DIY cost (£)	Simple payback (years)
Draught-proofing	25	200	8

Table 33: Approximate draught-proofing costs and payback.

there are huge potential savings available. A typical market price to insulate a semi-detached house is around £250, before grants and subsidies.

Grants for the installation of draught-proofing and other insulation measures are available from time to time, and their availability should be investigated before carrying out any work. In the UK, draught-proofing is one area where grants are available through the Government's Warmfront scheme, although eligibility criteria must be met.

Draught-proofing will make a home feel warmer and the comfort level will improve significantly once the draughts have been eliminated. Severe draughts can cause major discomfort in the home and in extreme situations, during harsh winters for example, this can be a real health risk for the elderly and very young. Older buildings, in particular, frequently have poorly fitting sash windows. A lower temperature is more tolerable in a draught-free atmosphere. Draught-proofing products also guard against the ingress of rain and snow, which can damage floor coverings, decoration and timber inside the building.

MATERIALS AND PRODUCTS

There is a wide and varied selection of draught-proofing materials available. Products carrying the British Standard Kite Mark BS7386 and installed in accordance with manufacturers' instructions can last up to twenty years. A twenty-year guarantee is available on British Standard-endorsed products supplied by manufacturers accredited by the Draught-proofing Advisory Association (DPAA). The Kite Mark approval means that the product should be able to account for seasonal variations in temperature and moisture content, guarantees a long life expectancy and infers that it is easy to install and maintain. A lower-quality product may last only a short length of time, which represents poor value for money. Product guarantees will not be valid if the product is not installed according to the manufacturer's instructions. If you are considering having the work done by a professional installer, they should be approved by the National Insulation Association (NIA). An NIA installer is trained to supply and fit the full range of products in accordance with the British Standard Code of Practice 7880.

If the source of a draught can be established, then it is fairly straightforward to provide a solution. There is a range of tailored products for specific applications – around windows (casement windows, sash windows, metal and timber window

Safety Tips

Draught-proofing is a straightforward activity and requires relatively few tools. Protective clothing is not always required, although as usual, when using cutting tools and ladders, health and safety issues should be recognized and addressed.

Building Regulations require that most fuel-burning appliances with more than 7kW output require permanent fixed ventilation. If you are concerned that you may be affecting the supply of air or ventilation associated with a combustion appliance or fire, consult a registered gas installer before proceeding with any draught-proofing installation.

Never block the flue or vents associated with a fire which is in use – this is very dangerous. If you are in any doubt consult a professional installer.

frames); external doors (including weather bars for door bottoms); internal doors, particularly kitchens, bathrooms and main living areas; loft trap doors; and even for letterboxes, keyholes and cat flaps! Floors are another area to address when draught-proofing; see Chapter 6. Products are made in many materials, which can be painted, and most are designed to merge with their surroundings.

If you decide to exhaustively draught-proof and insulate your home, avoid sealing kitchen and bathroom windows, to allow steam to escape and to encourage sufficient ventilation. In these rooms the seal should be fitted to the inside doors.

REDUCING OR ERADICATING DRAUGHTS

Household draughts are most obvious on cold windy days when the outside air manages to find its way through the fabric of the building, displacing and cooling the warmer air inside and often causing discomfort to the occupants.

Draughts frequently arise around the frames of external doors and windows. This is usually due to either poorly fitting doors or windows, or seasonal temperature changes, which lead to the frames expanding and contracting relative to the walls. Timber expands or contracts depending on the moisture content of the air. This can be minimized or eliminated by fitting new hardwood or uPVC doors and window frames. Draughts can also arise due to gaps under the window sills. They are also found where services such as gas pipes, drains, pipework, electricity cables and waste pipes come through the walls of a building.

Draughts are usually easy to feel, but it can be much harder to pinpoint their source. One way is to wet the back of your hand and pass it over the

A smoking splint being used to locate draughts around a window.

Older, single-glazed sash windows can be a source of draughts.

area where you suspect a draught may be originating. You should be able to sense a noticeable drop in temperature when the draught is located. The source of more difficult draughts can be located using a smoke pencil or smouldering match.

Sealing Gaps around Door and Window Frames

Gaps appear around door frames and window frames for a variety of reasons, such as poor installation, wood twisting and buckling, and wall settlement. The solutions are relatively straightforward since small gaps can be filled with exterior sealing mastic or filler. Larger gaps can be addressed with sand and cement mix, suitably supported with a wooden batten until it sets.

Older properties, or buildings with replacement windows or doors, sometimes have wide cracks and gaps around the frames, which can lead to

draughts. If these are too large to fill using mastic, then expanding polyurethane foam sealer may be the answer. It is available in aerosol cans and it can be used to fill any opening or crack, such as the hole left after the removal of an overflow pipe. Once the foam has been applied and has set hard, it can be trimmed with a craft knife or junior hacksaw blade. The surface can then be finished off using a suitable mastic or filler as required. A word of caution: expanding foam can be very messy and tricky to apply for a DIY enthusiast. The foam will expand to many times its original volume once it has been applied and, if not supported until it sets, it will fall back out of the hole.

Sealing cracks around the sides and top of a door frame using mastic and a caulking gun.

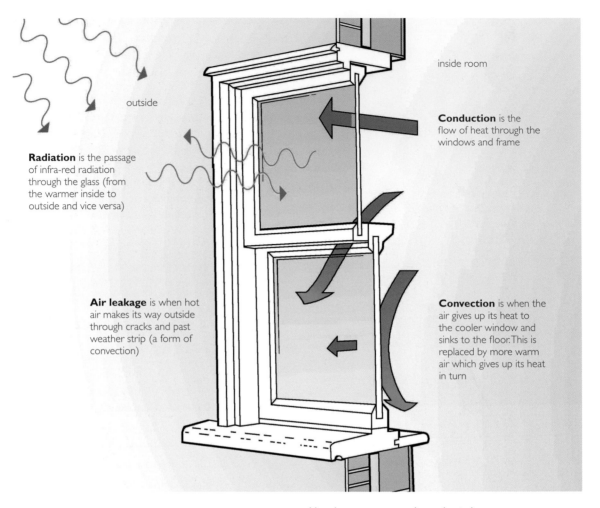

outside

Radiation is the passage of infra-red radiation through the glass (from the warmer inside to outside and vice versa)

inside room

Conduction is the flow of heat through the windows and frame

Air leakage is when hot air makes its way outside through cracks and past weather strip (a form of convection)

Convection is when the air gives up its heat to the cooler window and sinks to the floor. This is replaced by more warm air which gives up its heat in turn

Heat-loss routes around a sash window.

Windows

Draught-proofing Casement Windows

Windows that open can be draught-proofed using draught-proofing strips that adhere to the internal surfaces of the window frame. They are designed to fill the gap between the window and the frame. Draught-proofing strips come in two main varieties: self-adhesive foam strips, and metal and plastic strips with brushes or rubber wipers attached. The foam strips are cheap and easy to install, but they may not last as long as other products. Metal or plastic strips with brushes or wipers attached require more effort to fit and cost a little more, but are longer-lasting.

A neat job is essential, so make sure the draught-proofing strip is the right size to fill the gap in the window. If the strip is too big it will get compressed and damaged and the window may not close properly. If it is too small there will still be a gap and draughts will continue to get in.

Draught-Proofing Sash Windows

Sash windows are notoriously draughty and can rattle noisily when the wind blows, but they are very straightforward to seal and the application of some draught-proofing will eliminate draughts and at the same time help keep them silent.

For the sealing to be effective, sash windows require a range of draught-proofing products to be fitted to the various components of the window.

Draught-proof strip fitted to double-glazed sash windows.
Draught-proofing brush strip indicated with >.

The area where the window closes at the top and bottom of the frames can be sealed with a simple self-adhesive compressible strip. This can be applied directly to the window, although it is important to make sure that the strip does not foul on the latch when the window is closed.

Draughts coming from around the sliding edges are less severe and can be addressed using a brush strip fixed to the frame right down the edge of the sliding part of the window. The brushes are applied to the inside edge of the lower sash and to the outside edge for the upper window. The brush strips will have pre-drilled holes and panel pins can be inserted through these to secure them to the frame.

The most difficult part of the window to treat is the gap between the two sliding sashes. In this case a self-adhesive 'V' strip can be applied and this will automatically seal any gap when the windows are closed.

Sash Window Refurbishment

Some companies provide a sash window refurbishment service and can supply new beading that has brush draught seals already fitted. Although this is a non-DIY application, the refurbishment will ensure that the windows are highly draught-proofed, and will slide smoothly. It can, however, be rather costly to get sash window refurbishment carried out.

Sealing Gaps below Window Sills

Gaps can form below window sills for a variety of reasons and the solutions are straightforward. Small gaps can be filled with a sand and cement mix or exterior sealing mastic, applied with a caulking gun. Larger gaps can also be addressed with a sand and cement mix, suitably shored up with a wooden batten until it hardens. Expanding polyurethane foam can be used to fill a large gaping space and this can be finished off with external mastic or external filler.

Doors

Draught-proofing fitted to external doors can prevent heat loss and it is inexpensive and simple to fit. There are a number of areas that require attention, including the gaps at the bottom, the top and along both door edges. Gaps around the edges can be closed with brush or wiper draught excluders.

Draught-Proofing External Doors

Strong draughts can originate from the gap between the bottom of the door and the floor or carpet strip. This gap is most effectively sealed using door strip or a threshold draught excluder. External doors will need weatherproof excluders and these are commonly available to fit most doors. They can be purchased in lengths and trimmed to suit. Doors are not designed to be a tight fit in their frames as the changing seasonal moisture content of the wood will make them swell, causing them to jam and stick at certain times of the year. Rather, a gap of around 2 to 3mm should exist all the way around the door so that it can close and open smoothly

in the frame. This gap, however, is a source of heat loss and it can be successfully draught-proofed using DIY solutions.

Customized Door-Sealing Kits

Exterior door kits are available to make a good job of sealing an external door. They have a number of components including door strips. The kits may also include a metal trim, which acts as a barrier to rain ingress, as well as a weather bar, fitted with a tubular draught excluder made from rubber or plastic. This will prevent driving rain forcing its way under the door into the house.

The metal trim is fixed to the outside face of the door, positioned to overhang the gap at the bottom. It is important to make sure the trim does not foul when the door is opened or closed. Arched vinyl-insert draught excluders rely on a flexible plastic or rubber arch forming a seal along the bottom of an external door. They are fixed in place to the floor or threshold to ensure a good seal.

If there is a big draughty gap at the bottom of an external or internal door, then the draught can be stemmed by using a draught excluder in the shape of a long roll positioned behind the door on the floor, along the gap.

Having addressed the gap at the bottom, you should turn your attention to the sides and gap along the top of doors. Many people fit foam strips to external doors but this is usually not a great success and they are much better suited to internal doors. Sealing kits for external doors will perform much better. They consist of aluminium metal formers that hold a rubber or plastic sealing strip against the front face of the door when closed. These strips are fitted on the door frame to seal along both sides of the door and across the top. The strips can be mitre-cut at the corners to make a neat fit. Three strips will be provided in the kit. The short strip is fitted to the top of the door frame to seal the gap above the door. Fitting the strips is very straightforward:

1 Measure each section of door strip to suit the door frame and cut to the correct length using a junior hacksaw.
2 Locate each section and hold it in the correct

position on the door frame. The strip has a series of pre-drilled holes, which allow the position of the fixing screws (or pins) to be marked on the frame.

3 Make pilot holes in the frame using a bradawl. The holes in the draught strip permit slight adjustment in the position of the strip to give a good seal against the door. Once the pilot holes have been made, the strip can be screwed in place on the frame.

4 Pins or screws are provided. Screws permit easier adjustment of the strip during final positioning.

5 Follow a similar procedure to fit the second strip along the closing edge of the door frame, taking care to ensure that there is a neat fit where it meets the top strip at the corner.

6 The third strip is applied to seal the hinged edge of the door. The rubber wiper in this strip is sometimes curved (it will be identified in the kit) and care should be taken to ensure that it does not foul on the edge of the door when the door is closed.

Door Strips for Internal Draught-Proofing

Internal doors need draught-proofing if they lead to a room that is not normally heated, such as a spare room or kitchen. Doors to unheated rooms should be kept closed as much as possible to prevent the cold air from moving into the heated living areas of the house. Internal doors between two heated rooms will not require draught-proofing since warm air circulation between two heated rooms is perfectly acceptable.

Draught-sealing the gap at the bottom of internal doors and the inside of external doors can be accomplished with door strips. In their simplest form, these are flexible strips of plastic or rubber, which seal against the floor covering or carpet strip when the door is closed in the frame. The seal is provided by rubber or plastic strips, held in place within a crimped rigid metal or hard plastic former.

Attachment to the door is straightforward:

1 Measure the door strip to suit the door and cut to the correct length using a junior hacksaw.

Fitting a draught excluder to an external wooden door. As a first step, measure the length of draught strip required along the top and height of the door.

Cut the draught strip to the required size using a junior hacksaw.

Secure the draught strip in place using small nails or screw nails.

Make sure that the door closes evenly along the strip.

Mitre the edges of the draught strip at the join between the long-edge strip and the strip along the top edge of the door.

2 It should then be located and held in the right position on the bottom of the door. The strip has a series of pre-drilled holes, which allow the position of the fixing screws to be marked on the door.

3 Once the pilot holes have been made using a bradawl, the strip can be screwed in place on the door face. The holes in the door strip are usually slightly adjustable (in the vertical plane), to allow the strip to make a neat seal against the floor covering. (The more even and level the floor covering is, the better the seal will be.)

Always ensure that the strip is the correct length so that it does not get trapped in the frame, either at the hinge side or on the closing side when the door is operated. The screws can be slackened and the strip adjusted to make sure it is sealing well along its length.

Brush Excluders for Internal Doors
Brush excluders are also suitable draught strips that are readily available. They consist of nylon bristles crimped in a rigid metal or plastic former to make what looks like a long brush in a thin strip. Brush seals will work well with uneven or rougher floor coverings. DIY installation is very similar to above:

1 Cut the excluder to the correct length to suit the door, using a hacksaw.
2 Crimp or seal the cut edges with strong pliers or with a 'tap' with a small hammer to prevent the brushes falling out.
3 Mark the locating holes on the door using the pre-drilled holes in the strip as a guide. Start the holes with a bradawl.
4 Fasten the strip to the face of the door using the screws provided and adjust the strip height above the floor covering, to ensure a good seal.

Brush strips can also be fitted to sliding doors.

VENTILATION AND HEAT RECOVERY SYSTEMS

In the past, buildings were constructed to allow air leakage around windows, door frames and through the general fabric of the building, so that sufficient air movement was available to provide adequate ventilation. As the air in the building heats, it rises through the structure, eventually making its way outside through the various leakage points. As this air leaves, it draws in fresh, cooler air from the lower parts of the building. This flow of air is referred to as the 'stack effect'. The hot air leaving the building is an uncontrolled heat loss and in windy or gusty weather the loss increases.

As described above, ventilation usually occurs in a passive manner, relying on the wind, or perhaps changes in temperature between the inside and outside, to provide the movement of air through a building. Ventilation can also be driven or forced, using wall- or window-mounted fans to extract the air content of a room to the outside through a duct.

Air Changes and Controlled Air Flow

In the case of most buildings, the air inside the building is usually hotter and more polluted with smells and fumes than the air outside. Since most people spend the vast majority of their time inside buildings, internal air quality becomes an important issue. Furnishings (plastics, carpets, curtains, and so on) and the range of products used in the kitchen and bathroom (sprays, cleaners, bleaches, and so on) introduce a wide variety of airborne vapours, which can be removed by a ventilation system. Showers, baths and cooking activities pump moisture into the air and, unless this is controlled, problems can arise through condensation, damp and mould growth. Even with an extractor fan, cooking generates significant quantities of moisture in the house and, unless the extractor is venting to the outside, the fumes and smoke will be retained within the building.

Many modern buildings suffer from condensation, that is, water forming on and running down windows and walls on cold days. This is largely due to inadequate ventilation and lack of air flow and has been addressed in the 2006 edition of the *Building Regulations – Approved Document F* (Great Britain version). Boilers, fires and indoor stoves require adequate ventilation to provide oxygen for proper combustion and this is specified in the Building Regulations.

Airtightness and Air Leakage

As the amount of insulation in buildings increases, then the leakage of air becomes a more significant source of heat loss. The aim with new buildings is to increase their 'airtightness', which will result in reduced indoor air quality, with lower volumes of fresh air entering the building. To counteract this, ventilation systems have been introduced, which can control the number of 'air changes' in a building. However, the ventilation system itself then becomes a significant source of heat loss, so it is a good idea to recover some of this heat through a heat recovery system. These systems can ventilate a single room – for example, a kitchen or bathroom – or a whole house, and they can operate with or without heat recovery. Airtightness testing is now mandatory for new developments of over two dwelling units. A sample of each type of dwelling must be tested and be within the air leakage rate stated in the dwelling's SAP calculations. For one or two units, airtightness testing is not mandatory, but an 'assumed' air leakage rate above the industry norm must be made. Often, it is simpler and more cost-effective for builders to demonstrate a lower air leakage rate than to find more complex ways to demonstrate energy saving.

PREVENTING DRAUGHTS FROM FIREPLACES, KEYHOLES AND OVERFLOWS

Unused Fireplaces

It is not unusual for a fireplace to lie unused for a period of time, for example, over the summer months.

Area	Living space	Bathrooms	Kitchens	Bedrooms
Pollutant source	Carpets Perfumes Sprays Cleaners Polishing and dusting aerosols Flame-retardant coatings Tobacco smoke Smoke from open fires Gas fire emissions Wall insulation	Bathroom sprays and aerosols Deodorants Hairsprays Detergents, soaps and perfumes Cleaning agents and bleaches Chipboard flooring Powders (talc)	Kitchen sprays and aerosols Cooking odours Food odours (good and bad) Air fresheners Detergents and soaps Cleaning agents and bleaches Chipboard flooring Fabric conditioners	VOCs from pesticides Perfumes Deodorant sprays Shaving toiletries Carpets Soap powders

Table 34: Sources of indoor pollution.
(Source: Residential Ventilation Association, Indoor Air Quality Statement (July 2006))

There are various ways of blocking up an unused open-flue fireplace. The simplest is to place several sheets of crumpled newspaper in the chimney cavity of the fireplace. Another method is to cut a piece of flame-retardant polystyrene to fit the cavity; if it is a tight fit, it should remain in place once it has been positioned. A hole of around 50mm diameter should be cut in the polystyrene to allow adequate room ventilation. Either of these methods will also protect against rain, soot or dirt coming down the chimney, which could spoil a carpet or floor covering. A chimney balloon – an inflatable cushion designed to block the chimney – is another useful way to prevent chimney draughts. Fitting a cap to the chimney pot will also help to prevent draughts, and stop rain and birds entering the chimney.

Caution: any obstruction placed in the chimney or fireplace cavity must be removed before the fire is re-lit, otherwise a chimney fire may well result. Never block the flue or vents associated with a fire that is in use since this is very dangerous. If there is any doubt concerning the ventilation air flow relating to a combustion appliance, consult a Gas Safe engineer immediately.

Keyholes

Although it may not seem to be significant, a keyhole in an external door can be the source of a

Keyholes can be draught-proofed using custom brass fittings.

strong draught. The solution to a draughty keyhole is very straightforward and easy to apply. Decorative keyhole covers are designed to suit a wide range of existing decors and are available in most DIY outlets. For a lock that is only opened from the inside, or one which is infrequently operated, apply some duck tape or heavy-duty insulation tape over the opening on the outside of the lock. This will stop draughts and also act as a barrier to insects.

Overflows and Vent Pipes

In windy conditions, the overflow pipe from a toilet cistern or cold-water storage tank can allow

Simple DIY draught cap fitted to toilet or water-tank overflow pipe. The plastic flap is held in place on the overflow pipe using cable clips.

draughts to bring cold air into the house. In prolonged cold periods this can encourage pipes to freeze. One simple solution is to seal an overflow pipe using a cover flap cut from metal or plastic, with a simple hinge created from the same material. The flap can be held in place on the overflow pipe using a jubilee clip or a plastic cable fastener. Any gap between the overflow pipe and the wall should be sealed with a sand and cement mix or with mastic filler.

CHAPTER 9

Energy-Efficient Glazing

Triple-glazed window unit showing three panes (each pane stamped with a Kite Mark). (Budget Conservatories Ltd, budget-conservatories.co.uk/contact.htm)

Around 15 to 18 per cent of the heat that escapes from a building is lost through windows. Installing energy-efficient glazing is an effective way of lowering energy bills, reducing heat loss and making a property more soundproof. Most people are familiar with double-glazed windows that use two sheets of glass with an air gap between them; it is this gap that creates an insulating barrier to heat loss. Triple-glazed windows have three sheets of glass with two air gaps. Either type of window can deliver a much lower heat loss than a single-glazed window, although very often triple-glazing will not provide a significant advantage over good double-glazing. The type of glass used in the window, the gas between the panes and the frame construction will decide how effective the window is at retaining heat in a room. Performance also depends on how the windows affect the quantity of sunlight that passes through the glass and also how much air can leak around the frame.

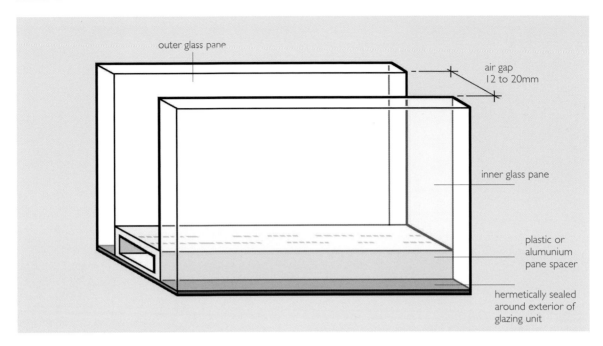

Section through a uPVC double-glazed sealed window unit.

ADVANTAGES OF ENERGY-EFFICIENT GLAZING

Double-glazing has a range of advantages. Replacing all of a building's single-glazed windows with energy-efficient glazing could save around £135 per year on energy bills (source: EST) and this would also result in a smaller carbon footprint. Replacement glazing also means fewer draughts, which leads to a more comfortable home. Double-glazing will also lessen unwanted external noise in the rooms and can reduce condensation build-up on the inside of windows.

Replacement glazing systems are available in a variety of styles and most offer the choice of wood, uPVC and metal frames. The costs and savings for energy-efficient window systems will vary for each home, depending on the window size and design, frame material and choice of installer. Typical costs savings are shown in Table 35.

Another benefit to uPVC windows is the fact that they require very little maintenance – they can be wiped down with water and a mild detergent and will generally not buckle or discolour. On the other hand, some hardwood-framed double-glazing units

Double-glazing system cost (£)	Savings from lower energy bills (£/year)	Carbon dioxide savings (kg CO_2/year)	Payback on investment (years)
2,000–4,000	135	720	15–30

Table 35: Typical saving and payback on double-glazing.
(Source: Energy Saving Trust)

require frequent re-varnishing, or the application of a protective coating on a regular basis. Replacement glazing can also make the appearance of a building more attractive, enhancing its market value.

SELECTING ENERGY-EFFICIENT REPLACEMENT WINDOWS

Energy-efficient window systems are available with frames made from wood, uPVC or metal, and double- or triple-glazing. The glass itself may be treated with special coatings to help improve the thermal properties. The size of the glazing gap between the panes can also vary, usually in the range from 6mm to 26mm. The gas in the glazing gap can be selected on the basis of its insulation properties. Some locations

Modern designs include fully draught-proofed sash windows with argon-filled double-glazed units. (Budget Conservatories Ltd, budget-conservatories.co.uk/contact.htm)

within a dwelling require tempered or safety glass to be fitted in glazing units (see the relevant Building Regulations).

The most energy-efficient glass in a double-glazed unit is known as low-emissivity (low-E), E glass or K Glass. This has an undetectable coating of metal oxide, normally on the internal surfaces of the glass, next to the gap. This is referred to as an Insulating

window energy ratings

Windows can now carry an energy rating similar to that given to electrical goods. Any window with a 'C' rating or higher is deemed to be energy efficient.

A window with an 'A'. rating is the most energy efficient.

icosave A+ glass units are used by many of Ireland's leading window companies to attain an 'A' rating.

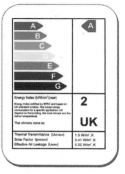

EN 1279
Lic. No. 7002

BS EN1279 part 2 and 3 accreditation is required by the British Fenestration Rating Council (BFRC), who award Window Energy Ratings

GlassSeal is one of only a small number of leading sealed unit manufacturers with EN1279 Part 2 & 3 Kitemark certification.

energy saving trust

The Energy Saving Trust (EST) is a non-profit organisation promoting energy efficiency in the home.

According to the Energy Saving Trust, Energy Saving Recommended double glazing can cut heat loss through windows by half and by replacing leaky, poorly fitting window frames, you'll be cutting down on draughts and improving the comfort of your home.

Window-rating badges indicate the energy efficiency of the glazing system. (Budget Conservatories Ltd, budget-conservatories.co.uk/contact.htm)

Glass Unit (IGU). The coating lets sunlight and heat into the room but reduces the amount of heat that can escape back out again. Air acts as a good insulation material between the panes but high-efficiency glazing can also use gases such as argon, xenon or krypton in the gap.

All double-glazed window units have pane spacers set around the inside edges, to keep the two panes of glass apart. For a more efficient window,

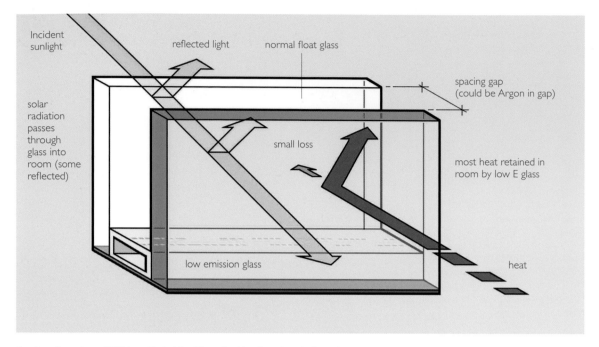

Section through a uPVC Low-Emissivity Glass double-glazed sealed window unit.

look for pane spacers containing little or no metal, often known as 'warm edge' spacers. The energy-efficiency performance of new window systems can be checked by looking for the 'Energy Saving Trust Recommended' logo and or the BFRC Energy Label; the Energy Saving Trust endorses any windows rated 'C' or above. The higher the energy rating (with 'A' representing the best), the more energy-efficient the glazing and the higher its Window Energy Rating (WER). Unfortunately, at the moment there is no obligation for window manufacturers to label their products; however, by opting for a high-rated window you know you will be buying the most efficient. 'A'-rated double- and tripled-glazed windows are available.

The frame you select depends very much on the design of the building and on personal taste. There are windows available in each of the energy ratings in all frame materials:

• White plastic or uPVC frames are the most common type. They last a long time and can be recycled.
• Wooden frames can have a lower environmental

impact than uPVC but require maintenance. They are often required in conservation areas where the original windows were timber-framed.
• Aluminium or steel frames are slim and long-lasting although they may corrode and require maintenance. They can be recycled.
• Composite frames have an inner timber frame covered with aluminium or plastic. This reduces the need for maintenance and keeps the frame weatherproof.
• Frames and sashes can be made from the materials detailed in Table 36.

GLAZING VENTILATION

As a general rule, double-glazing will improve problems associated with ventilation such as condensation on windows. However, because replacement windows will be more airtight than the original single-glazed frames, condensation might occur where it was not previously a problem. To improve the level of ventilation in the room, most replacement windows will have trickle vents incorporated into the frame to facilitate a small controlled air flow.

Material	Thermal resistance	Durability	Maintenance	Cost	Recycled content	Comment
Wood	Very good	Variable	High	High	Low	Shrinks and swells with humidity changes
Vinyl or uPVC	Very good	Good*	Low	Low	Very low	Harmful emissions if burned
Aluminium	Bad**	Good	Very low	Low	Typically >95%	Used in most large structures
Steel	Medium	Superior	Very low	High	>98%	Usually welded at corner joints
Fibreglass	Very good	Very good*	Very low	High	Medium	

Table 36: Window frame options and their properties.
*Vinyl (uPVC) and fibreglass frames perform well in accelerated weathering tests. Since vinyl is not as strong as other materials, frames are reinforced with metal (normally aluminium) or composite materials to improve their structural strength.
** Modern metal window frames are typically separated by a thermal break made of a non-conducting material. This greatly increases thermal resistance, while retaining virtually all of the structural strength. Composite window frames combine a range of different materials to obtain the desirable aesthetics of one material with the functional benefits of another.

Although not significant, condensation can sometimes occur on the outside pane of low-emissivity glazing. This is because low-E glass reflects heat back into the home and as a result the outside pane remains cool and condensation can build up in cold weather.

Performance of low-energy glazing. Double-/triple-glazing, low-E glass and argon filling provide the best results.

GAS-FILLED WINDOWS

Most multi-paned window units are filled with air or are flushed with dry nitrogen prior to sealing. Rather than having air between the panes, gas-filled windows have another gas within the sealed glazing space. Triple-spaced panes will have two sealed gas-filled gaps.

Glazing Gap

Early double-glazed units had an air gap of around 6mm between the panes of glass and, as the systems have developed, the gap has increased through 12mm and 16mm to the current gap of around 20mm. A gap of between 16mm to 20mm is generally regarded as the optimum limit because it was found that increasing the gap allowed the air inside the space to circulate, thereby reducing the thermal performance of the unit. The glazing gap can be agreed at the time of purchase. A wider gap will require a wider frame, which may incur extra cost. Table 37 illustrates the effect that increasing the gap will have on the U-value.

Using Inert Gases in the Glazing Gap

The best insulation between two (or more) panes of glass would be a vacuum, but evacuating the space and sealing the gap is difficult. Filling the gap between the glass panes with gases that are denser than air, such as krypton, argon or xenon, reduces the heat flow across the glazing unit by minimizing the convection currents within the glazing space. Krypton, xenon and argon are inert, harmless gases that are present in air, and glazed units require special attention to the sealing process in order to prevent the gases leaking out. In high-efficiency windows, gas filling and low-E glass are combined to provide best all-round insulation performance. Argon, krypton and xenon gas are denser than air, so they reduce the sound transmission across the glazing unit, making rooms quieter. When argon, the most frequently used gas, is combined in a sealed unit with low-emissivity K or E glass, the glazing unit will score high in a thermal efficiency audit, such as is required under the EPC scheme.

Table 37 is presented for illustrative purposes only and shows some typical U-values for glazing units. It also illustrates the effect of using Pilkington K glass, argon gas filling, and the effect of varying the glazing gap width. U-value is the measurement of heat transfer through a building material such as glass, wood, brick, and so on (see Chapter 2 for a fuller explanation). In the UK, U-values are quoted as W/m²K and lowest values are best.

In the UK, figures are determined in accordance with the requirements of the standard BS EN673: 1998 for 'normal' exposure conditions. U-values are rounded to the nearest 0.1W/m²K, as described in clause 9 of the standard. The total overall U-value of a window can be calculated taking into account the

Installation Safety Tips

(See also Chapter 11.)
- Before attempting any work from a ladder, make sure that you feel comfortable at a height. The feet of the ladder must be resting on a firm and level surface, and the ladder base should be set at the correct angle, so that if you lean backwards at the top, the ladder will not topple. Have someone with a foot on the bottom rung, making certain that the ladder is secure.
- Scaffolding may be required in some glazing-system replacement work and should always be assembled in accordance with the supplier's instructions.
- Tools which require mains voltage outdoors should not be used when it is damp or wet. When using drills or electric equipment outside always ensure that a residual current device (RCD) is used.
- Use safety nets to catch falling glass and materials. Clearly the cutting hazard associated with glass makes this extremely important and calls for extra care during installation.
- When working with glass or glazed units, particular care is required to ensure that breakages do not occur.
- Wear tool straps that can be fitted to heavy tools such as hammers and chisels.
- Wear the correct protective clothing when carrying out the work.

insulation of the glazing, the spacer and frame. As can be seen, there is very little difference between a 16mm and 20mm glazing gap.

It should be noted that adding argon gas alone has very little effect in improving the U-value. When argon is combined with K glass there is a significant improvement. Pilkington is one of a number of glass suppliers and K glass is used in this example for illustration only. (Source: Double Glazing-UK: double-glazing-uk.co.uk/newestlinks.asp and Pilkington Glass: pilkington.com)

Other Considerations

For homes with a large amount of window area, the improvement in U-value through the use of energy-efficient glazing can cut energy costs significantly. It is critically important that the gases are inserted into the window carefully to ensure a good fill and that the glazing units are well sealed and handled

Glass product specification	Glazing gap width		
	12mm	16mm	20mm
Optifloat/air/Optifloat U-value (W/m²k)	2.9	2.7	2.8
Optifloat/argon/Optifloat U-value (W/m²k)	2.7	2.6	2.6
Optifloat/air/Pilkington K Glass U-value (W/m²k)	1.9	1.7	1.8
Optifloat/argon/Pilkington K Glass U-value (W/m²k)	1.6	1.5	1.5
Overall width of Insulight Unit (mm)	20	24	28

Table 37: The impact of glazing gap width and of gas filling on U-value.
Note: U-values based upon 4mm Pilkington Optifloat thickness. (Optifloat is the brand name given by Pilkington to 'normal' float glass. Insulight is the brand name given to the insulated glazing unit by Pilkington.)

carefully during transportation and installation to prevent the gas escaping. It is expected that the gas will remain in the glazed unit for the lifetime of the seals, which in most instances is ten to fifteen years. Around 1 per cent gas leakage per annum is considered acceptable. Argon filling will incur an extra cost of around £12 per square metre of glazing; other gases are denser but more expensive, which means that the payback time on gas-filled replacement glazing will be longer.

DIY INSTALLATION OF ENERGY-EFFICIENT WINDOWS

The process of installing double- or triple-glazed uPVC units is similar to that of installing wooden-framed glazing, but, unlike wooden frames, uPVC frames will need space to expand and contract to a much higher degree.

First, always check with your local building control office as to whether or not the glazing work requires a building control service. Also check with the local planning department if the external appearance of a building will be modified by the installation of replacement windows, as planning permission may be necessary.

When moving or installing glazed units, take care not to disturb or break the seal. It is very easy to damage the corner of a glazed unit during handling. In air-spaced or gas-filled glazing units, a broken seal will lead to failure of the glazing unit and this will result in condensation forming between the panes. Smaller frames are clearly much easier to tackle than a large glazed unit and, if there is a programme to replace all the windows in a building, it is recommended that you start with a small downstairs unit before moving to a larger upstairs window.

The following steps should help a DIY enthusiast to tackle a replacement glazing installation:

1 Begin by removing the opening sections of the existing window. *Carefully* remove all the existing glazing.
2 With the glazing removed, cut through the sides of the existing window frame at a 45-degree angle. Then pry the frame away from the wall with a jemmy. This will permit the top and bottom

The first step in installing a new window unit is to remove the old frame. Once the opening casement windows have been removed, then the existing frame is sawn through at the corners. (Budget Conservatories Ltd, budget-conservatories.co.uk/contact.htm)

sections of the frame to be pulled away from the brickwork.

3 In kitchens and bathrooms, tiles may be stuck to the window frame because of the tile adhesive and this can lead to broken tiles when the frame is removed. Remove any indoor wall-tile adhesive and grout with a hacksaw blade. It is a good idea to carefully remove tiles which butt on to the window frame or which form an internal window sill.
4 Clear out any residual fixings and materials from the old window and then insert the replacement frame in the opening. (A uPVC window will be

The old wooden frame is removed using a prising bar (or jemmy). (Budget Conservatories Ltd, budget-conservatories. co.uk/contact.htm)

Having positioned the new window frame in the gap and checked it for plumb and level, the new frame is drilled through and screwed securely to the wall using the appropriate fischers. (Budget Conservatories Ltd, budget-conservatories.co.uk/contact.htm)

slightly smaller than the gap and plastic packers can be used to position the window level, vertically plumb and central within the opening.)

5 Once the window is properly located and held in place, use a power drill to drill an 8mm fixing hole right through the frame into the wall masonry.

6 There are special fixings available for new uPVC windows and doors, known in the trade as 'fischers'. The most common sizes are 8 x 100mm, 8 x 120mm or 8 x 140mm. When fitting windows and/or doors, bear in mind that the 'fischer' should penetrate the brickwork by at least 30mm. A Number 3 Pozi-drive screwdriver bit should always be used when doing up fixings. A Number 2 Pozi-drive bit can be used for just about everything else in window fitting, but not for doing up fixings. Most system suppliers (i.e. the uPVC extrusion company) specify that no fixing should be closer than 150mm to a uPVC weld, and that fixing centres should be no more that 600mm apart.

7 It is important not to over-tighten fixings; they just need to be 'nipped up'. This is because uPVC windows need to be able to move, and expand and contract with the different seasonal humidity and temperatures.

8 To seal and finish the new windows ('caulking'), silicone mastic sealants are applied using special mastic applicators or caulking guns. To apply the mastic, 'push forward' along the line you want to seal rather than feeding the sealant in by pulling away from the gap. It is important to cut the nozzle straight across to give the required hole size, and not to cut it across at an angle as is often suggested. Practise on a couple of pieces of wood held at 45 degrees to each other and hold the gun at 45 degrees to the joint that is being sealed.

9 There is no need to change internal window board sills. This can cause much disruption to the decoration and can mean losing plaster around the window board. The internal window board or indoor 'window sill' is not really a part of the window, although it may have a tongue on it which will be jointed into a groove in the bottom of the window sill. This tongue is normally cut off with a saw when removing the old frame. A length

The new frame is then sealed around its external edges using silicon mastic and then weatherproof trim is fitted. 'Head drips' should be put in place to stop the rain running into the frame from the wall. (Budget Conservatories Ltd, budget-conservatories.co.uk/contact.htm)

of quadrant beading can be stuck in place with mastic to make a neat joint between the new window and the interior window board.

10 When caulking indoors use water-based acrylic decorator's filler and try to get the gaps filled and even between the original plaster line and the new window. Use a spare packer to scrape off any excess filler, followed by a damp cloth to give the required finish.

11 The 'horns' are the extended part of the exterior window sill, which often go further across the width outdoors than the window itself. It is best if the exterior sill extends some 50mm more at each end of the window frame. It is aesthetically more pleasing and also serves the purpose of ensuring less dampness will penetrate indoors.

12 The 'head drips' are the projecting trim over the top of the window. These are designed to deflect water that is running down the window from the brickwork above. These should always be fitted.

13 Never rest a glass sealed unit on its edge on concrete, as this will very likely 'shell' and the glass might crack as it is handled.

The frame is prepared for the glazing unit using glazing blocks. These blocks will ensure that the glazing unit sits level and in the correct position. (Budget Conservatories Ltd, budget-conservatories.co.uk/contact.htm)

The new frame is sealed around its external edges using silicon mastic and weatherproof trim is fitted. (Budget Conservatories Ltd, budget-conservatories.co.uk/contact.htm)

The new glazing unit is positioned in the frame on the glazing blocks. (Budget Conservatories Ltd, budget-conservatories.co.uk/contact.htm)

14 The double-glazed sealed unit should sit on glazing blocks, not directly on the frame itself, and panes should be supported equally to prevent slippage. Glazing blocks should be of the 'bridge' type, which means that water getting past the outer gaskets (as happens in practice) will have a route to escape. It is important that the correct glazing blocks to suit the window system are used. Check with the supplier.

15 The bottom of the framework will be drained, either through holes that are hidden from view, or through drainage holes on the front of the frame.

16 The perimeter of the glazed unit will be well ventilated within the frame, as air enters and circulates from the drainage holes.

17 Clip in the window beading, which holds the glazing unit in the frame and prevents most of the water ingress. This will be supplied with a 'wedge gasket'. Most glazing units have strong double-sided tape that will hold them firmly in the frame to improve security.

18 In most windows the glazing unit is sealed to the frame using the wedge gasket, black flexible rubber that takes up the gap between the glazing and the frame. The gasket should not be cut too short, and it is prudent to allow approximately 25mm extra. When fitting, it should be eased into position from both ends. Make sure there are clear instructions available from the supplier and request a demonstration on how to fit the wedge gasket before starting the installation. This part of the operation can be troublesome for a DIY enthusiast.

19 Also ask the window supplier to demonstrate how to fit the beading and practise the technique before leaving the supplier, since the fitting varies from system to system.

20 Do not run a sealant line along the outside gap between sill and frame; this should be left clear for the concealed drainage to work. However, make absolutely certain that every frame is sealed at the bottom from front to back where it rests on the sill and at the ends of the window frame, or water could run below the frame and cause dampness to the fabric of the building.

DIY replacement of existing glazing with new energy-efficient glazed windows is a challenging project even for an experienced DIY enthusiast. If you are prepared to undertake the challenge, there are a number of real advantages beyond the significant

The wedge gasket seal and beading (beads) are fitted to the inside of the window frame. The glazed unit is now firmly secured in the uPVC frame. (Budget Conservatories Ltd, budget-conservatories. co.uk/contact.htm)

saving in installation costs. Control of the quality of the work will be in your hands and the cost saving will allow more windows to be upgraded; indeed it might be possible to go for better quality or more expensive glazing options such as lead lights.

It is worth remembering that, if you opt for DIY, there will be no installer guarantee. Regardless of who completes the installation, the local building control office will need to be informed and they will need to complete inspections (costs will be incurred for this service). If things do not go according to plan, any mistakes can be very expensive, so plan in detail and work carefully and safely.

MAINTAINING REPLACEMENT WINDOWS

The frames for replacement glazing should last for more than twenty-five years and, since windows are not replaced on a frequent basis, it is worth installing glazing with a good energy rating. Double- and triple-glazed windows will need attention if the glazing unit seal fails. Seal failure is normally indicated by the appearance of condensation between the panes, and glazing unit replacement can be done at a reasonable cost without replacing the frame. Most

glazed units will last for around ten to fifteen years before the seals fail, although modern seals can last longer. As with installation, glazing units should only be replaced by registered installers or the work should be checked through the building control process if you are considering DIY replacements.

BUILDING REGULATIONS AND GLAZING

When considering an alteration or modification to your property, it is vital to understand the requirements of the Building Regulations. Replacement glazing must be installed correctly and it must comply with the relevant Regulations:

- Specifically for England and Wales, according to the Building Regulations, Part L1 Conservation of Fuel and Power, the energy-efficient glazing window you use must attain the required U-value. This can be achieved in a few ways but you may be asked to prove that the glass you use is of a recognized quality or make, and to provide the calculations to show how the U-value will be attained.
- New and replacement windows must meet certain energy-efficiency requirements: new windows

(for example, in an extension, or where there was not previously a window) must be at least Window Energy Rating (WER) band D rated or U-value 1.8W/m²K.

- In England and Wales, replacement window systems must be at least WER band E or U-value 2.0W/m²K or centre pane U-value 1.2W/m²K.
- In Scotland, replacement window systems must be at least WER band D or U-value 1.8W/m²K or centre pane U-value 1.2W/m²K.
- In Northern Ireland, replacement window systems must be at least WER band E or U-value 2.0W/m²K or centre pane U-value 1.2W/m²K.
- Building Regulations, Part N1 Glazing Protection Against Impact, sets down the rules governing the height of windows and the type of glass used in them.
- Other regulations may also come into force when changing windows and doors. These may include structural regulations found in Approved Document A, which deals with whether the support above a window is suitable for that window; Approved Document B, which deals with how occupants may escape in the event of a fire; Approved Document F, which assesses whether the new installations provide enough ventilation; Approved Document K, which deals with how high the window sills are and how much protection there is to stop people falling out of the window.
- If you live in a Conservation Area, have an Article 4 Direction on your property or have a listed building, additional regulations are likely to apply. Before you do any work, make sure you check with your local planning office. An Article 4 Direction removes the right of permitted development, meaning that you will have to apply for planning permission before replacing any windows. This is frequently applied in Conservation Areas. Repair work, such as replacement glazing or repair of rotten or damaged frames, is not subject to Building Regulation approval.
- If you intend to replace your windows on a DIY basis, you must contact your Local Council (or Authority) building control service and tell them. They will ask for dates when you plan to complete the work and you will need to arrange for

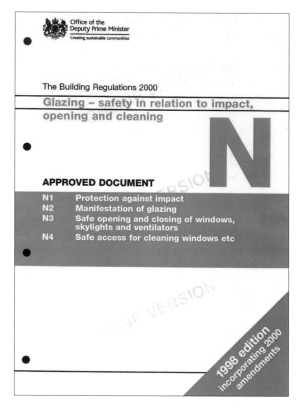

The relevant sections of the Building Regulations are L1 Conservation of fuel and power and N1 Glazing protection against impact (E&W). In addition, you must also ensure that replacement windows and doors are no less suitable than the existing windows and doors in relation to the following regulations: A1 Structure, B1 Means of escape in fire, F1 Means of ventilation, J2 Combustion appliances and fuel storage systems, K2 Protection from falling, M2 Access and facilities for disabled people. (Her Majesty's Stationery Office, 2010, under PSI licence)

them to visit your home during and after the installation to ensure the work is carried out in accordance with the relevant regulations.

- In England and Wales, it is against the law to fit windows and doors that do not comply with the Building Regulations and are fitted in a way that cannot be approved by building control. If you try to sell your property without the correct certificates you may well find yourself in serious difficulties. In the rest of the UK and Ireland, check the regional situation with your Local Council or Local Authority.

OTHER OPTIONS TO IMPROVE GLAZING PERFORMANCE

If double-glazing cannot be installed for any reason – for example, if the building is in a Conservation Area or is listed – there are other options to improve the thermal performance of the windows, most of which are possible through DIY.

Heavy Curtains

Curtains lined with a layer of heavy material can reduce heat loss from a room through the windows and at the same time help reduce draughts.

Secondary Glazing

Secondary glazing is an ideal solution if you are unable to remove or replace the existing glazing for planning or other reasons. Low-emissivity glass is also available for secondary glazing, and this will improve the performance. Secondary glazing involves fitting a secondary frame, complete with panes of glass, inside the existing window reveal.

Secondary glazing is likely to be less effective than replacement windows because the installation will not be as well sealed, although it will be considerably cheaper to install than full replacement glazing. A number of companies offer good-quality secondary-glazing solutions and some of these are available for DIY installation. Secondary glazing is supplied to suit individual applications and it can be specified simply by providing widths, height, style (for example, two-panel vertical slider, three-panel horizontal slider, hinged unit, and so on) and the quantity required. These companies provide good instructions on how to measure up the secondary glazing units.

Secondary glazing installed on a wooden casement window. (Granada Secondary Glazing Systems Ltd, gsecg.com/ products_3.html)

Magnetic DIY Secondary Glazing – A Low-Cost Solution

A DIY magnetic secondary-glazing kit is probably one of the simplest and speediest ways to double-glaze a window. This form of secondary glazing is simple to remove and replace, as required, and the only tools needed for installation are a pair of scissors and a tape measure. The magnetic fixing comes in two self-adhesive parts: a magnetic strip (with a white adhesive backing) to stick to the pre-cut clear plastic sheet, and a metal strip (which comes in white but can be over-painted) to stick to the window frame.

Each kit contains magnetic tape with a white adhesive backing, 12.5mm wide x 1.5mm thick x 30m long, as well as steel tape with a white face, also supplied with an adhesive backing, 12.5mm wide x 0.4mm x 30m long. Each secondary-glazing kit has enough magnetic tape to cover 30m of window frame.

These kits are widely available and generally work well, although it is advisable to go for products at the higher end of the market, which will have stronger, more permanent magnetic strips with good-quality adhesive. Kits generally cost around £40.00.

	Savings against energy costs (£ /year)	Carbon dioxide savings (kg CO_2/year)	Payback on investment (years)
Secondary glazing	85	460	7–10

Table 38: Typical saving and payback on secondary glazing.
(Source: Energy Saving Trust)

CHAPTER 10

Insulating Tanks, Pipework and Installing Radiator Foil

The costs of tank jackets, pipe insulation and radiator foils are low, but the savings can be excellent over time. These are some of the easiest and most cost-effective ways to save money on energy bills through DIY insulation.

The preceding chapters have addressed the main heat loss areas in buildings, but there are other important, but less significant, sources of heat loss, which include the hot-water cylinder and the associated hot-water pipework, the central-heating boiler and the radiators. Insulation can help reduce the heat lost in these areas and they are easy DIY

Tools and Equipment

Sharp craft or cutting knife, straight-edge ruler (1m), scissors (to cut pipe lagging, radiator foil and pipe foam), claw hammer, long measuring tape, access ladder and steps, range of screwdrivers with flat-blade and cross-head points, junior hacksaw (to cut foam), pencils, PVC adhesive tape to seal foam joints.

Safety Tips

Pipe lagging and tank insulation are straightforward activities and require relatively few tools. Although protective clothing is not really essential, when using cutting tools and ladders (to gain entry to a loft), health and safety concerns are of utmost importance.

The best method of cutting plastic radiator foil is by using scissors or a craft knife. Craft knife blades are very sharp and care in handling and cutting is essential. Caution should be exercised when cutting the plastic moulded radiator panels so that the panel does not split.

Handy Hints

Radiator foil is sometimes best fitted with the radiator removed from the wall. Marking the outline of the radiator on the wall before it is removed will assist in getting the panel cut to the correct size. When removing a radiator, care should be taken to drain the contents (normally very dirty water) into a container and to protect the surrounding furnishings and carpets accordingly.

Measure	Cost	Annual saving	Payback	Carbon dioxide (CO_2) saving
Hot-water jacket	£12	£35	< 6 months	190kg
Pipe insulation	£10	£10	1 year	60kg
Radiator foil	£3–4 per panel	£5–25	c. 1 year	55–100kg
Boiler jacket	£39	£60–70 (estimated)	< 1 year	100kg (estimated)

Table 39: Costs and savings for insulation products.
(Source: Energy Saving Trust. Boiler jacket savings are estimated values.)

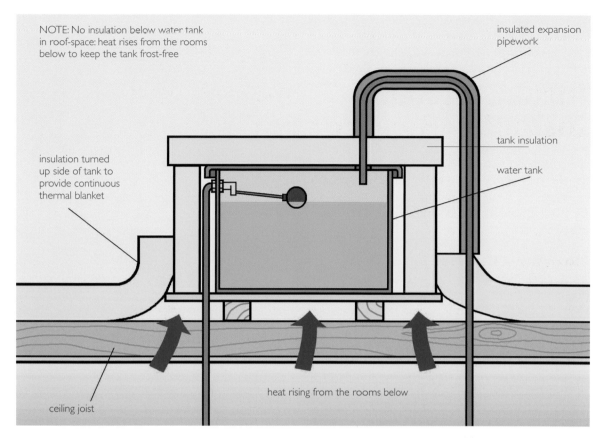

NOTE: No insulation below water tank in roof-space: heat rises from the rooms below to keep the tank frost-free

insulated expansion pipework

tank insulation

water tank

insulation turned up side of tank to provide continuous thermal blanket

heat rising from the rooms below

ceiling joist

Water-storage and header tanks in lofts should be within the loft insulation envelope, although insulation should not be placed below the cold-water tank but brought up to the sides of the tank. This will allow heat to rise from the rooms below and will keep the tank frost-free.

targets. Undertaking the work is straightforward, carries little risk and is relatively inexpensive. No protective clothing other than overalls need be worn, and no special precautions need to be taken, although care is needed when working around hot pipes, using ladders and when working in lofts.

INSULATING HOT-WATER CYLINDERS

Most hot-water cylinders are located in an airing cupboard in the bathroom or on the landing and it is generally considered that there is one major advantage to an unlagged hot-water cylinder – that it heats the airing cupboard and surrounding areas.

Insulation jackets for both the cold-water header tank and the central-heating header tank (small pack) are simple to fit, held in place with ties. The jackets are plastic covered, mineral wool insulation and are suitable for tanks with lids. (Homeseal Insulation Installers, Magherafelt, NI, homesealni. co.uk)

In fact, a lagged cylinder will provide ample heat in an enclosed airing cupboard, whereas an unlagged cylinder will lose heat wastefully. Usually, that heat is lost to the roof-space, or to the outside through the bathroom window and external wall.

Insulation jackets, typically of around 227 litres capacity, are available for the main and central-heating cold-water header tanks in the roof-space (see the illustration on page 157), and these help prevent the cold water in these tanks from freezing. Generally, the insulation, consisting of natural glass wool, is supplied as a two-piece wrap-round jacket, suitable for most types of circular (and square) cold-water storage tanks.

Hot-Water Cylinder Jackets

Water cylinder jackets are made from individual pockets of mineral-fibre insulation, 75 to 100mm thick, supported within three or four plastic segmented pockets. The pockets are tapered and connected together at the top so that they can hang over the tank (like a tea cosy). The jacket is held in place using a number of strap ties around the girth of the tank. They come in a variety of sizes and a simple measurement of the approximate height and circumference of the cylinder will help identify the correct size to buy. The quality can be guaranteed by checking that the jacket carries the British Standard Kite Mark. The hot-water cylinder thermostat should be set at 60 degree centigrade (140 degrees Fahrenheit); a higher setting will waste energy and a lower setting may lead to a risk of the formation of *legionella* bacteria.

DIY Fitting a Cylinder Jacket

Begin by threading the tapered ends of the jacket segments on to a length of string or cloth tape (usually provided) and tie it round the pipe at the top of the cylinder. Distribute the segments evenly around the cylinder and then wrap the strap ties around it to hold the jacket in place, without pulling the ties too tightly.

The cylinder should be completely covered by the jacket, with no gaps in the lagging to prevent the heat leaking away. It is good practice to obtain a jacket that is oversized rather use than one that is too small.

Hot-water cylinder jacket fitted to a 200-litre cylinder.

Ensure that the cable running to the immersion heater and any cabling to sensors or thermostats does not become trapped between the insulation and the cylinder.

Pre-Insulated Hot-Water Cylinders

If a replacement cylinder is required, always ensure that it is of the pre-insulated, high-efficiency variety. These are available with at least 50mm of insulation already fitted and in a range of capacities, normally around 140 to 220 litres. Pipework around the cylinder should be lagged using fibre pipe insulation (available as rolls) or foam plastic tubing, paying particular attention to the hot-water draw-off pipework.

High-Efficiency Hot-Water Cylinders

There are at least three different types of hot-water cylinder installed in most buildings: the 'stock average' cylinder, the 'British Standard' cylinder and the 'high-performance' cylinder. The stock average cylinder has been defined by a combination of survey data on insulation and expert opinion on the mixture of tank types in the stock. The British Standard and high-performance types are described in 'Central-Heating System Specifications', CHeSS (Energy Efficiency Best Practice Programme General Information Leaflet 59) (feta.co.uk/rva/downloads/gil72.pdf).

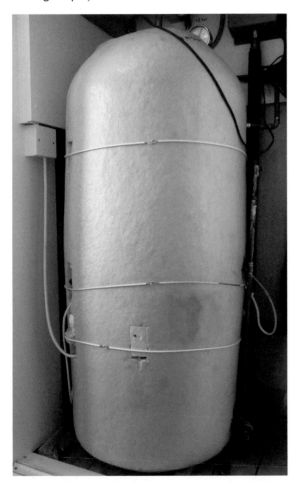

Pre-insulated hot-water cylinder. This 200-litre cylinder has around 50mm of polystyrene insulation factory-fitted to the outside of the tank.

Where the water is heated from a gas-fired boiler, research has demonstrated that, in a property with no primary pipework insulation, the energy saved by replacing a stock average cylinder with a high-performance insulated cylinder is 994kWh/year. In a property with insulated primary pipework, the saving achieved by replacing a stock average cylinder with a high-performance cylinder is 533kWh/year. In a new house, the energy saved by installing a high-performance cylinder rather than a British Standard cylinder is 153kWh/year. For dwellings with water heated by an electric immersion heater the savings are 181kWh/year for replacing a stock average with a high-performance cylinder and 39kWh/year for installing a high-performance rather than a British Standard cylinder. (Source: Energy Saving Trust, September 2009.)

LAGGING PIPES

Pipework and cold-water tank insulation. Note the joints in the pipe insulation foam have been taped to prevent heat loss. (Homeseal Insulation Installers, Magherafelt, NI, homesealni.co.uk)

Hot-water pipes can contribute to the warmth of rooms and it makes little sense to insulate pipe runs if they pass through a living space. However, cold-water pipes located in unheated areas of a building, where they could freeze, should certainly be lagged. Pipework can be wrapped in lagging bandages and there are a number of different types, including a variety that is backed with reflective foil. The most common type of pipe insulation, which is specifically designed for the purpose, is expanded foam plastic tubing. This works particularly well where pipes run close to a wall. Tube insulation is manufactured to fit pipes of different diameters and foam plastic varies in thickness from 12mm to 20mm. The thicker the insulation the better, subject to space constraints.

Foam pipe insulation can be adjusted to suit bends. The joints can be taped to ensure that heat cannot leak out.

Foam pipe insulation is available in a range of diameters. It comes already cut through on one side, which allows it to be fitted to pipes already in situ.

The foam plastic tubes are open along their length, and can be sprung in place over the pipe. For longer pipe runs the foam plastic lengths can be butted together end-to-end, and the joints sealed with PVC adhesive tape. Pipes that pass through ceilings or between rooms should be insulated along the whole section of pipe and should not be stopped short.

It is good practice to ensure that pipe bends are also fully insulated. This can be achieved by cutting small segments out of the foam in order to bend the plastic lagging easily around the pipe bend, and to close and seal the joints with tape. Where two pipes

Foam pipe insulation can also be carefully cut to suit 'T' joints and the joint can be taped for sealing.

are joined with an elbow fitting, the ends of the two lengths of tube can be mitred, then butted together and sealed with tape. T-joints can be lagged by cutting lengths of foam plastic tubing to fit around the

T-joint, linking them with a shaped butt joint, and then sealed with tape. The aim of the exercise is to make sure that there are no exposed lengths of metal pipework through which heat can escape and, of course, it is desirable to produce a neat job.

Customized insulation is now available for a range of applications. This pre-formed insulation will protect an outside tap from frost damage.

REFLECTIVE RADIATOR FOIL

Radiators attached to an outside wall can lose up to 25 per cent of their heat through that wall. Reflective foil fitted between the radiator and the wall will reflect around 50 per cent of the heat back into the room and away from the wall. Radiator panels are thin silver plastic moulded panels with adhesive tape on the wall side to facilitate attachment. Reflective foil material is available in rolls, sheets or as pre-formed panels or tiles. Installation is easier when the radiator has been removed from the wall, perhaps during room decoration, although it is possible to install foil with the radiator in place, as described below. Radiator foil panels should not be applied behind radiators fitted to internal wall surfaces.

The total energy saving from radiator panels can be calculated knowing the savings on a square metre (m^2) basis for each panel, which is generally assumed to be around 100kWh/m^2/year. Therefore, a radiator panel with a surface area of 0.3 square metres could achieve energy savings of 30kWh/year. Counting the total number of panels installed and the area of each will allow the overall energy savings to be predicted for a dwelling by multiplying the total area by the energy saving factor.

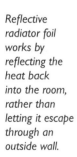

Reflective radiator foil works by reflecting the heat back into the room, rather than letting it escape through an outside wall.

It is good practice to 'bleed' radiators from time to time to remove unwanted air from the heating system, thereby keeping radiators working at their maximum output. The heating system should be switched off when the radiators are being bled in order to prevent more air being drawn into the system.

The procedure for the DIY Installation of radiator foil (with the radiator in place) is as follows:

1 Turn off the radiator and measure it, making a note of the position of the brackets.
2 Using a sharp trimming knife or scissors, cut the reflective sheet or panel to size, ensuring that it is slightly smaller than the radiator all round.
3 Cut narrow slots to fit over the radiator wall-fixing brackets.
4 If the material does not come with double-sided adhesive tape already fitted, tape can be applied as required. Alternatively, apply heavy-duty fungicidal wallpaper paste to the back of the foil and then slide it in place behind the radiator.

5 Make sure the shiny side is pointing towards the radiator.
6 Smooth it on to the wall with a wooden batten or a small roller (such as might be used for painting behind radiators).
7 If paste is used, allow it to dry before turning the radiator on again.

BOILER INSULATION JACKETS

As with hot-water cylinders, an uninsulated boiler can waste heat if it is not located within a living space, such as a kitchen or utility room. Boilers in boiler houses or garages, for example, can lose significant heat to their surroundings and are generally regarded as a source of wasted energy. Some boilers come mounted in a metal case with insulation pre-fitted in the factory, but the vast majority do not and these will benefit from a boiler insulation jacket. A boiler jacket is fitted to a boiler in a similar manner to the hot-water cylinder jacket.

Reflective radiator foil works by reflecting the heat back into the room, rather than letting it escape through an outside wall.

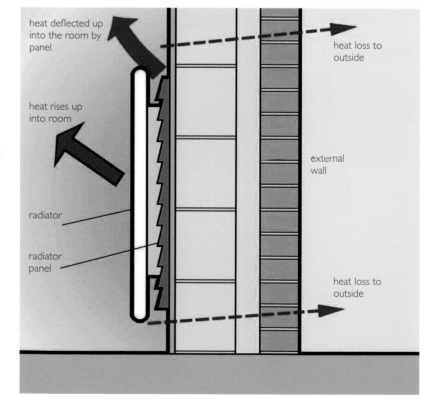

CHAPTER 11

Tools and Equipment, Protective Clothing and Safety

The golden rule when planning a job is to step back before you start and take some moments to consider the risks and how you should prevent them. A little extra time at this stage can save a lot of trouble later on. Safety really is everyone's responsibility: think for a moment about how a DIY injury caused by lack of foresight could affect you, your family, your friends, and your work.

PERSONAL PROTECTIVE EQUIPMENT (PPE)

Personal protective equipment (PPE) is a term that covers a range of clothing and protective items that are worn to afford protection when working with materials and equipment. When handling or working with materials that could be irritant or harmful, it is important to wear appropriate body protection. One of the easiest ways to protect clothing and cover most of the body is to wear overalls, which can be either heavy-duty or lightweight and disposable. When laying rolls of glass-fibre insulation, for example, a set of disposable coveralls including an integrated hood, worn with a face mask and latex gloves, will afford good protection against the small particles in the air. Some jobs do not require overalls and a set of bibs and braces may be more appropriate. Safety advice is often issued with dangerous substances and packaging usually incorporates hazard signage, so take the time to look for and read any advice before proceeding.

Protective clothing should be worn when needed. Rougher work, such as crawling under floors, will require heavy-duty overalls and head covering. Lighter jobs such as loft insulation and draught-proofing will usually only require 'disposable coveralls' to be worn.

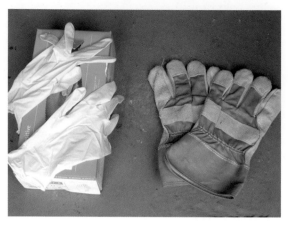

Hand protection. Latex gloves should be worn when moving or laying insulation materials. Rougher work involving hammers, chisels or construction materials will require sturdier gloves.

Foot protection. Safety boots with toe-cap protection should be worn for all external work. Work in lofts and under floors can be done using sturdy trainers.

Many DIY jobs require lifting heavy items and this is an area that needs special attention. The simple rule of lifting is that, when an object is heavy, large or awkward to get hold of, you should get help. Talk to your lift partner about how you will lift, for example, 'Lift when I say 3; 1-2-3', and where you will be lifting to. Try to use a cart, conveyor, pallet truck, or electric or hand-powered hoist, or any other mechanical equipment. Lifting accounts for nearly one million injuries a year, so take your time and be careful.

A well-fitted back support, similar in design to those used by weight-lifters, can help protect and support the back when moving or lifting a range of materials. They are not, however, a substitute for getting help with lifting, where appropriate.

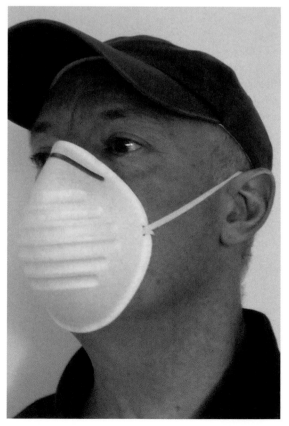

Disposable safety masks cost only a few pence and can be bought in packs.

Tool belts or tool aprons can be an invaluable aid when a range of tools is required, especially when work is being carried out in awkward spots, such as in lofts or at height on ladders. Tool aprons have a range of holsters and pockets that hold tools securely, as well as accessories, such as screws, nails, small brackets, and so on, and this can reduce repeated trips up and down stairs or ladders. Some tool belts have the facility to carry cordless power tools such as drills and spare batteries.

For jobs that require constant kneeling, such as the rolling out of insulation or floorboard preparation or repair, there are a range of padded knee protectors. Some come with impact-absorbing gel in a hard plastic contoured pad for added protection.

TOOLS AND EQUIPMENT

With activities ranging from the straightforward installation of draught-proofing strips to the full attachment of external cladding panels and installation of double-glazed windows, DIY energy-efficiency work embraces the full range of tools and equipment, from the simple screwdriver to a complete set of power tools. Although in practice most jobs can be tackled as DIY, providing the enthusiast has the appropriate skills, equipment and knowledge, there are certain activities that should be left to the professionals. The complexity

A set of wood chisels will come in very handy when working on any job involving timber.

Wood and rubber mallets are essential for most of the DIY activities covered here.

or specialized nature of the work involved, or the safety issues involved, may make it inappropriate for the DIY practitioner and you need to be realistic about this.

Special Tools and Equipment

Some activities, such as the removal of floorboards, can benefit from specialist tools. Other activities, such as cavity-wall insulation, are probably best carried out by specialist contractors who will have the required materials, pumps, drills, and so on, to do the job safely and efficiently.

Table 41 summarizes the special tools that may be needed when undertaking DIY energy-efficiency and insulation jobs.

Activity /Job	Principal tools and equipment required	Note (Chapter)	Recommended protective equipment and clothing required
Installing draught-proofing strips	Screwdrivers (Phillip's/straight bladed, range of sizes) Hammer Hacksaw/junior hacksaw Bradawl Drill and small bits Pencil/marker Measuring tape	After marking positions using pre-drilled holes as a template, holes are started with the awl and screws fitted. Strips are cut to length with hacksaw (Chapter 8)	Goggles should be worn if hammering nails into walls or concrete
Installing underfloor insulation	Screwdrivers Wood chisel (range of sizes) Bolster chisels Wood saw Pad saw Crowbar Hammer Staple gun (electrically operated) Inspection lamps with wandering leads	Floorboards require to be lifted, trapdoor cut, insulation suspended beneath joists using netting. Alternatively foil-backed insulation attached to joists by staple gun (Chapter 6)	Knee pads, overalls, possibly goggles, possibly gloves
Installing roof-space insulation (rolls of fibre glass or equivalent)	Inspection lamps plus wandering leads Craft knife Heavy-duty scissors Measuring tape Knee pads Face masks	Insulation purchased in rolls can be a straightforward DIY activity (Chapter 7)	Knee pads, overalls or plastic coveralls, face mask, gloves and goggles
Installing thermal insulation blanket/ polystyrene board over/under and between roof rafters	Inspection lamps plus wandering leads Craft knife Heavy-duty scissors Measuring tape Electrically powered staple gun	Installing roof insulation between the rafters as blankets or as polystyrene blocks is a straightforward DIY job. Roof removal and installation of insulation above the rafters is a more complex, specialist activity (Chapter 7)	Knee pads, overalls or plastic coveralls, gloves, face mask, safety shoes/boots and goggles
Installing external wall insulation and cladding	Scaffolding, ladders, electrically powered drill, masonry drill bits	Although this is possible as a DIY job, recommend using specialist installer to complete this job (Chapter 5)	Overalls Gloves Safety shoes/boots Hard hat Goggles Face mask
Installing internal wall insulation (dry lining)	Raised working platforms (internal), ladders, electrically powered drill, masonry drill bits	Although this is possible as a DIY job, recommend using specialist installer to complete this job (Chapter 5)	Overalls Gloves Safety shoes/boots Goggles Face mask
Cavity-wall insulation	This is generally considered to be a specialist job involving heavy-duty drills, ladders, possibly scaffolding and requires pumps and injectors to get the insulation material into the wall cavity. Possibly a *borescope* will be required to inspect for voids and bridging	Although this is feasible as a DIY activity, it may be cheaper (depending on grant availability) and a lot less hassle to use a specialist installer to complete this job (Chapter 5)	Knee pads Hard hat Overalls or plastic coveralls Gloves Safety shoes/boots Goggles
Replacement glazing	Scaffolding, ladders, electrically powered drill, masonry drill bits	Window removal and replacement (Chapter 9)	Knee pads Overalls or plastic coveralls Gloves Goggles Safety shoes/boots
Insulating pipework, hot-water tanks and installing radiator foil	Screwdrivers (Phillip's/straight bladed, range of sizes) Hammer Hacksaw/junior hacksaw Bradawl Drill and small bits Pencil/marker Measuring tape	Straightforward DIY activity. (Chapter 10)	Goggles should be worn if hammering nails into walls or concrete. Care should also be taken when using sharp knives to cut the foam insulation on pipes

Activity/Job	Special-purpose tool
Installation of underfloor insulation	Floorboard saw, floorboard cutting attachment for circular saw or possibly circular saw. Electronic cable and pipework detector
Cavity-wall insulation	Heavy-duty industrial power drill and masonry bits to cut at least a 10mm hole right through the external wall skin to the cavity. Borescope to inspect insulation fill pattern in cavity
External cladding of walls	Scaffolding, heavy duty power drill and masonry bits
Internal dry lining of walls	Electronic cable and pipework detector

Table 41: A sample of special purpose tools required in insulation jobs.
Note: hiring from a tool-hire centre represents an affordable way to access the necessary specialist professional tools and equipment.

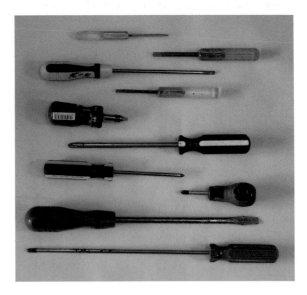

A selection of flat-bladed and cross-head screwdrivers are essential for all aspects of DIY work.

Safety Considerations When Using Tools and Equipment

It is easy to choose to use the wrong tool if the correct one is not immediately to hand, but avoid having to improvise. From a safety point of view it pays to check a tool before it is put to use – this means a simple rudimentary visual inspection for fitness for purpose. Never use a tool that has a loose head or handle, or has a cutting blade that is broken or badly worn. When purchasing new tools, check the labels and always choose the ones that are made to a British or European standard, or which have an approved quality and safety mark.

Depending on the tool and its function, it may be necessary to read the instructions before use. This is especially true if the tool is new or has been hired for a specific job. It is good practice to get a full demonstration of the workings of an unfamiliar tool from the hire retailer. There are also a wealth of websites available whereby you can download a

OPPOSITE:

Table 40: Typical tools required to perform DIY insulation jobs.

Bolster, cold, flat-blade and pointed chisels. They should be kept sharp and free from burs, which can be removed using an angle grinder or grinding wheel.

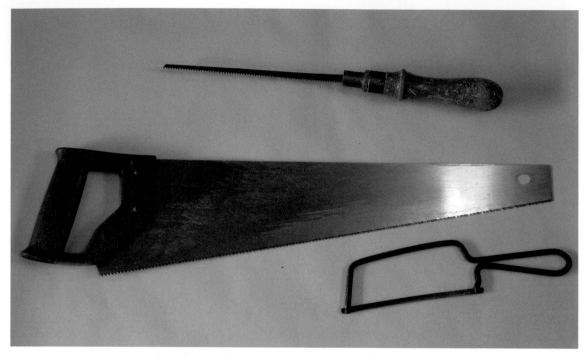

A hack saw, pad saw and wood saw are all essential tools for DIY work

A range of hammers including claw and club hammers. Claw hammers are particularly useful when levering nails from wood and floorboards.

short video demonstration of the equipment and task you are attempting. Any tradesman will advise you to keep tools in a good, clean condition, es-pecially electrically powered tools. Those provided with cover guards – for example, sharp tools such as chisels or knives – should always have the covers fitted when not in use. The purchase of a Residual Current Device (RCD) that plugs into the power tools plug is recommended (see below).

A well-organized toolbox with a tidy internal layout will ensure that everything is easily available when required. The correct protective clothing must be worn at all times and sometimes specialist work will necessitate a safety helmet, dust masks or, in some cases, ear protection. Most jobs, especially where materials handling is involved, require strong shoes, overalls and gloves.

USING LADDERS

The ladder is one of the most frequently used and abused pieces of equipment, and its inappropriate use is one of the leading causes of DIY accidents. Working above the ground using step ladders, ladders or scaffolding is often taken for granted and insecure or dangerously positioned ladders can lead to serious DIY disasters. There are a few very necessary golden rules which come into play when working above ground level:

- It is good practice to have someone with you standing at the bottom or holding the ladder, or at the very least inform someone of what you are doing. Wear sensible shoes when working on ladders, never sandals or bare feet.
- The bottom of the ladder, which should preferably have non-slip feet, should rest on a hard, level surface. Similarly, the top should rest against a solid surface. Never prop a ladder against glass, a window sill or guttering, and where necessary use a pre-fitted stand-off.
- Slipping ladders are a primary cause of accidents so, where possible, secure both the bottom and top parts of the ladder to something firm and strong with ropes or straps. In difficult situations it is possible to create an anchor point, for example, a screw-in loop or eyelet, on a wall to which a ladder can be secured.
- Always move or extend a ladder rather than risk over-reaching. When moving a ladder to a new position ask someone to help wherever possible.
- The angle at which a ladder is placed against a wall is very important. A safe angle means that the distance of the foot of the ladder from the wall is one-quarter of the ladder's height. A good rule of thumb is that a 6m ladder should be 1.5m away from the wall at the bottom.
- Get a ladder that fits your purpose. There are a multitude of different designs of ladder for different jobs, and each is designed to take different weights, so make sure you factor in your weight and the weight of the equipment and materials you may be carrying.

For some work to be undertaken at a height – for example, the fitting of external insulation and cladding to an outside wall, upstairs windows replacement, or any work around roofs – a ladder will not be suitable. Cladding panels and insulation boards can be quite large and therefore difficult to manoeuvre and secure when on a ladder, so it would

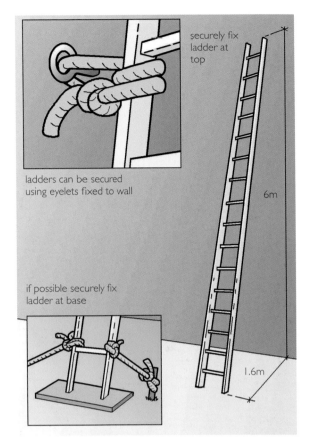

securely fix ladder at top

ladders can be secured using eyelets fixed to wall

6m

if possible securely fix ladder at base

1.6m

Ladders should be safely set against walls and tied at the top where possible.

be safer and more appropriate to use scaffolding in these cases.

The proper erection of scaffolding is generally considered to be a professional activity that should only be attempted on a DIY basis if you feel fully confident that you know what you are doing. It is recommended that, before you attempt to erect scaffolding, you discuss the requirements with a professional; most companies are happy to do this. Transporting scaffolding to and from the depot will require a van, so it may be less problematic to get the scaffolding delivered, erected and dismantled professionally.

If you do decide to attempt scaffolding for DIY work, it can be hired. On collection of the equipment, check that all the necessary components have

Scaffolding should be inspected before every climb. Ladders should be tied securely when they are used in conjunction with scaffolding.

been supplied. Scaffolding is relatively straightforward to erect, but a full understanding of what is involved should be received from the hire company before assembly. Make sure the proper number of wooden platforms and kick boards have been supplied and that these fit properly on to the scaffolding runs. When erected, the structure should be stable and well secured on firm, level ground. Scaffolding with a 1.3m-square base should be tied to a building (using secure anchor points) once the height exceeds 3.25m. Kick boards should always be installed around the platform.

When working on scaffolding, it is good practice to wear a safety helmet, particularly when there is the possibility that others may be working above you. Gloves should also be worn as much as possible, even though they may make some aspects of the work a little cumbersome.

CARE WITH ELECTRICITY

Without care and proper attention, electricity is a potential killer and should always be treated with respect. This is one area of DIY where, if there is any doubt at all, you should call in a fully qualified professional. Energy-efficiency devices will generally use less electricity than standard appliances, but they need to be fitted to the same standard and with the same consideration for safety as any other electrical appliance.

Water can conduct electricity and this means it is very dangerous to have water, in any form, close to a source of electricity. This is an especially important consideration, even when carrying out seemingly harmless tasks, such as washing down walls. When undertaking this type of work it is imperative that the electricity is turned off first. Never use electrical equipment or tools outside when it is raining or in circumstances where they will get wet, and never use electrical plugs, sockets or equipment that have become wet, unless you are totally sure that they have completely dried out.

In recent years many new homes have been constructed with circuit-breaker trip switches. Any

A power drill with a range of speeds will be an invaluable, if not essential, aid to the full range of DIY activities.

dampness or water around the building can mean that these switches operate or trip, to cut off the electricity supply. If you cannot avoid working with electrical appliances outdoors, you should use a residual current device (RCD). This automatically cuts off the power supply in the case of a fault,

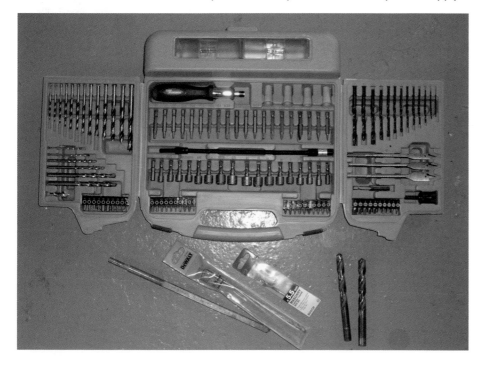

A range of wood and masonry drill bits are essential for most types of DIY work. Larger holes cut through brick or masonry usually require a power drill with a hammer action, as well as hardened masonry drills and extra long bits.

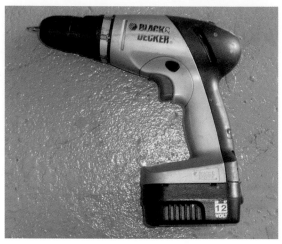

A masonry power drill is an essential tool where holes need to be drilled through or into walls. Jobs such as external- or internal-wall insulation and CWI require masonry drills with a range of bits up to 20mm in diameter.

A battery-powered screwdriver/drill will prove invaluable for the full range of DIY activities. More powerful 18V units are now available, which can drill holes up to 5mm in metal. The advantage is the lack of power cord, which means they are particularly well suited to outdoor jobs and working in inaccessible locations.

A residual current device (RCD) offers protection when an electrical fault occurs.

such as a cut cable, excessive dampness or a circuit malfunction.

Another potential source of electrical problems involves the heating up of extension reels and cables when they are used to connect appliances to an electricity supply. Best practice is to make sure that they are completely uncoiled or unwound from their reel before use, to prevent them overheating. Powerful devices, such as drills and electric heaters, can draw heavy current and these are more likely to cause the cables to overheat. Rechargeable battery-powered cordless tools are now widely available and batteries are powerful enough to allow the equipment to be employed in a range of situations, where previously mains connection was essential.

Another common problem is an overloaded socket and care should always be taken not to use too many plugs or adaptors. It is good practice regularly to check the condition of a plug: that it is not damaged in any way and that the connections inside are tight, and that the cord grip is securely gripping on the external cable sheath rather than just clamping the wires inside the cable.

Plugs must contain the correct fuse for the device they are designed to protect. If a fuse blows, switch off the power and unplug the appliance before trying to find the fault. If in doubt, call an electrician. Determine the correct fuse rating for the appliance or tool by checking the manufacturer's recommendations, or by looking at the recommended rating, which should appear on the device. Always replace damaged plugs or kinked or frayed cables and flexes connected to tools and appliances.

The same principles apply to a mains fuse in a consumer unit: first, switch off at the mains supply before removing a blown fuse, and, if the fuse is fuse wire rather than a cartridge fuse, replace the blown fuse with the correct rating of fuse wire, after you have determined why it blew in the first place. If you cannot easily establish why a fuse blew or if it blows repeatedly, call in an electrician. When working with unfamiliar consumer units, always assume that the current is live; even when you think you have switched off a circuit, test it before attempting any work.

GAS APPLIANCES AND WORKING WITH GAS

Work on gas equipment should be carried out only by Gas Safe (formerly CORGI) registered engineers. There are a few golden rules to follow for safety, especially for DIY enthusiasts:

- Never attempt to work on gas appliances yourself. It will not save you money and it could cost you your life. Always use a Gas Safe registered engineer (see page 183).
- If anyone other than a Gas Safe registered engineer carries out gas work in your home, you could be risking the safety of your family and your property.
- Badly fitted gas appliances can lead to fires, explosions, gas leaks and carbon monoxide poisoning. Such incidents killed eighteen people in the UK during 2009 and hospitalized a further 310.

Liquefied petroleum gas (LPG) cylinders can be used to run a wide variety of home appliances, for example, gas cookers, gas fires and tumble driers. These are generally very safe, but certain precautions should be taken when replacing or fitting

the cylinders to the gas regulators and pipework distribution system. It is good practice always to fit new cylinders in the open air. Never smoke or work near a naked flame when changing a cylinder and remember that electrical power tools can give off sparks as part of their normal operation. They should always be used well away from gas containers and appliances.

LPG appliances should be used only in well-ventilated areas as the gas is heavy and highly flammable, and will not easily disperse in the event of a leak. LPG has a distinctive smell; if you smell it, turn off the gas supply at the cylinder immediately and ask an expert to check the appliance. Leaks commonly occur around the regulator, which attaches to the top of the cylinder, and it is also worth checking for leaks around pipe couplings and bends where screwed connections are used.

Leaks can be detected by applying soapy water with a soft brush over all the connections. The source of the leak will be identified by frothy bubbles forming at the point of the leak. Gas hoses should also be checked regularly and it is good practice to replace them if they are ageing or cracked. Empty and spare LPG cylinders should be stored in a secure and well-ventilated area outside the house, but not below ground level. When LPG gas repairs are necessary, they should always be carried out by a properly qualified and registered Gas Safe engineer. Repairs should never be attempted on leaky or faulty gas cylinders.

WORKING SAFELY OUTDOORS

The DIY installation of equipment around the external parts of the home and in garages can be surprisingly hazardous. Electrically powered DIY equipment, such as drills, sanders and saws, demand particular care when in use outdoors, possibly in damp surroundings, and they should always be used with a residual current device (RCD) or power breaker.

One of the most common mishaps with these appliances is cutting the cable. It is good practice to feed the cable over your shoulder with the bulk of the reel safely behind your body, and always keep the appliance in front of the cable. Never attempt to clean or adjust electrical tools whilst they are still plugged in. Switch off first, unplug, and clean by wiping with a cloth. Do not wash the appliance, or spray, or direct water on to it, especially with a power washer. When working outside, particularly with electrical equipment, always wear strong shoes or boots. Wear the correct protective clothing, including eye and ear protection where appropriate, particularly if drilling into walls using electrical tools or when spraying chemicals or foam insulation. Details of the correct clothing are given in the relevant chapters and summarized in Table 40 on pages 164–5.

If potentially harmful or hazardous materials need to be handled as part of a job, it might be advisable to contact the Council or your Local Authority to get the correct advice on how to handle and dispose of these materials. This would apply in the case of, for example, asbestos, some insulating materials, paints, solvents and lead.

BASIC FIRST AID

The key thing to remember when administering first aid is not to do anything to put yourself in danger. One accident is bad enough and by rushing in you could exacerbate the problem. Accidents do happen, even to the most safety-conscious worker. The following gives some basic advice on what to do:

Your first aid box should always be well stocked to cover minor accidents.

- Assess the seriousness of the situation as calmly as possible.
- If someone is injured, your first priority is to get help, if you can, and remove any continuing danger if it is safe to do so; for instance, in the case of electric shock, turn off the electricity immediately.
- If you are in any doubt, call the emergency services or a doctor.
- Do not move the patient unless necessary.
- Clean minor cuts and grazes with water; the use of antiseptic is not recommended.
- In the case of potentially harmful fluids and materials, always carefully read and follow the instructions on the label. If a harmful fluid has been ingested, best advice is not to give any food or drink in an attempt to dilute the effects. Make a note of the toxin and the amount consumed, call 999 and ask for advice from the operator.
- Always call the emergency services in all cases of unconsciousness, drowsiness or sickness, poisoning, severe bleeding or bleeding from the ear, bad burns, or intense pain. Never try to induce sickness, and never put your hands into the mouth.
- In the case of severe bleeding, elevate the damaged limb (if possible) and press a clean pad firmly on the cut. A clean, folded handkerchief is suitable if a first aid kit is not available. If the cut contains a foreign body, such as a splintered stick or glass, apply pressure *around* the wound and seek medical assistance. For a deep, wide or dirty cut, or a wound containing a foreign body, immediately call for assistance.
- Burns and scalds, especially all chemical burns, require hospital treatment. Minor burns should be held under running cold water for at least ten minutes. Because skin can swell, remove any belts or jewellery, but do not attempt to move any clothing that is stuck to the burn. To minimize the risk of infection, burns can be covered with a clean cloth (such as a large handkerchief or pillowcase) or clingfilm. Never use butter or oil on a burn; leave it untreated and call for assistance.

As DIY work inevitably carries a degree of risk, it is a good idea to take a simple first aid course so that you are better prepared for any accidents.

Guidance on the Specification and Installation of Insulation and Energy-Efficient Products and Equipment

In the following guidance, reference is made to relevant British Standards or other appropriate notes. An overview of British Standards is available at the BSI website (bsonline/technindex.co.uk), where copies of the Standards may also be ordered.

Much of the following information has been gathered from the performance specifications for the various government and utility energy-efficiency support schemes, such as the Carbon Emissions Reduction Target (CERT) in England and Wales, the Home Energy Efficiency Scheme (HEES) in Scotland and Wales and the Northern Ireland Sustainable Energy Programme (NISEP). A list of 'Energy Saving Recommended' (ESR) products and appliances can be viewed on the Energy Saving Trust's website, at the following link: est.org.uk/myhome/efficientproducts/recommended.

GUIDANCE ON LOFT INSULATION PRODUCTS AND INSTALLATION

Loft insulation should ideally be installed to a depth of at least 270mm, although in some circumstances it may be physically impossible to install to such a depth. Loft insulation will generally last the lifetime of the building – at least thirty years. Insulation installed to 270mm ensures that the loft has a U-value of 0.16W/m^{2}K, based on the product installed having a thermal resistance (r-value or lambda) of 0.044W/mK.

Loft insulation products should be compliant with the following British or European Standards:

- BS EN 13162:2001 – 'Thermal insulation products for buildings. Factory-made mineral wool (MW) products'. This document details the standards that loft insulation materials should meet for installation in buildings.
- BS EN 5803 Part 5:1985 – 'Thermal insulation for use in pitched roof-spaces in dwellings. Specification for installation of man-made mineral fibre and cellulose fibre insulation'. This standard specifies the guidance for installing loft insulation in pitched roof dwellings.

It is good practice where space and access permit to include loft boarding, in order to provide safe access to the cold-water tank (see Chapter 7). It is also recommended that loft hatches should be insulated and draught-sealed. In addition to these requirements, good practice when insulating roof-spaces requires the insulation of the cold-water tank and associated pipework (see Chapter 10). The relevant British Standard is:

- BS 5422: 2001 – 'Method for specifying thermal insulation materials for pipes, tanks, vessels, ductwork and equipment operating within the temperature range -40 degrees centigrade to +700 degrees centigrade'.

There are a couple of guides produced by the Energy Saving Trust relating to best practice when installing loft insulation:

- 'Energy-efficient refurbishment of existing housing (GPG155/CE83, November 2007)'. energysavingtrust.org.uk/business/Global-Data/ Publications/Energy-efficient-refurbishment-of-existing-housing-CE83-GPG155
- 'Practical refurbishment of solid-walled houses (CE184, March 2006)'. greenspec.co.uk/documents/refurb/solid-walledhouses.pdf

Both publications state that insulation above the height of the joists should be laid across the joists where appropriate.

SOLID-WALL INSULATION PRODUCTS AND INSTALLATION

Best practice for solid-wall insulation recommends an improvement to the U-value of 0.35W/m²K. Energy Saving Trust guidance strongly encourages applicants to install to this level, where practical. Solid-wall installation (internal or external) is typically installed to achieve U-values of 0.35W/m²K, 0.37W/m²K and 0.45W/m²K when installed on a wall with a U-value of 2.1W/m²K or higher (for example, a 220mm solid brick wall). (Source: Energy Saving Trust.)

A number of technical standards and specific requirements apply and it is recommended that solid-wall insulation materials should conform to the following British or European Standards:

- BS EN 13914-1:2005 – 'Design, preparation and application of external rendering and internal plastering – Part 1: External rendering'. This standard specifies the materials, aspects of design, mixes and methods of application of cement-based renderings to all common types of new and old backgrounds. It also includes advice on the inspection and repair of defective renderings.
- BS 8212:1995 – 'Code of practice for dry-lining and partitioning using gypsum plasterboard'.

This standard contains recommendations for materials, design backgrounds and insulation of dry-lining to walls, ceilings and partitioning.
- When solid-wall insulation is composed of material for which no British or European Standard exists, it is recommended that the material should be certified by the British Board of Agrément (BBA), or another UKAS-accredited Technical Approval Body, to establish the thermal performance.

Further details on products that can be used to attain the best practice improvement are provided in the following publications:

- Energy-efficient refurbishment of existing housing (GPG155/CE83, November 2007).
- External insulation systems for walls of dwellings (GPG293/CE118, March 2006).

The following guides provide advice on solid-wall installations:

- Practical refurbishment of solid-walled houses (CE184, March 2006).
- Internal-wall insulation in existing housing – a guide for specifiers and contractors (GPG138/CE17, January 2008).

GUIDANCE ON CAVITY-WALL INSULATION (CWI) PRODUCTS AND INSTALLATION

Energy savings achieved using CWI differ considerably between homes constructed pre-1976 and those constructed post-1976. It is recommended that any materials used should be certified by an appropriate UKAS-accredited certification body and must conform to the following British Standards:

- BS EN 13162:2001 – 'Thermal insulation products for buildings. Factory-made mineral wool (MW) products. Specification.' This standard replaces the current BS6232.
- BS 5617:1985 – For UF foam insulation, 'Specification for urea-formaldehyde (UF) foam systems

suitable for thermal insulation of cavity walls with masonry or concrete inner and outer leaves'.

- BS 5618:1985 – 'Code of practice for thermal insulation of cavity walls (with masonry or concrete inner and outer leaves) by filling with UF foam systems'.

Generally, a twenty-five-year guarantee must be provided to the customer when CWI work has been completed. The technical requirements of CWI installation are outlined in the following documents published by the Cavity Insulation Guarantee Agency (CIGA) (ciga.co.uk/):

- Assessor's Guide: Suitability of external walls for filling with cavity-wall insulation. Part 1 existing buildings, Version 1.0, December 2003.
- Technician's Guide to Best Practice – Installing cavity-wall insulation, Version 2, July 2002.
- Technician's Guide to Best Practice – Flues, chimneys and combustion air ventilators, Version 3.0, May 2006.
- Conservatories, Technical Guidance Note, Version 1.0, July 2007.
- Ventilators, Technical Guidance Note, Version 1.0, September 2007.

DRAUGHT-PROOFING PRODUCTS AND INSULATION

Draught-proofing measures are assumed to last at least ten years. The following British Standards are relevant to the materials used for draught-proofing:

- BS 7386: 1997 – 'Specification for draught strips for the draught control of existing doors and windows in housing'. This Standard specifies the requirements for products to fit the common types of installed doors and windows in housing not originally designed to incorporate draught stripping.
- BS 7880:1997 – 'Code of practice for draught control of existing doors and windows in housing using draught strips'. This standard specifies the requirements when installing draught-proofing.

HOT-WATER TANK INSULATION PRODUCTS AND INSTALLATION

There are a couple of relevant documents relating to hot-water tank insulation:

- BS 5615: 1985 – 'Specification for insulating jackets for domestic hot-water storage cylinders'. This Standard specifies the performance, in terms of the maximum permitted heat loss, the materials, design and marking of jackets for cylinders to BS699 and BS1566.
- The British Standard for high-efficiency hot-water cylinders (including high-performance types) is described in 'Central-Heating System Specifications', CHeSS (Energy Efficiency Best Practice Programme General Information Leaflet 59) (feta.co.uk/rva/downloads/gil72.pdf).

CENTRAL-HEATING BOILERS AND CONTROLS – PRODUCTS AND INSTALLATION

It is recommended that boilers installed should be SEDBUK 'A'-rated models. The SEDBUK database can be viewed at sedbuk.com/, indicating the energy efficiency of all currently available boilers. The generally assumed lifetime for boilers is fifteen years, although they may last considerably longer in some instances. It is recommended that the installation of boilers must meet the best practice guidance set out in CHeSS (Energy Efficiency Best Practice Programme General Information Leaflet 59).

Several British Standards also apply:

- BS 5440 Part 1: 2000 – 'Installation and maintenance of flues and ventilation for gas appliances of rated input not exceeding 70kW net (1st, 2nd and 3rd family gases). Specification for installation and maintenance of flues'.
- BS 5440 Part 2: 2000 – 'Installation and maintenance of flues and ventilation for gas appliances of rated input not exceeding 70kW net (1st, 2nd and 3rd family gases). Specification for installation and maintenance of ventilation for gas appliances'.
- BS 6798: 2000 – 'Specification for installation of gas-fired boilers of rated input not exceeding

70kW net'.

- BS 5449: 1990 – 'Specification for forced circulation hot-water central-heating systems for domestic premises'.
- BS 7671: 2001 – 'Requirements for electrical installations, IEE wiring regulations, 16th Edition'.

BOILER INSTALLATIONS

There are a number of best practice guidelines which relate to the installation of boilers of differing fuel types:

- Energy Efficiency Best Practice in Housing Domestic Heating By Oil: Boiler Systems (CE29, January 2008).
- Energy Efficiency Best Practice in Housing Domestic Heating By Gas: Boiler Systems (CE30, January 2008).
- Energy Efficiency Best Practice in Housing Domestic Heating: Solid Fuel Systems (CE47, March 2005).

HEATING CONTROLS

In general it is recommended that heating controls must be installed in line with the best practice guidance provided in CHeSS (Energy Efficiency Best Practice Programme General Information Leaflet 59).

There are a range of heating control applications and devices:

- hot-water tank thermostat;
- room thermostat;
- roomstat and thermostatic radiator valves (TRVs);
- TRVs without a roomstat;
- delayed start roomstat and TRVs;
- intelligent heating controls and TRVs.

The installation of heating controls is set out in 'Central-Heating System Specifications – CHeSS (CE51, June 2008)'. Such installations will meet the standards outlined in the guidelines to the Building Regulations 2000 (Scotland 2004) as amended. The guidance note can be obtained from the Energy Sav-

ing Trust's Energy Efficiency Publication Hotline on 0845 120 7799 or by visiting energysavingtrust.org.uk/housingbuildings.

Heating controls should be installed in accordance with the following Standards:

- BS 7671:2008 – 'Requirements for electrical installations, IEE wiring regulations, 17th Edition'.
- BS 5449:1990 – 'Specification for forced circulation hot water central-heating systems for domestic purposes'.

The Energy Saving Trust has published the following guides for information on the different types of controls available, including descriptions of their advanced functions:

- Energy Efficiency Best Practice in Housing Domestic Heating By Oil: Boiler Systems (CE29, January 2008).
- Energy Efficiency Best Practice in Housing Domestic Heating By Gas: Boiler Systems (CE30, January 2008).
- Energy Efficiency Best Practice in Housing Domestic Heating: Solid Fuel Systems (CE47, March 2005).
- The best practice guidance set out in the CheSS document states that TRVs should be fitted on all radiators in a dwelling except in rooms where there is a room thermostat.

SELECTION AND INSTALLATION OF ENERGY-EFFICIENT LIGHTING

Although not strictly associated with insulation, details of best practice lighting guidance have been included for completeness. New legislation, in the form of the Energy End Use Products Directive, came into force in the UK as of September 2009. This legislation will have a significant impact on lighting.

Compact Fluorescent Lamps (CFLs)

The Energy Saving Trust maintains a listing of CFLs that have achieved Energy Saving Recommended (ESR) status under the Energy Saving Trust's ESR

Programme. These lamps have been tested in accordance with the requirements of the Energy Saving Trust's lamp specification. A list of ESR-approved lighting products can be viewed on the Energy Saving Trust's website: est.org.uk/myhome/efficient-products/recommended

Luminaires

It is recommended that luminaires should only use CFLs that are displayed on the Energy Saving Trust's approved CFL list. These lamps have been tested in accordance with the requirements of the Energy Saving Trust's lamp specification. The ballast used in conjunction with the recommended CFL must meet the requirements of Energy Saving Trust's luminaire Specification. Energy efficient luminaires meeting the requirements of this specification are eligible for use of the ESR logo. Details of endorsed luminaires are available from the EST.

Halogen Lamps

A wide range of energy-saving versions of halogen lamps is now available in the UK and Ireland.

Light-Emitting Diode (LED) Lighting

LED lighting that is suitable for domestic applications is now being developed by a wide range of manufacturers. The most common LED products available are replacements for existing halogen reflector lamps (spotlights). The benefits are low power consumption and an extremely long lifetime. The Energy Saving Trust has recently extended the scope of the ESR scheme to include LEDs. As of May 2009 there are no LED products endorsed but this is expected to change in the coming period.

SELECTION OF ENERGY-EFFICIENT APPLIANCES

There are a number of guidelines and recommendations for energy-efficient appliances and products. As a general rule, efficient cold and wet appliances should be energy saving recommended (ESR). The website of the Energy Saving Trust has a list of ESR appliances, including products such as energy-efficient washing machines, fridges, freezers, and so on: est.org.uk/myhome/efficientproducts/recommended.

Relevant Legislation

The following is not exhaustive, but some of the legislation noted may apply to the range of activities (including DIY) carried out as part of an insulation or improvement scheme. The legislation can be reviewed at hmso.gov.uk/.

It is vital to be aware of the health and safety implications of any work (see Chapter 11), and it is the responsibility of the homeowner or contractor to ensure that the work has been carried out in accordance with the appropriate legislation, and that there is full compliance with the Building Regulations.

CONSTRUCTION (HEALTH SAFETY & WELFARE) REGULATIONS 1996

These regulations are aimed at protecting the health, safety and welfare of everyone who carries out construction work. They also give protection to other people who may be affected by the work.

BUILDING REGULATIONS 2000 AND BUILDING (APPROVED INSPECTORS ETC.) REGULATIONS 2000

Building Regulations are made under The Building Act 1984, and apply in England and Wales. They set standards for the design and construction of buildings to ensure safety and health for people in or about those buildings. They also include require-

ments to ensure that fuel and power is conserved and facilities are provided for people, including those with disabilities, to access and move around inside buildings. Similar legislation applies in other regions of the UK and in Ireland.

THE BUILDING ACT 1984

The Building Act 1984 is the enabling Act under which the Building Regulations have been made. The Secretary of State, under the power given in the Building Act 1984, may for any purposes of

- securing the health, safety, welfare and convenience of persons in or about buildings and of others who may be affected by buildings or matters connected with buildings;
- furthering the conservation of fuel and power;
- preventing waste, undue consumption, misuse or contamination of water;
- furthering the protection or enhancement of the environment;
- facilitating sustainable development, or
- furthering the prevention or detection of crime,
- make regulations with respect to the design and construction of buildings, demolition of buildings, and the provision of services, fittings and equipment in or in connection with buildings.

THE PARTY WALL ETC. ACT 1996

Some types of work carried out to a property may not be controlled by the Building Regulations, but may be covered by the Third Party Wall etc. Act 1996. This is a separate piece of legislation with different requirements to the Building Regulations. The Party Wall etc. Act makes provision in respect of party walls and excavation and construction in proximity to certain buildings or structures. There will be some instances in which both the Party Wall etc. Act and the Building Regulations apply to the work being carried out.

HEALTH AND SAFETY AT WORK ACT 1974

(HASAWA) provides a wide, embracing, enabling framework for health, safety and welfare in the UK. Similar legislation applies in Ireland.

THE BUILDING (LOCAL AUTHORITY CHARGES) REGULATIONS 1998

These regulations enable Local Authorities in England and Wales to charge for carrying out their statutory building control functions relating to the Building Regulations.

VOLUNTARY NATIONAL STANDARD: CODE FOR SUSTAINABLE HOMES

The Code for Sustainable Homes is a voluntary national standard introduced by the Government in April 2007, to improve the overall sustainability of new homes in England. It sets a single framework within which the home-building industry can design and construct homes to higher environmental standards. Where it is used, the code gives new homebuyers information about the environmental impact and the potential running costs of their new home, and offers builders a tool with which to differentiate themselves in sustainability terms. It is expected that other regions of the UK and Ireland will introduce similar legislation in the near future.

THE CONSTRUCTION PRODUCTS REGULATIONS 1991

The Construction Products Directive (89/106/EEC), which introduced CE marking for construction products, is implemented in the UK through the Construction Products Regulations (SI 1991/1620). These state that products must be fit for their intended purpose, and that a correctly carried out CE marking is one way of demonstrating this. There is no legal requirement under the UK Regulations for products to be CE marked before they can be put on the UK market or used in construction works.

CONSTRUCTION DESIGN AND MANAGEMENT (CDM) REGULATIONS 1994

These regulations have been produced to ensure that health, safety and environmental issues are addressed during the life-cycle of a building or plant.

CONTROL OF SUBSTANCES HAZARDOUS TO HEALTH 1994 (COSHH)

This legislation prohibits work involving exposure to hazardous materials (chemicals, microorganisms, gases, and so on) unless a 'suitable and sufficient' assessment of these exposures has been carried out.

NOISE AT WORK REGULATIONS 1989

These regulations aim to protect workers from the risk of hearing damage due to excessive noise.

ELECTRICITY AT WORK REGULATIONS 1989

The purpose of these regulations is to ensure precautions are taken against the risk of death or personal injury from electricity in work activities.

OZONE DEPLETING SUBSTANCES (ODS) REGULATION 2000

This regulation affects users, producers, applicants, maintenance and servicing engineers, and those involved in the disposal of all ODS. These include chlorofluorocarbons (CFCs), hydrochlorofluorocarbons (HCFCs), halons, 1,1,1 trichloroethane, carbon tetrachloride and bromochloromethane (CBM). These substances are mainly used in refrigeration, air-conditioning, foam-blowing, as solvents and in fire fighting. Some of the materials described above may be encountered in the course of DIY insulation activities.

ENVIRONMENTAL PROTECTION ACT 1990

The aim of this Act is to ensure that any potential polluting process has an authorization from either the Environment Agency or the Local Authority and that control measures are in place to prevent, minimize or render harmless emissions into the surrounding environment.

Contacts and Links

ENERGY SAVING TRUST

Website and Advice Centres

energysavingtrust.org.uk/ has a list of professional installers, information on energy efficiency and insulation in housing, best-practice case studies.

EST Best Practice examples can be reviewed on est. org.uk/business/Business/Building-Professionals

Energy Saving Trust advice centres operate on a local basis on 0800 512 012 for free, impartial, one-to-one advice on saving energy in the home. The EST advisors will have information on available grants and utility company offers in your area and advisors will be able to recommend the most appropriate options. They can also explain any technical issues and put you in touch with local approved installers.

The Housing Energy Efficiency Best Practice programme is managed by the Energy Saving Trust (EST). GPG 155 (available on feta.co.uk/rva/downloads/gpg155.pdf) was produced by BRE on behalf of EST. BRE best practice examples: projects.bre.co.uk/ConDiv/structfireeng/default.htm

Publications

Practical Refurbishment of Solid-Walled Houses (CE184), EST, 2006

Energy Efficient Loft Conversions (CE120), EST, 2004

Energy Efficient Refurbishment of Existing Housing (CE83), EST, 2004

Refurbishment of Dwellings – A Summary of Best Practice, EST, 2004

EST Domestic Energy Efficiency Primer, ISBN: GPG171

CLIMATE CHANGE AND GRANTS

For the latest climate-change conclusions and information: ipcc.ch/

To receive the Carbon Emissions Reduction Target (CERT) update, either by email or post, send your contact details to: cert@ofgem.gov.uk

Warm Wales is a community insulation/sustainable activities initiative: warmwales.org.uk

National Insulation Association (NIA), phone 08451 636363, website: nationalinsulationassociation.org.uk/

Warm Front: warmfront.co.uk/

In the Republic of Ireland grants are available through the Sustainable Energy Authority for Ireland (SEAI), 1800 250 204, warmerhomes@sei.ie, Home Energy Scheme website: sei.ie/Power_of_One/Grants_Available/

Green Grants Machine (greengrantsmachine.co.uk/) is a good source of information on insulation and other grants and sends out a regular newsletter by email.

Grant-Aided Heating Installers' Network (GAHIN): gainassociation.org.uk/

CALCULATING HEAT LOSS

engineeringtoolbox.com/heat-loss-buildings-d_113.htm

diydata.com/planning/ch_design/sizing.php

tombling.com/heaters/heatloss.htm

National Energy Action (NEA) (nea.org.uk), publication, *Energy in the Home* (ISBN: 0 948371 25 0)

Federation of Authorized Energy Rating Organizations (SAP Assessors): faero.co.uk

SAP 2005 for dwellings up to 450m²: bre.co.uk
SBEM (Simplified Building Energy Model): ncm.bre.co.uk
SEDBUK (Boiler efficiency data): sedbuk.com

BUILDING CONTROL AND PLANNING

In England and Wales, building control matters are covered on: communities.gov.uk/planningandbuilding/Building_Regulations
In Scotland, building control matters are covered on: scotland.gov.uk/Topics/Built-Environment/Building/Building-standards
In Northern Ireland information on building control is available on: buildingcontrol-ni.com/site.default.asp?secid=home
In Ireland the relevant legislation is under the Building Standards as set down in the Building Control Act (2007). This is the responsibility of the Department of Environment, Heritage and Local Government (DEHLG) based in Dublin: environ.ie/en/DevelopmentandHousing/buildingstandards/
The Construction Industry Council (CIC) (cic.org.uk/home/index.shtml) is the representative forum for the professional bodies, research organizations and specialist business associations in the construction industry.
The window standards organization FENSA (Fenestration Self-Assessment Scheme) (fensa.org.uk) has a list of registered installers of windows.
The Party Wall etc. Act 1996: opsi.gov.uk/acts/acts1996/Ukpga_19960040_en_1
The Building Regulations 2000: opsi.gov.uk/si/si2000/20002531.htm
Approved Documents: communities.gov.uk/index/asp?id=1164177
Airtightness Testing and Measurement: attma.org/member_list.htm
BRE Certification: brecertification.co.uk
An explanatory booklet is available on the Building Regulations and the Impact of the Party Wall etc. Act 1996 at odpm.gov.uk
Communities.gov.uk/documents/planningandbuilding/pdf/133214.pdf
For current wiring regulations: simplifydiy.com/building-works

FINDING PRODUCTS AND SERVICES

To find a builder, architect or chartered surveyor near you: simplifydiy.com/
HETAS (hetas.co.uk) is the official body recognized by Government to approve solid-fuel domestic heating appliances (boilers, cookers, open fires and stoves and room-heaters), and fuels and services. It holds a register of competent installers and servicing businesses and lists in its Official Guide factory-made chimneys, carbon monoxide detectors and alarms suitable for use with solid fuel.
Making structural changes to your property and regulations and permissions for extensions: simplifydiy.com/planningpermission

INSULATION MATERIALS, PRODUCTS AND SUPPLIERS

National Insulation Association (NIA), 2 Vimy Court, Vimy Road, Leighton Buzzard, Beds, LU7 1FG, Tel: 0845I 636363, Fax: 01525 854918, website: nationalinsulationassociation.org.uk/householder/householder-nia.html
The Green Guide to specification (BRE) is an excellent site with information on insulation products and materials: bre.co.uk/greenguide/
NGS Greenspec is an excellent guide to specification of insulation materials: greenspec.co.uk
Insulated Render and Cladding Association: inca-ltd.org.uk
Information on perlite as an insulation material: Perlite.net or Schundler.com
Suppliers include: just-insulation.com, william-sinclair.co.uk, celotex.co.uk, jablite.co.uk/adl/, insulation.kingspan.com/enviro/default.htm, knaufinsulation.co.uk, rockwoolinsulation.co.uk/sw47799.asp, sheffins.co.uk, celcon.co.uk, topblock.co.uk, thermalite.co.uk/default.aspx, xtratherm.com, springvale.com
For details on spray insulation: spray-insulation.co.uk/Insulation_material_comparison.htm

Publications

Clarke et al., *Thermal Improvement of Existing Dwellings*, University of Strathclyde, 2005 (BRE) Thermal

Insulation: Avoiding Risks, C. Stirling, BRE Press, 2001
Installing Thermal Insulation, BRE Press, 2006

DIY GUIDANCE

DIY guidance from Which (Consumers' Association): which-local.co.uk
Helpful DIY insulation guides and video instructions: easy2diy/com/cm/easy/diy_ht_index.asp?page_id=35720202
jmhomeowner.com/insulation/projects/attic.asp
Web-based DIY forums with some useful discussion topics: askjeff.co.uk and lets-do-diy.com
Draught-Proofing Advisory Association (DPAA) LTD, PO Box 12, Haslemere, Surrey GU27 3AH. Tel: 01428 654011, Fax: 01428 651401, email: dpaassociation@aol.com

FLOORING AND WINDOWS

Flooring

For information on flooring and floor coverings: floorideas.co.uk, healthyflooring.org, comebacktocarpet.com, greenbuildingforum.co.uk, timberwise.co.uk

Windows

A number of websites offer a huge selection of shutters, electric awnings, bespoke blinds, roller blinds, roman blinds, vertical blinds, venetian blinds and canopies, including superiorblinds.co.uk and blindsuk.net
Energy Saving Trust (EST) Recommended scheme accredits double-glazing products that are 'C'-rated or above, in other words, better than the current Building Regulations standard.
The British Fenestration Ratings Council (BFRC) rates all energy-efficient windows in the UK and lists all energy-efficient windows, their frame material and energy rating: bfrc.org/consumer/index.aspx
Using an installer who is a member of a Trade Association has two benefits: first, it will protect your consumer rights; second, it will ensure that the company is competent to do the job. The Fenestration Self-Assessment Association (FENSA) (fensa.co.uk/

FENSAHomeownerHome.aspx) lists all registered installers. It has been set up by the Glass and Glazing Federation in conjunction with other industry bodies (with Government encouragement), in response to the current Building Regulations for England and Wales. FENSA guarantees that its installers and frames comply with Building Regulations.
Certass is another scheme that registers and approves installers: certass.co.uk/postcode-search.html
The Glass and Glazing Federation (GGF) is a trade association representing companies who make, supply or fit glass and glass-related products. This includes replacement windows, energy-efficient windows, doors, conservatories, hardware for these products, and all aspects of glass, including double-glazed units, safety glazing, fire-resistant glass, emergency glazing, decorative glass, secondary glazing, and solar control applied films and sealants. The GGF can provide details of installers in your area. For more information visit ggf.org.uk (Glass and Glazing Federation, 54 Ayres Street, London SE1 1EU, Telephone: 020 7939 9101).
For advice on fitting energy-efficient glazing: thewindowman.co.uk/air-gap.htm

SAFETY

Gas Safe

gassaferegister.co.uk/learn/carbon_monoxide_kills.aspx
Register of Gas Safe engineers: gassaferegister.co.uk/about/gas_safe_register_engineers.aspx

First Aid

In all first aid situations always dial 999 and ask for assistance.
For first aid training: British Red Cross (redcrossfirstaidtraining.co.uk, and St John Ambulance Association (sja.org.uk).

Glossary

(Note: This listing contains some terms as defined in the Building Regulations.)

Air permeability
The air leakage rate per unit area of the building fabric, measured in m^3/m^2 per hour at 50Pa excess pressure.

Ammonium phosphate
Used as a flame retardant in a range of plastic materials and insulation products.

Anthropogenic
Effects, processes or materials that are derived from human activities, as opposed to those occurring without human influence. The term is often used in the context of climate change, which is produced as an unintentional by-product of otherwise purposeful human activities.

Area of Outstanding (Natural) Beauty (AONB)
Designated areas of the countryside, the primary purpose of which is to conserve and enhance the natural beauty of the landscape. There are two secondary aims: to meet the need for quiet enjoyment of the countryside and to have regard for the interests of those who live and work there. In order to achieve these aims, AONBs rely on planning controls and practical countryside management.

Article 4 Direction
Article 4 Directions are issued by a council in circumstances where specific control over development is required, primarily where the character of an area of acknowledged importance would be threatened. They are, therefore, most commonly applied to Conservation Areas.

Batts
Pre-cut lengths of insulation, usually mineral wool or similar, generally available in a range of lengths and thicknesses.

BER
The Building (carbon dioxide) Emissions Rate in kg/m^2 per year, as calculated by the National Calculation Methodology (NCM); one implementation for non-dwellings is the Simplified Building Energy Model (SBEM).

Biocide
A chemical substance capable of killing living organisms. Biocides are commonly used in medicine, agriculture, forestry and in industry, where they prevent the fouling of water and oil pipelines. Some biocides are also employed as anti-fouling agents or disinfectants: chlorine, for example, is used as a short-life biocide in industrial water treatment and as a disinfectant in swimming pools.

Building Control Body
A local authority or approved inspector licensed to control compliance with the Building Regulations.

Bulk density
A property of powders, granules and other 'divided' solids. It is defined as the mass of many particles of the material divided by the total volume they occupy. The total volume includes particle volume, inter-particle void volume and internal pore volume. Bulk density is not an intrinsic property of a material and it can change depending on how the material is handled.

Carbon footprint
A measure of the impact of certain activities on the environment and in particular on climate change. It

relates to the amount of greenhouse gases produced through burning fossil fuels for electricity, heating, transportation, and so on. It is a measurement of all the greenhouse gases produced individually or as a group, or company, and has units of tonnes (or kg) of carbon dioxide equivalent.

Casement windows

Hinged windows set in a fixed frame. In the 1930s their popularity increased and they took over from the sash window as the window of choice in housing.

Caulking

Refers, in this instance, to the application of flexible sealing compounds to close up gaps in buildings and other structures against water, air, dust, insects, or as a component in fire-stopping.

Central-heating system

A heating system that includes a boiler, pipework, radiators and controls. The boiler can be fired from a range of fuels including gas, oil, coal, biomass and LPG.

CFCs

Organic compounds that contain carbon, chlorine and fluorine. A common sub-class is the hydrochlorofluorocarbons (HCFCs), which contain hydrogen as well. They are also commonly known as freon. Many CFCs have been widely used as refrigerants, propellants (in aerosol applications), and solvents. The manufacture of such compounds is being phased out by the Montreal Protocol because they contribute to ozone depletion.

Cladding

In building construction, siding or cladding may refer to the application of one material over another to provide a skin or layer intended to protect against the effects of the weather, or for aesthetic purposes. Cladding does not necessarily have to be waterproof but it may form a protective covering which serves to direct water or wind safely in order to control run-off and prevent infiltration into the building structure.

Clean Air Act

Legislation relating to the reduction of smog and air pollution in general. Its enforcement has contributed to an improvement in human health and longer life spans.

Combined Cycle Gas Turbine (CCGT)

'Combined cycle' refers to the use of a power-producing engine or plant that employs more than one thermodynamic cycle. Conventional fossil-fuelled power stations use the Rankine Cycle and they are only able to use a portion of the energy from their fuel (usually less than 30 per cent). The balance of the fuel's energy is generally carried away as waste heat in the hot exhaust gases or in the condenser cooling water in the case of a power station. Combining two or more thermodynamic cycles, such as the Gas Turbine Cycle and Rankine Cycle, results in an improved overall efficiency of around 55 per cent for a modern CCGT.

Condensation, Interstitial

Interstitial condensation occurs when warm, moist air from inside a building penetrates into a wall, roof or floor construction and meets a cold surface. This causes the air to cool, lowering its capacity to carry moisture, and resulting in condensation on the cold surface. In time, the condensation can cause rotting of timber or corrosion of metal components. Structural damage may occur and it is likely to be invisible to the occupants of the building.

Condensing boiler

Type of boiler that is more efficient than a conventional boiler. It improves its efficiency by condensing out water from the flue gases and taking up the heat of condensation into the boiler water.

Consequential improvement

Improvement in energy efficiency of a building (or part of a building) as a consequence of other work being carried out, as required by Building Regulation 17D.

Conservation Area

An area or tract of land that has been awarded protected status in order to ensure that natural features, cultural heritage or biota are safeguarded. It may be a nature park, a land reclamation project, or other area. Conservation areas vary greatly in character, and may comprise the centre of a historic town or city, a fishing or mining village, eighteenth- and nineteenth-century suburbs, a model housing estate, a country house set in its historic park, or historic transport links and their environs, such as stretches of canal.

Conservatory

A structure that has at least 75 per cent of its roof and at least 50 per cent of its walls made of translucent material, and is thermally separated from the building to which it is attached.

Controlled fittings

Windows, roof windows and external doors in existing buildings (including vehicle doors and high-usage entrance doors).

Controlled services

Fixed heating, hot water, ventilation, air-conditioning and lighting systems in existing buildings.

Damp-proof membrane (DPM)

When laying a new concrete floor there must be a damp-proof membrane incorporated. If an existing floor does not have a DPM, then it should be sealed with heavy-duty moisture-curing polyurethane.

DER

Dwelling (carbon dioxide) emissions rate in kg/m^2 per year, as calculated by the Standard Assessment Procedure (SAP) energy rating 2005.

Design air permeability

The assumed air permeability included in the calculation of the DER of an unbuilt dwelling, or the BER of an unbuilt non-domestic building, at the design stage.

Design limits

The worst acceptable U-values and air permeability of the building fabric, the lowest acceptable efficiencies of space and water heating appliances, the worst acceptable specific fan power and heat recovery efficiencies of ventilation systems, and the minimum provision and/or efficacy of fixed internal and external lighting systems, in new buildings.

Distillate oil

A combustible hydrocarbon liquid sometimes called kerosene or paraffin. It is used as home heating fuel, as aviation fuel and also to power turbines for power generation.

Dwelling

A self-contained unit of residential accommodation designed to accommodate a single household.

Dwelling type

A set of dwellings of the same built form in which the same construction methods are used for each of the main elements, irrespective of small variations in floor area.

Emergency escape lighting

Lighting that provides illumination for the safety of people leaving an area or attempting to terminate a dangerous process before leaving an area.

Energy Performance of Buildings Directive (EPBD)

The Energy Performance of Buildings Directive, issued by the European Commission, requires all EU countries to enhance their Building Regulations and to introduce energy certification schemes for buildings. All countries are also required to have inspections of boilers and air-conditioners.

EST

Energy Saving Trust.

Fit-out work

Work to complete the internal partitioning and building services within the external envelope (shell) of a building to meet the specific needs of incoming occupants.

Fixed building services

Any part of, or any controls associated with, fixed systems for heating, hot water, air conditioning, mechanical ventilation, or internal or external lighting (excluding emergency escape lighting and specialist process lighting).

Formaldehyde

An organic compound known as an aldehyde. It is an important precursor to many other chemical compounds, especially for polymers, which are used in the manufacture of insulation materials. Exposure to formaldehyde is a significant consideration for human health due to its widespread use, toxicity and volatility.

Gas appliance

Gas-fuelled heater, fire or boiler.

Graphite barrier

Graphite can be used to enhance the thermal properties of a material and can be applied as a coating to the insulator to form an effective barrier to heat.

Halogens (or halogen elements)

A series of non-metal elements from Group 17 of the periodic table: fluorine (F), chlorine (Cl), bromine (Br), iodine (I), and astatine (At).

Historic building

A building that is officially 'listed' as being of special architectural or historic interest, or is located in a Conservation Area, a National Park, an Area of Outstanding Natural Beauty or a World Heritage Site.

Hygroscopic properties

Properties conferring a degree of humidity control, meaning that the insulation materials can absorb and release water without becoming ineffective.

Inert gas

An un-reactive gas, used in glazing because it will not react with the other materials in the glazing and its density will resist gas circulation in the glazing gap.

Infra-red image

A picture taken using an infra-red camera, which is representative of the temperature at which a body, such as a component of a house, is radiating heat. Brighter areas are generally radiating heat and darker areas are cooler.

Joists

Sawn softwood beams (100 x 50mm) that are used to support the floorboards and the floor load. They are connected to softwood wall plates (100 x 75mm), which spread the floor loading to the walls.

LZC

Low- and zero-carbon technologies.

Managed forests

Forests that are managed to provide wood for a variety of reasons, including amenity (tourism, walks), material for wood products and generating energy. As the forests are harvested, they are also re-planted to ensure a sustainable supply of wood. The wood that is derived from managed forests may be treated as 'carbon neutral' by some authorities.

Mansard roof

Also called simply a 'mansard' or a 'French roof', a four-sided hip roof characterized by two slopes on each of its sides, with the lower slope at a steeper angle and more vertical than the upper. It is punctured by dormer windows to create additional habitable space, such as a garret or attic room.

Material alteration

Work to an existing building that would result in the building or any part of it failing to comply with any relevant Building Regulations requirement when previously it did, or in it becoming less satisfactory in respect of such a requirement.

Material change of use

The conversion of a building into a dwelling or dwellings, or the addition of a dwelling to a building that already contains dwellings, or the conversion of a building to a hotel, boarding house, institution or public building, where previously it was not.

Means-testing

Assessment of the ability of a homeowner to pay for work, based on income and financial circumstances, and used in regard to the allocation of grants. Since the grant money available for insulation treatments is limited, some form of priority screening may be applied to ensure that those most in need are addressed first.

Minimum controls package

A package of controls specific to each technology that represents the minimum provision for controls to reduce carbon dioxide emissions associated with space heating, water heating or cooling.

National Calculation Methodology (NCM)

The UK national methodology, under the EPBD, for calculation of the energy performance of buildings; one implementation of the NCM is SBEM.

No-fines concrete

Concrete with no fine aggregates in it.

No-Fines House

House designed by the George Wimpey Construction Company, intended for the mass production of social housing and built in large numbers in the UK following the Second World War. With walls constructed using no-fines concrete, it is now one of the most common building designs in Britain.

No-fines wall

Wall constructed using no-fines concrete.

Non-domestic buildings

Offices, industrial or commercial premises and buildings.

PassivHaus

A specific construction standard for residential buildings, which have excellent comfort conditions in both winter and summer.

Petrochemicals

Chemical products derived from petroleum. Some chemical compounds made from petroleum are also obtained from other fossil fuels such as coal or natural gas, or renewable sources such as corn or sugar cane.

Phenol formaldehyde

A petrochemical derivative product that is well known for its use in the production of moulded products, including pool and snooker balls, laboratory countertops, and as coatings and adhesives. In the form of bakelite, it was the earliest commercial synthetic resin.

Polyolefin

A polymer produced from a simple olefin or alkene

as a monomer (building block). For example, polyethylene is the polyolefin produced by polymerizing the olefin ethylene. Polypropylene is another common polyolefin which is made from the olefin propylene.

Positive feedback

A response to a disturbance that acts to increase the magnitude of the perturbation. The effect of a positive feedback may or may not be desirable. 'Positive' refers to the direction of change rather than the desirability of the outcome. In this instance the outcome is undesirable for most, and will potentially result in catastrophic environmental change as a consequence.

Principal works

Works to an existing building that give rise to a requirement for consequential improvement of the energy efficiency of the building.

Recessed lighting

Lighting that is flush with the ceiling, with the lamp holder and wiring located out of sight above the ceiling.

Relative humidity

The amount of water vapour that exists in a gaseous mixture of air and water vapour.

Render

The name usually given to a coating of an aggregate, a binder and water, which is used on walls and ceilings for protection against the elements or for decoration. Also known as stucco.

Renovation (of a thermal element)

Provision of a new layer, or replacement of an existing layer, in the construction of a thermal element of an existing building.

Residual Current Device (RCD)

Similar to a Residual Current Circuit-Breaker (RCCB), an electrical safety device that disconnects a circuit whenever it detects that the electric current is not balanced between the energized conductor and the return neutral conductor. Such an imbalance is sometimes caused by current leakage through the body of a person who is grounded and accidentally touching the energized part of the circuit. A lethal shock can be the result. RCDs are designed to disconnect quickly enough to mitigate the harm caused by such shocks, although they are not intended to provide protection against overload or short-circuit conditions.

Room for residential purposes

A room or a suite of rooms that is not a dwelling and is used by one or more persons to live and sleep (including rooms in hostels, hotels, boarding houses, halls of residence and residential homes). It is separated from the rest of the building by a lockable door, but is not designed to be occupied by a single household.

SAP (Standard Assessment Procedure)

The national calculation methodology for the energy rating of domestic buildings in England, Wales and Northern Ireland.

Sash window

A sash window or hung sash window is usually in two parts (or sashes) that overlap slightly, and slide up and down inside the frame. The one or more movable panels or 'sashes' hold panes of glass that are often separated from other panes (or 'lights') by narrow muntin bars. Although any window with this style of glazing is technically a 'sash', the term is used almost exclusively to refer to windows where the glazed panels are opened by sliding vertically or horizontally. Styles include 'Yorkshire light', sliding sash or sash and case (so called because the counterweights are concealed in a box case). Nowadays, most new double-hung sash windows use spring balances to support the sashes, but traditionally, counterweights held in boxes on either side of the window were used.

SBEM

The Simplified Building Energy Model (the national calculation methodology for non-domestic buildings).

Seasonal efficiency

The estimated ratio of the heat input (based on the gross calorific value of the fuel) to the heat output of a heat-generating appliance (for example, a boiler) over the heating season.

SEDBUK (Seasonal Efficiency of Domestic Boilers in the UK)

A database of seasonal efficiencies at boilers.org.uk.

Service

In the context of this book, this term refers to electricity, gas, water.

Simple payback

The amount of time taken to recover an initial investment in improved energy efficiency through fuel cost savings (excluding VAT).

Sleeper walls

Three or four courses of honeycombed masonry brickwork spaced at 2m and ventilated. Sleeper walls spread the load on and support floors.

Solum

Underfloor space or void, ventilated to prevent the timbers rotting.

Space-heating system

The complete system that is installed to provide heating to a space, including the heating appliance or plant, and the heat distribution and emission mechanism.

Statutory requirements

A legal necessity that must be complied with.

Stirling engine

Heat engine that operates by cyclic compression and expansion of a working fluid (usually air or other gas), at different temperature levels, such that there is a net conversion of heat energy to mechanical work. Invented by Robert Stirling in 1816, it has the potential to be much more efficient than a gasoline or diesel engine.

Styrene

A colourless oily liquid that evaporates easily and has a sweet smell, although high concentrations produce a less pleasant odour. Styrene is the precursor to polystyrene and several copolymers. It is used to manufacture a range of materials used in rubber, plastic, insulation, fibreglass, pipes, car and boat parts, food containers, and carpet backing.

TER

The Target (carbon dioxide) Emissions Rate in kg/m^2 per yr, as calculated by SAP (for dwellings up to 450m^2 floor area), or by SBEM (for all other buildings).

Thermal bridge

An area of reduced insulation within the construction of a wall, roof or floor, at the junction of a wall with another wall, or a roof or floor, or around an opening such as a window, roof window or external door.

Thermal element

A wall, floor or roof of an existing building that separates the internal conditioned space from the external environment, or from an unheated space.

Timber-frame construction

A building comprising a pre-formed timber load-bearing inner framework with a brick or pre-cast concrete outer skin. Sometimes an outer wooden skin is also used.

Total useful floor area

The total floor area of all enclosed spaces in a building measured to the internal faces of the external walls.

Vapour barrier

An impermeable layer designed to prevent the transfer of moisture between two adjacent spaces within a building, through walls, ceilings or floor assemblies. Generally, the layer is a sheet of tough plastic or foil, or similar material (typically 100g polythene sheet). In reality, many of the materials are only vapour retarders, as they have varying degrees of permeability.

Ventilated facade

A facade or outer face of a building may be ventilated (through the use of suitable airbricks or vents) to prevent the ingress of moisture or damp.

Wet central-heating systems

A central-heating system that uses a boiler and a system of pipes to supply radiators in rooms and corridors with hot water, in order to distribute heat throughout a building.

Index